Oxford and Cambridge

Twentieth Century Architecture 11

Oxford and

Edited by
Elain Harwood
Alan Powers and
Otto Saumarez Smith

The Twentieth Century Society
2013

Cambridge

Twentieth Century Architecture is published by the Twentieth Century Society, 70 Cowcross Street, London EC1M 6EJ

© The authors, 2013. The views expressed in *Oxford and Cambridge* are those of the authors, and not necessarily those of the Twentieth Century Society

Number 11 | 2013 | ISBN 978-0-9556687-3-9

Twentieth Century Architecture Editors:
Elain Harwood, Alan Powers, Otto Saumarez Smith (guest editor)
Text Editor:
Alison Boyd
Twentieth Century Society Publications Committee:
As above, plus Tim Brittain-Catlin, Barnabas Calder, Susannah Charlton, Mark Eastment, Alistair Fair, Geraint Franklin, Fiona MacCarthy, Simon Wartnaby, Charlotte Newman and the Society's Trustees

Designed and typeset by Esterson Associates
Printed by Butler Tanner & Dennis Ltd

Every effort has been made to contact copyright holders, and the editors would be glad to hear from those we failed to reach.

The Twentieth Century Society gratefully acknowledges the generous support of the Paul Mellon Centre for Studies in British Art, Marc Fitch Fund, All Souls College, Oxford, and sponsors of Elain Harwood in the Great North Run 2012 towards the publication of this journal. Individual authors have made their own acknowledgements at the end of their articles. We would also like to thank Nicholas Bullock, Adrian Forty, Holly Catford, James O. Davies, Sarah Duncan, Damian Grady, and all those who refereed the articles for publication

Maps of Oxford and Cambridge by Holly Catford

Aerial photographs of Oxford and Cambridge by Damian Grady/English Heritage

Frontispiece: Casson and Conder's Lady Mitchell Hall (RIBA Drawings and Archives Collections)

Contents

University buildings of Oxford

1. Wolfson College
2. Lady Margaret Hall
3. St Anthony's College
4. St Anne's College
5. St John's College
6. Mansfield College
7. St Cross Library
8. St Catherine's College
9. New Bodleian Library
10. Trinity College
11. Exeter College
12. New College
13. The Queen's College
14. Magdalene College
15. Brasenose College
16. Christ Church
17. Corpus Christi
18. Campion Hall
19. Merton College
20. Waynflete Building
21. Florey Building
22. St Hilda's College

- University buildings
- Modern Movement buildings of the 1950s and 1960s
- Traditional buildings of the 1950s and 1960s
- Buildings by Sir Giles Gilbert Scott

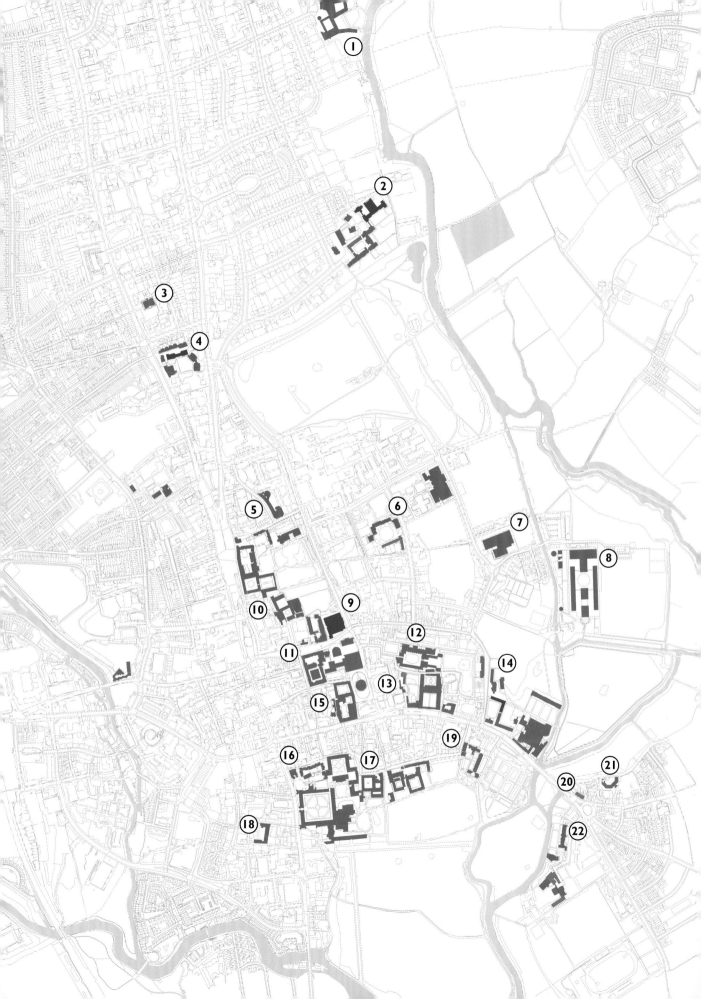

University buildings of Cambridge

1. Churchill College
2. Fitzwilliam College
3. New Hall (Murray Edwards College)
4. Castle Hill Lodge
5. Magdalene College
6. Jesus College
7. Christ's College
8. Trinity Hall
9. Clare Hall
10. University Library
11. New Court, Clare College
12. New Museums Building
13. Emmanuel College
14. History Faculty
15. Harvey Court
16. Raised Faculty Building
17. Newnham College
18. Queens' College
19. Graduate Centre
20. Pembroke College
21. Downing College
22. Department of Architecture, Scroope Terrace

● University buildings
● Modern Movement buildings of the 1950s and 1960s
● Traditional buildings of the 1950s and 1960s
● Buildings by Sir Giles Gilbert Scott

Contributors

Alan Berman was a founding partner of Berman Guedes Stretton Architects and Designers, who have been involved in numerous new buildings and restoration projects in Oxford, Cambridge and London. Following the publication of *James Stirling and the Red Trilogy*, Alan has been invited to write contributions to a number of journals and to lecture. He is currently engaged on a number of books: on Stirling's work in America, on a 5 building project in Oxford, and on aspects of post-war architecture.

Barnabas Calder is a historian of architecture specialising in Brutalism, High Tech and Postmodernism in Britain. He is writing an online complete works of Sir Denys Lasdun funded by the Graham Foundation, and a book on Brutalism to be published by William Heinemann. Follow him on Twitter @BrutalConcrete.

Simon Cornwell is a historian and collector of street lighting.

Alistair Fair is a Chancellor's Fellow in the School of Architecture and Landscape Architecture at the University of Edinburgh. His research focuses on the architectural history of public and institutional buildings since the late nineteenth century, in Britain and increasingly also in continental Europe and the USA. Recent publications include a book on theatre buildings, plus articles in *Architectural History* and the previous volume of this journal.

William Fawcett is an architect who studied architecture at Cambridge in the era of Sir Leslie Martin. He is now the Chadwick Fellow in Architecture at Pembroke College, Cambridge, and a director of Cambridge Architectural Research Ltd, where he has worked on conservation plans for twentieth century buildings including Reginald Blomfield's Usher Gallery in Lincoln, Owen Williams's Boots 'Wets' Factory and Denys Lasdun's University of East Anglia.

Elain Harwood is an architectural historian with English Heritage and co-editor of Twentieth Century Architecture and the Twentieth Century Architects monograph series. She is completing *Space, Hope and Brutalism, English Architecture 1945–1975* for Yale University Press through the Paul Mellon Centre and revising her guide to post-war listed buildings.

David Lewis is an architectural historian specialising in British and American architecture of the inter-war period. His master's dissertation focused on ecclesiastical designs by Edwin Lutyens. He is currently based at St John's College, Oxford, where he is writing a DPhil thesis on the architectural theories of Giles Gilbert Scott, which is funded by the Society of Architectural Historians of Great Britain's Jonathan Vickers Bursary.

Alan Powers was Professor of Architecture and Cultural History at the University of Greenwich until late 2012 and is currently working on a study of alternatives to Modernism in mid-twentieth century British architecture (funded during 2011–12 by the British Academy) and other book projects. He has published widely on art, architecture and design and curated many exhibitions. He was chairman of the Twentieth Century Society 2007–2012, and is one of the editors of Twentieth Century Architecture and the monograph series Twentieth Century Architects.

Otto Saumarez Smith is an architectural historian and journalist. He is writing a PhD on British architect-planners in the 1960s at St John's College, Cambridge, funded by the Kemp Scholarship. Other publications on post-war architecture in Cambridge include articles on Gillespie Kidd and Coia's Robinson College and Powell and Moya's Cripps Court in St John's.

Gavin Stamp, architectural historian, independent scholar and a former chairman of the Twentieth Century Society, went up to Cambridge in 1967 when he first encountered the University Library and soon grew to admire the architecture of Giles Gilbert Scott. His most recent books are *Britain's Lost Cities*, *Lost Victorian Britain* and *The Memorial to the Missing of the Somme*.

Geoffrey Tyack is a fellow of Kellogg College, Oxford, Director of the Stanford University Centre in Oxford, and a member of the Oxford University History Faculty. His books include *Oxford: an Architectural Guide* (OUP, 1998), *Modern Architecture in an Oxford College: St John's College 1945–2005* (OUP, 2005) and (with Simon Bradley) the second edition of the *Berkshire* volume in the Buildings of England series (Yale, 2010).

William Whyte is a fellow and tutor in history at St John's College, Oxford. He is the author of *Oxford Jackson* (2006), co-editor of *Nationalism and the Reshaping of Urban Communities in Europe* (2011) and recently produced a new edition of the 1910 RIBA Town Planning Conference Transactions.

Introduction
'A Pastiche or a Packing Case': Building in Twentieth-Century Oxford and Cambridge

William Whyte

Visiting Oxford in the early 1990s, the journalist Bill Bryson was not impressed. He found the cityscape needlessly compromised by intrusive modern architecture, and especially blamed the university for despoiling a once picturesque environment. Walking down Oxford's only remaining cobbled street, he took particular exception to the 'inescapable intrusion' he found at the end of the road. 'Is it an electrical substation?' he asked; 'A halfway house designed by the inmates? No, it is the Merton College Warden's Quarters, a little dash of mindless sixties excrescence foisted on an otherwise largely flawless street.' And he went on:

> What a remarkable series of improbabilities were necessary to its construction. First, some architects had to design it, had to wander through a city steeped in 800 years of architectural tradition, and with great care conceive of a structure that looked like a toaster with windows. Then a committee of finely educated minds at Merton had to show the most extraordinary indifference to their responsibilities to posterity and say to themselves, 'You know, we've been putting up handsome buildings since 1264; let's have an ugly one for a change.' Then the planning authorities had to say, 'Well, why not? Plenty worse in Basildon.' Then the whole of the city – students, dons, shopkeepers, office workers, members of the Oxford Preservation Trust – had to acquiesce and not kick up a fuss.

It was, he concluded, far from the only product of a 'mad seizure' which had 'gripped the city's planners, architects and college authorities in the 1960s and 1970s'. Only this could explain what he saw.[1]

Bryson's response to the previously little noticed Warden's Lodgings at Merton is noteworthy in general and in particular. By choosing to single out the buildings of the 1960s for criticism he is, it must be said, in good company. Architectural historians have equally expressed contempt for much erected then. In his standard work on the architecture of Oxford, for example, Geoffrey Tyack notes the 'bizarre impracticality' of James Stirling's Florey Building (1968–71) and the 'numbing banality' of Lionel Esher's work at Exeter College (1964) before going on to condemn the 'disastrously inappropriate' Wayneflete Building for Magdalen College (1960–1) by Booth, Ledboer, and Pinckheard.[2] 'Only an architect blinded by non-visual dogma', observes J. Mordaunt Crook, 'could commit an atrocity like the Sacher Building in Longwall Street, Oxford (David Roberts, 1961–2)'.[3] Writers on Cambridge have voiced similar emotions about designs of the same period, with James Lees-Milne dismissing Richard Sheppard's Churchill College (1958–68) as a 'beastly building, like an enormous public lavatory', and the rather more voluble historian David Cannadine describing Stirling's History

Faculty (1963–7) as nothing less than 'a monstrosity – dry-as-dust implausibly clad in the leaking raiment of high-as-tech. Part bunker, part factory, part greenhouse, all folly... ugly, strident, unpopular, aggressive, unwelcoming, antihumanist and anti-architecture'.[4]

As this suggests, it is not hard to find people willing to attack the products of the late Modern Movement. In that sense, Bill Bryson's few paragraphs simply serve as a précis of other, longer, more scholarly condemnations.[5] It is also worth remarking that exactly the same sort of criticism was levelled against the neo-Georgian architecture of the preceding decades from the late-1950s onwards.[6] The vocal critics of the Modern Movement in Oxbridge can consequently be seen as participants in a much longer-running debate which stretches back at least until the nineteenth century and which has been characterised by a recurring belief that almost all interventions in the architecture of each city are grossly inappropriate.[7] Indeed, to a certain extent, as Howard Colvin and Frank Salmon have shown, the impact of changes in taste on the buildings of Oxford and Cambridge is an important theme which can – and should – be traced throughout their history, from the earliest times until today.[8]

It is, however, Bill Bryson's particular choice of building to attack which deserves our fullest attention. Inadvertently, perhaps, in selecting the Merton Warden's Lodgings, he had rather brilliantly identified a structure whose past, present, and future helps to illuminate many of the issues that this volume of Twentieth Century Architecture explores. In 1908 the warden of Merton moved into a 'flamboyant mansion' built by Basil Champneys in the sort of free-Renaissance style that had become all but ubiquitous at Oxford in the previous generation.[9] Within a few decades this enormous house had become an embarrassment: 'hopelessly impractical' and seriously unfashionable, with Evelyn Waugh suggesting that work by the same architect in nearby Oriel College was so execrable that it should be destroyed, preferably with dynamite.[10] By the mid-1940s it had become clear that a new lodgings was needed, and so Merton turned to T. Harold Hughes, a respectable and traditionalist architect responsible for some pared-down Gothic work at neighbouring Corpus Christi, which Pevsner, not inaccurately, dismissed as '1927–9 … and looks 1900'.[11] Hughes drew up plans for a neo-Georgian building only a few doors down from the existing Lodgings, next to – and incorporating – an early eighteenth-century summer house. His death in 1949 brought that project to a halt with Merton approaching a new architect, the middle-aged but almost wholly untried Raymond Erith, in the hope of solving their problem. Erith's expansive Regency revival proposals were, however, considered excessively expensive and in May 1950 the whole idea of new accommodation for the head of the college appeared to have been abandoned for good.[12]

Another decade would pass before Merton broached the subject again, this time employing the noted conservation architect Emil Godfrey to prepare a scheme for the conversion of the sixteenth-century Postmasters Hall, just across the road from the College's main entrance.[13] It was when this, too, proved too costly that he returned to the site first proposed by Hughes at the end of Merton Street, designing the modern brick building that Bill Bryson found so abhorrent.[14] But the story does not stop there, for at the turn of the twenty-first century Merton changed its mind again, hiring another firm best-known for its conservation work – Acanthus Clews – to restore, refurbish, and reface Godfrey's now much-loathed Warden's Lodgings. Rejecting a self-consciously modernist proposal, the college opted for an alternative, more self-effacing, deliberately astylar approach. This quiet, undemonstrative, unostentatious new façade was unveiled in the summer of 2010 in the presence of a celebrity – no less than Bill Bryson himself.[15]

In a little over a century, then, Merton had built two Warden's Lodgings, abandoned one and refaced the other, and employed no fewer than five architectural practices to produce more than half a dozen different proposals. This is nothing compared to the 'indecision at Magdalen' described by Howard Colvin, in which one eighteenth-century Oxford College commissioned a score of designers, who drew up a bewildering

Fig 2. The refaced Warden's Lodgings (image courtesy of Acanthus Clews)

succession of abandoned plans.[16] Nor was it the only time that the fellows of Merton showed similar qualms about buildings commissioned by their predecessors. After all, Harold Hughes had first come to the college in the 1920s to remodel a work of William Butterfield's which had come to be seen as 'glaring, ugly, pretentious' and 'one of the great eyesores of Oxford'.[17] In an act described at the time as 'curiously tasteless and wanton', he removed one storey, added two wings, and covered up the characteristic Gothic Revival details, producing, in the words of Goodhart-Rendel, an effect as 'slavishly Tudor as a modern public house'.[18] Given the importance subsequently accorded to Butterfield, this was in many respects a much more significant change than the later loss of Emil Godfrey's boxy façade. Nor is the evolution of architectural taste revealed in these different versions of the Warden's Lodgings at all remarkable.

To move, in the years after 1900, from free-Renaissance to neo-Georgian, then from self-consciously modern to something more determinedly contextual is to follow a very well-trodden path.

Indeed, it is the very ordinariness of the experience outlined at Merton that makes it so telling. Unlike those institutions which have been the subject of previous studies, it never had any intention of making a bold architectural statement. Merton was not a new foundation with a reputation to make, like Churchill, which was intended to be as much a national monument as a Cambridge college.[19] It was not a place that wanted to symbolize a break with the past, like St John's College, Oxford, where a putsch in 1956 replaced Edward Maufe with the Architects' Co-Partnership.[20] Moreover, the Warden's Lodgings was a minor project, initially conceived as little more than the extension of an existing summerhouse and then as the conversion of a still older, vernacular building. In the words of the Warden himself, it was 'a task demanding scholarship and taste rather than creative genius' on the part of its architect.[21] In 1949, in fact, the art historian Tom Boase had observed 'this is the kind of job that Maufe does very well, but he may be somewhat too big a name to bring in'.[22] That the Warden of Merton between Harold Hughes' appointment and Emil Godfrey's production of an ultimately successful design remained the same notably reactionary Oxford philosopher, Geoffrey Mure, only makes this college more intriguing.[23] Here was an architectural approach that changed even when the putative inhabitant of the building in question did not. The case of the Warden's Lodgings at Merton thus allows us to explore three issues which run throughout this volume – and, in so doing, helps us to tease out what is distinctive about the twentieth-century architecture of Oxford and Cambridge.

The first of the issues that must be addressed is the role of the colleges and of the universities as architectural clients. This is not a simple question. Even to make a distinction between the two is potentially problematic. As Gilbert Ryle famously observed in *The Concept of Mind* (1949):

> A foreign visitor to Oxford or Cambridge is shown a number of colleges, libraries, playing fields, museums, scientific departments and administrative offices. He then asks, 'But where is the University? I have seen where the members of the Colleges live, where the Registrar works, where the scientists experiment and the rest. But I have not yet seen the University in which reside and work the members of your University.'

For Ryle, this was a classic – perhaps the classic – category mistake. 'The University', he went on to observe, 'is not another collateral institution, some ulterior counterpart to the colleges, laboratories and offices … . The University is just the way in which all that he has already seen is organized. When they are seen and when their co-ordination is understood, the University has been seen.'[24] Yet, although this was true enough conceptually, in legal and functional terms, Ryle's foreign visitor was on surer ground than his guide. In both Oxford and Cambridge, the colleges are autonomous institutions: so is the university. Thus, in Cambridge for example, it is perfectly possible for a university lecturer to have no college affiliation or for a college fellow to have no university post.[25] Each college is self-governing. The university is also self-governing; though most of those involved in its government are also part of one college or another. As the story of New Museums Site in Cambridge shows, this can mean that rival colleges compete for space and resources while the university competes with the colleges. Indeed, the growing distinction throughout the twentieth century between college and university is, in fact, best illustrated by the growth of those 'scientific departments and administrative offices' that Ryle mentioned, or indeed the laying out of campuses like the Sidgwick Site in Cambridge for humanities departments which increasingly included staff who might, but need not, be members of a college as well.

In this respect, Oxford and Cambridge differed enormously even from those institutions which sought to imitate them. In the US, for example, the twentieth century witnessed a move by some of the most influential universities to develop precisely the sort of collegiate life with which Oxbridge had become synonymous.[26] Yet even those Ivy League schools like Yale and Princeton which consequently built colleges did so in a way utterly unlike the decentralised and evolutionary development that had occurred over centuries in England. At Princeton, colleges formed only one part of the 'general plan' drawn up by Ralph Adams Cram after 1906 and were in fact intended to make the campus more uniform rather than less.[27] In Yale, the initial designs were all also produced by a single, university architect: James Gamble Rogers. When, after the Second World War, the tide of taste turned and his neo-Gothic confections were rejected, the university was able to move as one towards Modernism. That Yale is now notable for

Fig 3. Scheme by Raymond Erith painted by John Aldridge (Lucy Archer)

possessing buildings by some of the heroic names of high Modernism – Louis Kahn, Eero Saarinen, Philip Johnson, Skidmore, Owings and Merrill – was not really the result of different and competing institutions choosing different and competing architects, but rather the product of a decision taken centrally by the president of the university.[28]

The same factors distinguished Oxbridge from the newer universities in Britain. Although London and, to a certain extent, Durham were also collegiate, none of the others were.[29] By the time of the First World War it truly was a category mistake to distinguish between the departments and the university in Manchester, Liverpool, Leeds, or the other Redbricks. It was even a mistake to differentiate between the halls of residence and the university – for these were never intended to be autonomous institutions like Oxbridge colleges.[30] At the still newer 'Plateglass' universities founded in the 1950s and 1960s, the same was also true. Even those institutions, like Kent and York, which founded colleges never intended them to operate independently.[31] And the architectural implications of this unitary structure were significant. It made master planning for a whole institution possible. It meant that a relatively small group of people in committee, or sometimes working one-to-one with an architect, could determine the built environment for a whole institution. The fact that from the 1920s onwards most large capital projects were dependent on the support of the state, in the form of the University Grants Committee (UGC), ensured that certain norms were increasingly applied across the country.[32] By the 1960s the UGC had also evolved a uniform system for approving plans and a standard formula for assessing costs. Accommodation was measured against the SBU (or 'study-bedroom unit'); laboratories were laid out according to a fixed price for bench space.[33] Even buildings built by benefactions did not escape their attention; if the projected maintenance costs seemed abnormally high, then the UGC could veto the project.

True enough, this centralised model of control did not always produce coherence. At most universities, the story of the twentieth century is one of sudden stops and starts as master plan follows master plan, building follows building. In Birmingham alone,

there were at least half a dozen different campus layouts proposed between 1925 and 1957. None of them was ever satisfactorily completed.[34] It was also possible for institutions to hold out against their paymasters – as at Nottingham, where one vice-chancellor's commitment to neo-classicism in the 1950s defeated the UGC's insistent demands that he adopt something more contemporary.[35] But these examples also reveal the way in which Britain's modern universities – from Manchester to Sussex – could function as a series of single, unified institutional clients and as part of a wider network of architectural patrons, even if the end results reversed the settled conclusions of a previous generation of academics and administrators.

In 1900 Cambridge possessed 17 colleges while Oxford had 20. This meant that between the two, there were potentially 37 different architectural clients, in addition to the two universities themselves. As there were only four other universities in England at that time, this gave Oxbridge a disproportionate importance in the architecture of higher education. A century later, in 2000, Oxford had 39 colleges and Cambridge's total had risen to 31. With something like a hundred other universities also in existence, Oxbridge was no longer as central to the country's academic architecture as it had been. Indeed, as early as in 1953 the historian Denis Mack Smith had observed that 'the older universities have both of them moved far towards Redbrick, a direction symbolised by unexciting and efficient laboratory architecture'.[36] Nonetheless, the existence of dozens of multiple architectural clients – from the smallest college to the largest university department – undoubtedly created a very different environment from Britain's other universities. Oxford and Cambridge colleges, in particular, stood outside the financial arrangements which governed capital projects everywhere else – even in London and Durham. Their buildings were almost never funded by the UGC, but were paid for out of endowment income or benefaction or both.[37] This left poorer colleges exposed, but freed the richer from dependence on the Committee's bureaucratic systems and quinquennial accounting structures, which often forced other institutions to build even before they were quite sure what they wanted.[38] It also meant that they were not bound by the UGC's increasingly restrictive norms.

Oxbridge colleges were thus able to choose their own architects without reference to external authorities and to erect buildings to higher specifications, often with larger rooms and better quality materials, than the other universities. At Oxford's wealthy St John's in the 1950s, for example, the college spent more than £2000 per room on its new student accommodation, a vast sum when compared to the £726–£926 study-bedroom unit laid down by the UGC.[39] At Merton, this freedom meant a willingness to contemplate lodgings with room for resident servants and a private wine cellar, and even, in Raymond Erith's design, the creation of 'a sort of sham ruin'. 'I have often thought Oxford is rather unfortunate in having an inadequate history', he wrote. 'I have therefore taken the liberty of discovering some Roman remains in the foundations of your house … . The cost of this improvement would be negligible compared with what you will gain from living on top of a real (not an eighteenth-century version) Roman bath.' Erith argued that this sort of conjectural *jeu d'esprit* would improve the plan of the lodgings, though he also feared that the proposal sounded 'a bit whimsy' and added a note to the Warden: 'Keep this letter away from your Committee if you think it advisable.'[40] Had that committee been the UGC, rather than the one established by the college, such flights of fancy could probably not have been contemplated, let alone seriously considered.

The Merton lodgings also help highlight a second theme which runs through this volume: the process of commissioning itself. Throughout the twentieth century, the academics of Oxford and Cambridge were not unusual in finding themselves responsible for making important decisions about the architectural future of their institutions on the basis of very little knowledge and still less experience of architectural practice. Amongst non-architects, few indeed were those like the Cambridge English don Mansfield Forbes or the Oxford historian John Prestwich who were able to employ an architect to work on their homes.[41] Fewer still were those like Howard Colvin, who lacked architectural training but nonetheless designed his own house.[42] Little wonder that in 1960 Hugh Casson was warned off work in Cambridge by a taxi driver, who cautioned, 'Don't you build 'ere, sir, they'll muck you about something terrible.'[43] In the absence of real knowledge, experience, or contacts with the architectural world, universities across the country relied on intermediaries. At Leicester in the 1950s this meant John Summerson.[44] At Leeds the university turned to J. M. Richards, amongst others.[45] In the 1960s Leslie Martin became king-maker *extraordinaire*, doling out jobs at a dozen different institutions.[46]

But this model of patronage was not confined to what we might call the modernist moment, nor just to the civic and new universities. At Merton in 1949, the College's plans were thrown into disarray by the death of Harold Hughes. They had no intention of re-employing the only other architect with whom they were familiar. Sir Hubert Worthington's work for the College, a substantial set of buildings in a ponderous, rubble-walled Palladian style erected between 1939 and 1940, were widely loathed, with Warden Mure describing the entrance as 'Agamemnon's Tomb'.[47] Moreover, Worthington disliked the site that the College had chosen.[48] In desperation, Mure wrote to the RIBA: he also travelled to Cambridge, where he admired A. E. Richardson's Chancellor's Building for Christ's (1948) and pondered whether to approach him for the job.[49]

The decision to employ Raymond Erith was due to a most unlikely set of coincidences. It turned out that the Estates Bursar's brother-in-law was a publisher and a friend of Christopher Hussey, the chief architectural writer for *Country Life*. The brother-in-law in question, Ralph Arnold, wrote to Hussey, who suggested two names: the venerable Austen Hall, responsible for a large number of Edwardian Baroque banks or, 'if the college wished to have a young man', he recommended someone called 'Raymond Erith'.[50] A few days later, the Estates Bursar, Wilfrid Holland-Hibbert, passed the correspondence to the Warden; a little over a week after that, Mure wrote to Erith offering him the job.[51]

In some respects, all this vignette reveals is the smallness of the English cultural elite in the mid-twentieth century. It is notable, for example, that Wilfrid Holland-Hibbert was featured in Noel Annan's classic essay on the 'Intellectual Aristocracy', written in 1955 as a paean of praise to the tiny 'caucus' of inter-married academic families whom he believed were responsible for the nation's high culture. Still more tellingly, Holland-Hibbert did not even need to be named, but was simply described as 'the Bursar of Merton'.[52] More importantly, these highly-personalised patterns of architectural patronage help to explain much that seems puzzling about the particular decisions that individual colleges autonomously took. As David Lewis shows, in the case of the Jesuit Campion Hall in Oxford, it was advice from such unlikely acquaintances as the manager of Claridges and the society hostess Lady Horner which led to the dismissal of E. Bower Norris and the employment of Edwin Lutyens. More recently, David Finlay of Acanthus Clews attributes his firm's employment at Merton in 2009 to a shared relationship with the furniture designer Luke Hughes, who had previously worked with both the college and the architect, though on very different projects.[53] At least part of the reason that different institutions chose different firms – with college A taking up an architect just as college B was dismissing him – was often as much prosopographical as it was architectural.[54] It was due to networks of personal connection rather than educated aesthetic choice.

This question of personalities raises a third significant way of thinking about building in twentieth-century Oxford and Cambridge. For most architectural historians the story of Oxbridge architecture is one that can be best approached in stylistic terms.[55] It is also clear that distinctions of style were important for architects and their clients too. Nonetheless, the nature of the colleges as institutions and of their fellows as clients meant that fine distinctions of architectural philosophy and approach which would have been apparent to the architects themselves were often lost on their patrons. At The Queen's College, Oxford, it was apocryphally maintained that James Stirling owed his appointment in 1964 to the fact that the Scottish senior tutor approved of his name and another member of the building committee was unwilling to employ a rival architect 'with no turn-ups to his trousers'.[56] At Queens College, Cambridge, as Louise Campbell has shown, Basil Spence was the 'accidental beneficiary' of a vague 'wish to accommodate progressive opinion by commissioning a "modern" building', whatever that might happen to mean.[57]

Merton, again, provides a good example of this process at work. In his correspondence with the Warden, Erith was keen to establish that his early working drawings were just that. He offered several designs – none of which, he was clear, were satisfactory. 'Sketch No 1 was my first effort at pumping up a front to Merton Street', he wrote.

> I thought it had the defect of being too middle class, suitable for gentrified sort
> of people who had the maltings but not right for the Warden of Merton.
> So I pumped a bit harder and drew No 2 and some others, but I found the
> harder I pumped the worse it got. The building went two faced and squinted
> shiftily down Merton Street like an old sheep, and the more important I made it
> the less important it looked. So I made a tracing of No 2, which is Sketch No 3,
> just putting in the windows where they are and leaving out all the architect's
> flapdoodle … . If you don't at first see how much better No 3 is, shut your eyes
> and think of it. But perhaps it will not be so difficult for you to see that
> architecting is the ruin of architecture.

To reiterate the point, he went on: 'I must say this: don't let anybody judge the design by how it looks but by what it is, thinking of the plan and the site all the time. If it is right it will look right.'[58] Yet, of course, Erith was addressing his comments to a group of people who could not necessarily be expected to read a plan, much less to understand it, still less to be able to relate it to a site. As the warden counselled him a month later, 'A very important factor in carrying the C[ommi]tte[e] will be elevations that look attractive!'[59]

Eleven years after this exchange, in 1961, Mure's response to Emil Godfrey's proposals provide another insight into how architecture was understood by at least one client. In a memorandum rejecting the first set of plans, the Warden was extremely forceful and very revealing. 'One cannot nowadays get a house built which is not either a pastiche or a packing case', he observed.

> Less and less do I like imitations of the 17th or 18th century, and I assume that we may rule them out and confine ourselves to consider a packing case solution of the site … such as Mr Godfrey's model offers. This, like all buildings of its type, has the simplicity of flat insignificance; not of beauty unadorned, for it is no beauty … I could not be a party to erecting a house of this type on such a conspicuous site.[60]

Nearly a year's further work produced the version of the lodgings that was finally built: a design that the Warden himself came to support;[61] though Pevsner later observed that, just as Mure had worried it would, the building did indeed 'spectacularly interfere' with the rest of the street.[62]

The lodgings itself, however, is in many ways less important than the Warden's analysis of it. His assumption that architecture in the early 1960s had been reduced to a binary choice – 'pastiche' or 'packing case' – is extremely revealing. It speaks of a particular turning point in British architectural history; a time at the end of the 1950s and the beginning of the 1960s when many universities which had previously been committed to a form of neo-classicism abandoned that style in favour of something seen as more self-evidently modern.[63] What that actually amounted to was often unclear, with academics reduced to vague phrases about 'buildings … in contemporary style', with 'plain, severe, clean lines … red brick and glass'.[64] That architects themselves seemed equally uncertain about what the essence of this modern architecture might be only made matters worse.[65] Yet the change was real enough. It prompted the conservative Mure to abandon his earlier enthusiasm for the work of the staunchly traditionalist Albert Richardson in favour of something more self-consciously modernist. Still more strikingly, it also led him to believe that 'nowadays' such a decision was all but inevitable.

The change of tack at Merton and the terms in which it was debated do not, however, just delineate a particular moment in the history of taste, nor simply illustrate a more general process of change occurring in almost all British universities. They also help illuminate the environment in which colleges, departments and universities made decisions about what to build throughout the century. By 1900, Oxford and Cambridge had assumed their current status as national treasures, the focus of 'pilgrimage' by tourists seeking the dreaming spires or the beauties of the Backs.[66] 'If the foreign traveller were asked what he considers the most beautiful towns in England,' observed Nikolaus Pevsner in 1949, 'his answer would without doubt be Oxford and Cambridge. The truth of this answer will not be denied.'[67] This had, in fact, not always been the case – after all, at least one mid-Victorian visitor found Cambridge 'of all provincial English boroughs the most insignificant, the dullest and the ugliest'.[68] But the twentieth century celebration of both cities remained remarkably constant. Constant, too, was the analysis of their aesthetic effect. Their attraction, it was widely agreed, was not based on the impact of individual buildings;[69] rather, as Thomas Sharpe wrote in 1948, it was 'the relationships between them, either of harmony or complement, that have produced a great and homogenous work of art'.[70] It was the townscape, not the architecture that mattered: 'The organic development of a … unique combination of open space, architecture, paving, trees and grass. To move through this sequence of spaces is an experience without equal', as the architect Peter Chamberlin put it in 1960.[71]

It was within this context that the projects described in the present volume were conceived and built. The notion that Oxford and Cambridge each possessed a particular and powerful *genius loci* was inescapable for architect and client alike. It could be highly problematic; famously, Lionel Esher observed that Oxford 'gave him stagefright'.[72] But it also legitimated a wide range of different approaches, enabling clients to embrace change as part of the natural order of things. Whilst many other universities sought uniformity for much of the century, Oxbridge tended to value variety as intrinsic to the very essence of the city and university.[73] Moreover, discussions about architecture throughout the century were often debates over materials and massing in which issues of scale were more important than questions of style. At John's College, Oxford, in 1956 Howard Colvin urged that any new development demanded 'a frankly contemporary treatment which would make no concessions to the adjoining buildings except in such matters as scale and material'.[74] In thus stressing both style and substance, he was far from alone.[75] As a result, in Oxbridge, even high Modernism was always contextual because architects and their clients shared a fixed set of beliefs about the nature of the two universities and the cities in which they had made their home.

These assumptions have also undoubtedly shaped how buildings have been treated once they were built. To offend against the commonly-accepted understanding of the *genius loci* was hazardous. Butterfield's interventions at Oxford were covered up at Merton and vandalized at Keble, with undergraduates in the 1950s admitted to the Destroy Keble Society on production of a brick they had prised from the walls. His chapel at Balliol survived by sheer luck, though in narrowly escaping demolition, it did not avoid comprehensive refurbishment.[76] Similarly, James Stirling's work in Oxford and Cambridge always drew far more criticism than his equally avant-garde projects like the engineering building at Leicester. As Alan Berman observes, 'It seems telling that while Leicester suffered some of the technical problems of the others, there appears to have been no outcry from the engineers about this architecture. The dons of Oxford and Cambridge were probably doing what we all do: exaggerating the problems of something that offended their taste.'[77] Listing now preserves many of these buildings, meaning that Butterfield and Stirling are now officially recognised as spirits of the place. Yet it does not, of course, protect everyone or everything. It is striking, for example, that amongst the reasons adduced by the Department of Culture in 2010 for supporting the destruction of Howell, Killick, Partridge and Amis's 1966 Founder's Tower at St Anne's College, Oxford, was the belief that it did 'not relate well to adjoining buildings'.[78] The Twentieth Century Society expressed surprise at this conclusion, but it was, in truth, the product of a century's assumptions about the nature of Oxbridge architecture.

So too is the story of the Merton Warden's Lodgings. Ironically enough, given what happened to it, Emil Godfrey's project was an attempt at a sort of contextual Modernism: its scale deliberately diminutive in order to avoid dominating the streetscape or challenging the views of nearby Magdalen tower. The refacing of the lodgings in 2010 was simply another effort to help the house fit in, removing what a local writer described as 'one of Oxford's glaringly incongruous carbuncles' and replacing it with something 'more in keeping with the prevailing college vernacularities: a genuine response to respect the genius loci of Merton Street'.[79] Bill Bryson's attack on the building also shared these assumptions. It was not just because he disliked the architecture itself, but also because it seemed inappropriate that he so disapproved. The lodgings, then, was both built and rebuilt, defended and attacked, by people who fundamentally agreed about the nature of the environment, even if they fundamentally disagreed about the architecture itself. In that, as in so much else, it is a marvellous microcosm of building in Oxford and Cambridge.

1. Bill Bryson, *Notes From a Small Island*, London, Black Swan, 1995, pp.155–6.

2. Geoffrey Tyack, *Oxford: an architectural guide*, Oxford, Oxford Paperbacks, 1998, pp.325–6.

3. J. Mordant Crook, *The Dilemma of Style: architectural ideas from the picturesque to the post-modern*, London, John Murray, 1987, p.265.

4. Both quoted in Martin Garrett, *Cambridge: a cultural and literary history*, Oxford, Signal Books, 2004, pp.56, 58.

5. See David Watkin, *Morality and Architecture Revisited*, Chicago, University of Chicago Press, 2001, and more particularly James Stevens Curl, *The Erosion of Oxford*, Oxford, Oxford University Press, 1977, pp.66–67.

6. Philip Booth and Nicholas Taylor, *Cambridge New Architecture*, London, Leonard Hill, 1970; Lionel Brett, 'Universities: today', *Architectural Review*, vol.22, no.729, October 1957, pp.240–51; 'T.L.', 'Oxford University: new building exhibition', *Architects' Journal*, vol.129, 1959, p.398, no.3341, 12 March 1959, p.398.

7. William Whyte, *Oxford Jackson: architecture, education, status, and style, 1835–1924*, Oxford, University Press, 2006, esp. pp.91–101, 184–90.

8. Howard Colvin, *Unbuilt Oxford*, New Haven and London, Yale University Press, 1983; Frank Salmon, 'Howard Colvin's *Unbuilt Oxford* and the "might-have-beens" of architectural history', in Malcolm Airs and William Whyte, eds., *Architectural History After Colvin* (forthcoming).

9. David Watkin, *The Architecture of Basil Champneys*, Cambridge, Newnham College, 1989, p.35.

10. G. H. Martin and J. R. L. Highfield, *A History of Merton College*, Oxford, Oxford University Press, 1997, p.354; Edward Impey, 'The Rhodes Building at Oriel: dynamite or designate?', *Oxoniensia*, vol.76, 2011, pp.95–104, p.95.

11. Jennifer Sherwood and Nikolaus Pevner, *Oxfordshire*, Harmondsworth, Penguin, 1974, p.133.

12. Lucy Archer, *Raymond Erith: architect*, Burford, Cygnet Press, 1985, p.130.

13. Merton College Archive, 13.3 Committee reports 1946–68, Committee on the warden's Accommodation (16 December 1960).

14. Martin and Highfield, *History of Merton*, op. cit. pp.354–4.

15. I am very grateful to David Finlay of Acanthus Clews for speaking to me about this project.

16. Colvin, *Unbuilt Oxford*, op. cit. ch. 6.

17. Alan Bott, *Merton College: a short history of the buildings*, Oxford, Merton College, 1993, p.41; John Wells, quoted in Paul Thompson, *William Butterfield*, London, Routledge & Kegan Paul, 1971, p.413.

18. H. S. Goodhart-Rendel, *Vitruvian Nights: papers on architectural subjects*, London, Methuen, 1932, p.157.

19. Mark Goldie, *Corbusier Comes to Cambridge: post-war architecture and the competition to build Churchill College*, Cambridge, Churchill College, 2007.

20. Geoffrey Tyack, *Modern Architecture in an Oxford College: St John's College, 1945–2005*, Oxford, Oxford University Press, 2005, pp.22–4.

21. Merton College Archive Acc 2005/02 (Box 1): proposed new lodgings. G. R. G. Mure to RIBA Secretary, 9 December 1949.

22. T. S. R. Boase to Mure (17 November 1949), loc. cit.

23. *The Times*, no. 60478, 19 November 1979, p. 8. For his dislike of modern architecture, see M. G. R. Mure, *Retreat From Truth*, Oxford, Blackwell, 1958, pp.18–19.

24. Gilbert Ryle, *The Concept of Mind*, Chicago, University of Chicago Press, 2009, p.6.

25. C. N. L. Brooke, *History of the University of Cambridge*, vol.iv, Cambridge University Press.

26. Alex Duke, *Importing Oxbridge: English residential colleges and American universities*, New Haven and London, Yale University Press, 1996.

27. Paul Venable Turner, *Campus: an American planning tradition*, Cambridge, Mass., MIT Press, 1984, p.230.

28. Vincent Scully, Catherine Lynn, Erik Vogt and Paul Gildberger, *Yale in New Haven: architecture and urbanism*, New Haven and London, Yale University Press, 2004, esp. pp.263–354.

29. J. Mordaunt Crook, 'The Architectural Image', in F. M. L. Thompson, ed., *The University of London and the World of Learning, 1836–1986*, London, Hambledon Continuum, 1990, pp.1–34.

30. William Whyte, 'Halls of Residence at Britain's Civic Universities, 1870–1970', in Jane Hamlett, Lesley Hoskins and Rebecca Preston, eds., *Residential Institutions in Britain, 1725–1950: inmates and environments* (forthcoming).

31. Michael Beloff, *The Plateglass Universities*, London, Secker and Warburg, 1968.

32. *Methods Used by Universities of Contracting and of Recording and Controlling Expenditure*, 1956, Cmnd 9.

33. *Methods Used by Universities of Recording and Controlling Expenditure*, 1965, Cmnd 1235.

34. Eric Ives, Diane Drummond, and Leonard Schwartz, *The First Civic University: Birmingham, 1880–1980*, Birmingham, University of Birmingham, 2000, pp.430–40.

35. Peter Fawcett and Neil Jackson, *Campus Critique: the architecture of the University of Nottingham*, Nottingham, University of Nottingham, 1998, pp. 59–89.

36. Denis Mack Smith, 'The Changing University: a report on Cambridge today', *Encounter*, vol.6, no.5, 1953, pp.53–8, p.54.

37. For some exceptions, see Diane Kay, 'Architecture', in Brian Harrison, ed., *The History of the University of Oxford Volume viii: The Twentieth Century*, Oxford, Oxford University Press, 1994, pp.499–518, p.507.

38. Michael Cassidy, 'Pressure on University Building', *Official Architecture*, vol.30, no. 4, April 1967, pp.503–11.

39. Tyack, *Modern Architecture*, op. cit. p.39.

40. Merton College Archive, Acc 2005/02 (Box 1): Proposed new lodgings, Erith to Mure, 14 April 1950.

41. Elizabeth Darling, 'Finella, Mansfield Forbes, Raymond McGrath, and Modernist Architecture in Britain', *Journal of British Studies*, vol.50, 2011, pp.125–55; Kenneth Powell, *Ahrends, Burton and Koralek*, London, RIBA Publishing, 2012, p.57–8.

42. Richard Hewlings, 'A Scholar's Lair', *Country Life*, vol.202, no. 43, 22 October 2008, pp.60–63.

43. Hugh Casson, 'Bricks and Mortar-Boards' in *The Twentieth Century*, vol. 172, no. 1014, Summer 1962, p. 91.

44. Leicester University Archive, uncat. Bursarial notes, Summerson to Vice Chancellor, 19 March 1956.

45. William Whyte, 'The Modernist Moment at the University of Leeds, 1957–1977', *Historical Journal*, vol.51, 2008, pp.169–193.

46. Robert Proctor, 'Social Structures: Gillespie, Kidd, and Coia's Halls of Residence at the University of Hull', *Journal of the Society of Architectural Historians*, vol.67, 2008, pp.106–29; Peter Dormer and Stefan Muthesius, *Concrete and Open Skies: Architecture at the University of East Anglia, 1962–2000*, London, Unicorn Press, 2001, p.50.

47. Martin and Highfield, *History of Merton*, op. cit. p.354.

48. Merton College Archive, Acc 2005/02 (Box 1): Proposed new lodgings, Mure to Secretary of RIBA, 9 December 1949.

49. Mure to Secretary of RIBA, 13 December 1949, loc. cit.

50. Christopher Hussey to Ralph Arnold, 16 December 1949, loc. cit.

51. Holland-Hibbert to Mure, 23 December 1949; Mure to Erith, 4 January 1950, loc. cit.

52. Noel Annan, 'The Intellectual Aristocracy', in J. H. Plumb, ed., *Studies in Social History*, London, Books for Libraries Press, 1955, pp.243–243, 272.

53. Interview with David Finlay. 5 September 2012.

54. Tyack, *Modern Architecture*, op. cit., p. 91 provides a good example.

55. For an excellent recent example, see Otto Saumarez-Smith, 'Robinson College, Cambridge, and the Twilight of Collegiate Modernism, 1974–81', *Architectural History*, vol.55, 2012, pp.369–402.

56. Mark Girouard, *Big Jim: the life and work of James Stirling*, London, Pimlico, 2000, p.157.

57. Louise Campbell, 'Building on the Backs: Basil Spence, Queens' College Cambridge and university architecture at mid-century', *Architectural History*, vol.54, 2011, pp.383–405, p.386.

58. Merton College Archive, Acc 2005/02 (Box 1): Proposed new lodgings, Erith to Mure, 2 February 1950.

59. Mure to Erith, 15 March 1950, loc. cit.

60. Merton College Archive 13.3 Committee Reports 1946–86, Warden's Memorandum, 16 June 1961.

61. Committee on the Warden's Lodgings, 15 January 1962, loc. cit.

62. Sherwood and Pevsner, *Oxfordshire*, op. cit. pp.310–1; See also p.164.

63. William Whyte, 'Georgian: the other style in British university architecture', in Julian Holder and Elizabeth McKellar, eds, *Re-Appraising the Neo-Georgian 1880–1970* (forthcoming).

64. Leicester University Archive, Uncat. Minutes 1955–56, Buildings Advisory Committee, 3 November 1955.

65. John Gold, *The Practice of Modernism: Modern architects and urban transformation, 1954–1972*, London and New York, Routledge, 2007, pp.265–9.

66. *Inlander*, vol. 11, 1901, p.312.

67. Nikolaus Pevsner, *Visual planning and the Picturesque*, Los Angeles, Getty Publishing, 2010, p.51.

68. William Everett, *On the Cam*, Cambridge, Sever and Francis, 1865, p.11.

69. Nikolaus Pevsner in Philip Booth and Nicholas Taylor, eds., *Cambridge New Architecture*, London, Leonard Hill, 1970, p.7

70. Thomas Sharp, *Oxford Replanned*, Oxford, Oxford City Council, 1948, p.20.

71. *University of Leeds Development Plan*, London, privately published, 1960, p.47.

72. Quoted in Tyack, *Oxford*, op. cit. pp.325–6.

73. Thomas A. Gaines, *The Campus as a Work of Art*, New York, Praeger Publisher, 1991.

74. Quoted in Tyack, *Modern Architecture*, op. cit., p. 23.

75. Sharp, op. cit., p. 172.

76. Peter Howell, '"The Disastrous Deformation of Butterfield": Balliol College Chapel in the twentieth century', *Architectural History*, vol.44, 2001, pp.283–92.

77. Alan Berman, *Jim Stirling and the Red Trilogy: Three radical buildings*, London, Frances Lincoln, 2010, p.144.

78. http://www.architectsjournal. co.uk/Journals/1/Files/2010/7/16/ Decision%20Letter,%20EH,%20 Redacted.pdf (accessed 27 June 2012).

79. Tony Bintley, letter in *Oxford Times*, 19 January 2012.

I

Sir Giles Gilbert Scott in Oxbridge
Gavin Stamp

Sir Giles Gilbert Scott (1880–1960) was responsible for several important buildings erected in the two ancient English universities between the two World Wars. The last to be commissioned was Hartland House, an entrance and library block for the Society of Home Students in North Oxford. Begun in 1937, it was continued in 1949 but never completed. In his notorious attack on Oxbridge for the conservatism of its new architecture published in the *Architectural Review* in 1952, J. M. Richards singled out Scott's work at what by now had become St Anne's College as the

> most bizarre of all the new buildings I have claimed as whimsical-eclectic
> […]. The entrance facade, with its odd fenestration, its niggling stonework,
> and its doorway supported by strange totem-pole motifs, was completed a
> little while ago; the garden front, like a frilled fortress with its even stranger
> battlement motifs is but now on the point of completion. It will puzzle any
> future historian who may try to deduce from it the principles according to
> which architects worked in the mid-twentieth century.[1]

Like Sir Gilbert Scott in the previous century, Giles Scott worked in both Oxford and Cambridge. But whereas his grandfather's buildings were all resolutely Gothic, few of Giles Scott's were designed in the medieval manner in which he had been trained and for which he had come to fame by winning the competition for the Anglican Cathedral in Liverpool at the very beginning of the century. Some are neo-Georgian, one is early Christian or Byzantine in style, while the large new libraries he designed for both universities are in a personal modernistic manner, influenced by modern Swedish and American architecture and the ornamental manner now termed Art Deco. As far as the present historian is concerned, these various buildings are not at all puzzling but the works of a resourceful designer trying to respond with intelligence and integrity to changing conditions and new technologies while respecting the character of both ancient university towns.
He did this by modernising traditional forms and taking great care over the use of materials. He was concerned to please his clients – an honourable pursuit – and please them he did.

Scott's Oxbridge buildings – especially the two libraries – reflect the position he took in his inaugural speech as President of the Royal Institute of British Architects in 1933, that 'I hold no brief either for the extreme diehard Traditionalist or the extreme Modernist and it seems to me idle to compare styles and say that one is better than another'.[2] Scott sought compromise, or reconciliation, and this was an approach which proved to be particularly successful in both universities in the 1930s. When the RIBA visited Cambridge in 1933, Hugh Hughes – that local architect who would soon take up Modernism – wrote how

Fig 2. Clare College
Memorial Court in 1984
(author)

Here tradition marches side by side with cosmopolitanism. Lintols, apparently
unsupported, gleam through Gothic archways; high-pitched tile roofs, with
nothing within them, are over the heads of men splitting atoms or disentangling
cosmic rays; colleges like Italian cities of old vie with one another for the
services of Royal Academicians.[3]

Scott's venture into academic architecture began at Clare College, Cambridge. Earlier,
in 1911, having consulted T. G. Jackson, the college had proposed building a residential
block beyond the 'Backs' to the west of the River Cam (where so much later university
development would take place) and Reginald Blomfield, Edwin Lutyens and J. W.
Simpson were invited to submit designs. Ten years later, in 1921, the project was revived
but this time the building was also to serve as a war memorial to honour the 197 Clare
men who had died in the Great War. Scott seems to have been the only architect
considered. Why the college went to a designer who was then known only for
ecclesiastical work and who had no experience of designing a large residential or public
building is not recorded; it may possibly reflect the advice of Mansfield Forbes, the
Fellow of Clare who would later champion the young Raymond McGrath.

Scott's proposal was for a three-sided court, open to the west, with a central
memorial arch facing the old college buildings across the river.[4] The style adopted was
neo-Georgian, but Scott gave it distinction by using special silver-grey bricks (from
Ruabon) with Portland stone dressings, and the pitched roofs were covered in 'specially
made Italian tiles'. Scott described how 'elaboration of detail has been avoided, and an
attempt made to produce a quiet and dignified building'.[5] The repetitiveness
characteristic of neo-Georgian was avoided by having prominent open doorways facing
the court while on the exterior walls planes of brickwork slightly proud frame an elevated
window lighting the staircase behind. Each staircase allowed access to four sets of rooms
while the provision of basement bathrooms each to serve six sets made Memorial Court
almost luxurious by pre-war Cambridge standards.

Reviewing the completed building, the *Architect and Building News* considered that
'The grey bricks, snow white (not ivory) window sashes, and restrained use of stonework
combine in a most pleasant and unusual colour effect, and the general appearance of
reserve about the scheme inevitably recalls Carlyle's well-known remark on Chelsea

Hospital buildings'.[6] H. S. Goodhart-Rendel later observed that Clare Memorial Court 'was very much to the taste of its time and received loud applause' while for Nikolaus Pevsner, 'The scale is comfortable, and there is plenty of air and space. One need only in one's mind compare this building with the recent additions made by most other colleges to appreciate its superiority.'[7]

The most distinctive feature of the building was the central, axial memorial arch. For this, Scott adopted that restrained neo-classical manner which had become fashionable before the war and was known as 'neo-Grec'. He had used it before, in the house he had built for Arthur Stanley M.P. on the banks of the Thames in Pimlico in 1913–15, and it also manifested itself in the interiors of the similarly restrained neo-Georgian house he built for himself in Clarendon Place, Bayswater, in 1924–25 and, of course, in his contemporary Soanian design for the K2 telephone box. At Clare, the principal entablature, expressed in stone, is carried across the central arch as a lintel supported by an attenuated and stylised Corinthian order which frames an open porch. Pediments are so flattened as to be almost horizontal and enlivened with Greek detail. A proposal by Scott in 1925 to complete this feature with figures by the sculptor Frank Dobson came to nothing.

Work began on the principal, eastern range of Memorial Court in 1922, assisted by a generous donation by Col. Arthur S. Barham in memory of his son Wilfrid. It was formally opened on Armistice Day 1924. Three years later the college was ready to

Fig 3. Half-inch detail drawing of the War Memorial Arch at Clare College (RIBA Drawings and Archives Collections)

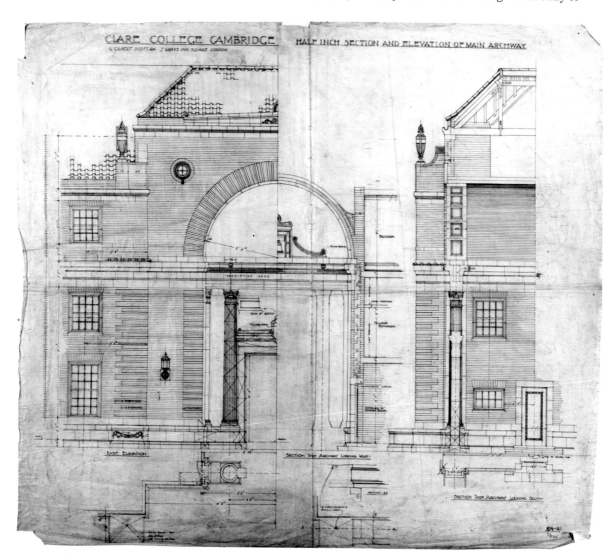

consider completing the scheme by building the two wings extending westwards and work began on them in 1928 to a slightly modified design. In 1931–32 these wings were taken further west, but on a different parallel alignment, thus narrowing the central space (and in 1953–55 further wings to the same design were constructed to the south to create Thirkhill Court). In 1927 the idea of closing the court with a western range had been mooted, but Scott soon rejected the idea, writing to the bursar that '… I feel it would be a great mistake to have a block of buildings across our West side, which would destroy all possibility of a long vista'.[8]

That long vista was to be centred on the new Cambridge University Library, which, since 1922, had been envisaged rising on the college's old cricket ground further to the west. In the event, Scott was to design that building as well, allowing him to consider Memorial Court and University Library as a unified conception. For half a century after the completion of the library in 1934 it was possible to see the entrance and tower of the University library as the axial termination of the view seen through the arch of Memorial Court. It was a dramatic vista unique in modern British architecture. Unfortunately, and despite the strenuous opposition of the (then) Thirties Society, Clare College chose to block that vista in 1986 by building a combined library and music room in a feeble and incoherent version of Scott's style in the middle of Memorial Court. This intervention gratuitously spoiled one of the finest creations in twentieth-century Cambridge and it is hard to understand, or to forgive.[9]

Recognising that the University Library could no longer expand on its confined central site in the Old Schools, the Library Syndicate had recommended in 1920 that a large new library building be erected elsewhere. The former cricket grounds across the Backs, then occupied by temporary hospital buildings, were eventually chosen as the location. Scott was asked to be the architect, without any competition, in 1923. Given that his buildings for Clare had not yet been completed, this may seem

Fig 4. Clare College Memorial Court seen from the top of the University Library tower in 1934 (*Country Life*)

Fig 5. Cambridge
University Library,
first design: perspective
by Cyril Farey, 1924
(Cambridge University
Library)

extraordinary and would seem to be the result of the intervention of Lord Esher, former Permanent Secretary at the Office of Works, politician, courtier and grandee. 'I went down to Cambridge yesterday, inspected the site, examined certain sketch plans, and talked the whole matter over with the Vice-Chancellor, the Master of Caius, and others', he informed the Duke of Devonshire, who was High Steward of the University.

> The site is an excellent one, immediately behind the new buildings of Clare. The sketch plans are by a man called Mitchell [...]. They will not do and would appeal to no one. We discussed the method of procedure, and it was resolved to ask you to join with us in approving the selection of Gilbert Scott to make a plan and a design for the new Library. We were all of us opposed to a competition. The choice of Scott was decided by the fact that he was the architect of the new buildings at Clare.[10]

Scott's first design for the library is recorded in a perspective by Cyril Farey made in 1924. He envisaged a long classical building, with lower wings extending its horizontal lines further, similar in materials and in style to his Clare buildings but with a central entrance behind a tetrastyle portico *in antis* and with vertical strips of glazing between piers, expressing the internal arrangement of tiers of open-access book stacks, rather than Georgian sashes. This dominating conception – probably derived from studying the design of American libraries such as the Stirling Library at Yale University – would be carried through to the final, executed design.[11] Inside, generous corridors would give access to the closely-connected catalogue room and large reading room which were specified by the Librarian.

Scott described his intentions in an appeal leaflet, in which he stressed that the open-access requirement for the Cambridge library was unusual so that there was little to be learned from American libraries in terms of general planning. 'At Cambridge the architectural treatment of the book-stack has to be boldly faced, as these features form the bulk of the building. The peculiar fenestration of a book-stack, with its very long narrow windows gives, however, to the exterior of these features a distinctive character, not without architectural qualities.' But, yet again, Scott emphasised reticence rather than display, an attitude which was typical of the gentlemanly 1920s. 'The aim has been to produce a quiet, dignified building, relying for its effect upon its main lines rather than upon elaboration of detail. This character seems to strike the right note for the library of an old University, and the anxiety to avoid any self-assertiveness has led to the omission of any prominent feature, such as a tower or dome.'[12]

Before work could go ahead, two problems had to be overcome. One was the siting and orientation of the building. Scott's first design envisaged the library being placed not on the axis of Memorial Court but further south on that of King's College Chapel. This, however, proved to be impossible because of the refusal by King's College to sell additional land to the University and to allow access through its Fellows' Garden (on which, after the Second World War, the college erected the reprehensibly mediocre Garden Hostel). Therefore, in 1924, Scott was faced with three choices: either redesigning the building, or turning it through ninety degrees so that it faced south with an approach from West Road, or moving it further north, 'keeping the centre of the Library on a line with the central axis of the new Clare buildings' – which is what was agreed the following year.[13]

The second, more intractable problem was to secure the funds to build the library. Eventually assistance was secured from the Rockefeller Foundation. Early in the decade the International Education Board founded by John D. Rockefeller, Junior, offered to fund medical research in Cambridge and in 1926 the Master of Caius, Sir Hugh Anderson, tried to interest the Americans in the library project. Unfortunately, Mr Rockefeller did not at first care for Scott's plans; 'the design for the library seems to me atrocious', he wrote to his agent. 'I would hate to be a party to the erection of such a building in so beautiful a surrounding, but then that is a detail'.[14] The consequence of this would be a radical change in the design.

The following year, the Librarian, A. F. Scholfield, was obliged to send Scott a tactful letter informing him that 'certain persons' wanted to give substantial financial help to the project, and that the 'modesty' aimed at by the architect was not helpful in fund-raising.

> One may say generally that the façade was thought not to be sufficiently imposing. ... Not that there is a want of dignity, but it is self-effacing, austere, and with no trace of richness. And it was partly its modesty, so to speak, partly its austerity that made it appear to our critics that this new Library was alien in spirit to the rest of the aggregate of buildings that make up the University of Cambridge. Partly too the grey brick and dark red tiles looked discrepant and cold to eyes accustomed to the red brick and green slates of St John's, of Jesus, of Magdalene, or the mellow stone of King's and of Trinity. [...] A fresh design for the facade was asked for.[15]

Scott at first responded that, 'My feeling is that modern university buildings rather suffer from over elaboration and that the best of the old buildings owe their charm to the quietness and simplicity of their treatment'. But he was an architect always responsive to his client's wishes and one who, as Goodhart-Rendel put it, was 'exceptionally sensitive to the tastes and aspirations of his contemporaries'.[16] He began to consider adding a tower to his design and using a warmer colour of brick. It may have been American influence, therefore, that made Scott, in the Cambridge context, move from the gentlemanly reticence and muted colours of the 1920s to the more assertive and flashy manner typical of the following decade. But Scott cannot have been averse to the notion of a vertical feature. In his revised design for the central tower at Liverpool, then rising, and with that for his church at Northfleet, he had shown that he was a master in creating powerful, distinctive and yet sensitively scaled towers, and he was then working on the one that would rise above the William Booth Memorial Building on Champion Hill in South London. He now seized the opportunity to create what is still the most dominant and recognisable landmark on the Cambridge skyline.

By the end of 1928, Scott had been refining his new design for a library with a central tower and now submitted a model of what would be his final scheme. 'As regards the design', he wrote to Scholfield, 'I feel more strongly than ever the need for a dominating feature in the centre, but I think the tower now shown is better in proportion than that previously submitted. I have made it lower and wider, giving a stronger and more reposeful character than the tall slender proportion indicated formerly. I think that

PROPOSED UNIVERSITY LIBRARY, CAMBRIDGE.

Fig 6. Cambridge
University Library,
early design with tower:
perspective, c.1927
(RIBA Drawings and
Archives Collections)

this type of tower will mark the Library from a distance in a quiet dignified manner, without being in any way aggressive.'[17] As Scott explained the following year, 'The site, situated as it is with no direct approach, is without any distinction, such as would naturally assist in giving prominence to the building; a tower has therefore been adopted, and this feature will not only give the necessary emphasis to the building, but will also serve as a vertical book-stack.'

Scott had also changed his mind about building materials, for the Library was now to be built of special small bricks, 'of a rather warmer shade than those used in the new buildings at Clare, and laid with wide joints'.[18] The building was also now raised from six to seven storeys in height. But Scott made one other significant change to his original design which might seem less happy. A perspective drawing of the Library survives with the tower rising above a projecting tetrastyle entrance portico. At some point this was replaced by a solid projecting pedimented bay with a large arched entrance below a row of four small windows. This feature may well seem unresolved, with the arch form discordant with the rectilinear ranges of tall brick piers which articulate the book-stack ranges on either side, while the flatness of this bay is not in harmony with the vertical treatment of both the wings and the tower above.

When the final design was ready, Scott together with Scholfield and the Library Syndicate were offered a visit to the United States by the Rockefeller Foundation to inspect American library buildings. They sailed on the Cunard Line's S.S. *Franconia* in September 1930. The buildings visited included the library of the New York Academy of Medicine by York and Sawyer; the 'useful library' by Charles Platt at Urbana, Illinois; the 'good library' by Albert Kahn at Ann Arbor; and the university libraries at Harvard and Yale. Scott was most impressed by the latter, originally designed by Bertram Goodhue and completed by James Gamble Rogers, for it was 'the last word in American libraries and from a practical working point of view has points of considerable interest. The Gothic book stack in this library is quite fine, but generally speaking, the building

Fig 7. Cambridge
University Library tower
in 1968; the concrete
lampposts were
removed soon
afterwards (author)

has had too much money spent on it and rather smells of money'. In fact, as Scott confessed to C. H. Reilly after the tour, 'I don't think that one learns very much from the point of view of planning, in view of the fact that one knew before going the planning of all the main libraries in America; it is interesting, however, to see their various gadgets and equipment, and of course they build regardless of expense'. And he subsequently told Scholfield that the visit to America had delayed work in Cambridge by at least six months.[19]

Work began on the foundations a year later, in September 1931, and the new University Library, filled with books, was opened by King George V in October 1934.[20] In his speech, he described the building as 'a power-house and a testing station of educational activities [… and] a workshop of new knowledge', rather overdoing the metaphors because of the celebrity of Scott's exactly contemporary work at Battersea Power Station.[21] The industrial comparison was often used in describing the new library, and Cambridge was clearly puzzled and disturbed by it, so different was it from the architecture of the old colleges and the Old Schools complex where the books had formerly been. Goodhart Rendel recalled how the building 'was arising in a curious form which was watched with mingled hope and anxiety' and a critic in the *Gownsman* noted that 'its main lines strongly resembled those of the Klingenburg power works in Berlin'.[22] For Olive Cook, writing after the Second World War,

> it looks like a cross between a public swimming bath and a warehouse; its huge proportions meaninglessly disturbed by the ungainly central tower. Within, it presents also a chilling contrast to the Library's old home. Gilded doors of angular design, not easily distinguishable from the entrance to an Odeon cinema, replace the finely carved pilasters and noble arches of the former building…[23]

As far as Nikolaus Pevsner was concerned, also writing in the 1950s, 'one is never sure whether the building was meant to be functional or for display; modern or traditional'.[24] But why cannot it have been both? With its open access shelving, rationally organised to make a powerful external expression of vertical window strips between giant pilasters, the Cambridge University Library works very well and is a pleasure to use. As was characteristic of the architect, the building is carefully and powerfully composed, but – as at Battersea Power Station – its monumental scale is humanised by the

Fig 8. Cambridge
University Library:
detail of south wing in
1984 (author)

careful placing of ornamental detail and the considered use of fine building materials.
The structure is faced with two-inch hand made bricks 'of a lightish Indian red' from
Great Missenden, Buckinghamshire, while the stone used for cornices and dressings is
Clipsham or Weldon. The roofs – and the top surfaces of the cornices – were laid with
special small Lombardic tiles. The same, rather exotic treatment and dramatic vertical
emphasis was given to the tower, 157 feet high, where, at a high level, gallery-like
openings are flanked by figures at the four corners representing the Four Winds of
Heaven carved by E. Carter Preston, the sculptor used by Scott at Liverpool.

Inside what one historian has appropriately described as an 'Assyrian palace'
the generous circulation spaces were given dados of blue and brown Hornton Wood
stone below the plain plastered walls.[25] The Entrance Hall, Catalogue Room and
Reading Room are placed on a central axis and everywhere 'simplicity is the keynote'.[26]
Colour and pattern was restricted to the noble Reading Room with its flat timber ceiling
above the rows of generous high-level arched windows, where the influence of modern
Swedish architecture is evident. Between these rooms are openwork doors of bronze
ornamented in a manner which is genuinely Art Deco; that is, the decorative manner
derived from the 1925 Paris Expo as reinterpreted by Scott. Although flawed as an overall
design when compared with the faultless assurance of Scott's churches, Cambridge
University Library is nevertheless one of Britain's most successful and representative
large institutional buildings of the inter-war decades.

Following the building of Clare's Memorial Court to so much acclaim, it was almost
inevitable that Scott would be approached by other colleges. In 1924, he was one of a
limited number of architects asked by King's College to submit designs for a new range
of buildings containing both residential accommodation and a new library. The college
had decided to demolish the existing 1820s Gothic library and Provost's Lodge by
William Wilkins and replace them with new buildings facing the Back Lawn running
from the Gibbs Building right to the River Cam. Scott proposed a long, tripartite
symmetrical range, with a wide central library raised up on Doric colonnades. This idea
– derived from the Wren Library at Trinity – was to allow access to a new Provost's

garden and Lodge behind. Low squat towers and lower wings were to frame the library range, that to the west completing the missing north range of Bodley's Court built in the early 1890s to the design of Scott's erstwhile partner at Liverpool Cathedral, G. F. Bodley. The style adopted was not that of Memorial Court but a suave Tudor-Gothic in rubble stone and ashlar, with a subtle, rather Spanish flourish in the profile of the parapets on the two towers. The whole design is strongly reminiscent of the school buildings by Leonard Stokes at Downside Abbey where Scott was then working and where the two squat towers would reappear when he extended them a few years later. The Fellows of King's College were evidently unimpressed, however, as they opted for a classical design by the Liverpool architects Lionel Budden and Herbert Rowse, although this was not built either.[27]

In the event, Scott's only other executed work in Cambridge were the two buildings faced in pale brown brick with wide flush mortar joints which stand at either end of the North Court at Trinity Hall. Built in 1934–36, they were designed in a simplified, well-mannered Tudor style, although a certain drama is provided by the external staircase rising to the first floor above the kitchen in the western wing; to quote Pevsner, these buildings are 'simple and conventional but by no means dull'.[28] They show how Scott could be discreet and self-effacing when required, as he had earlier demonstrated in the first buildings he was responsible for at the University of Oxford: an extension for Magdalen College.

The most recent addition to the architecture of this college was the long range of St Swithun's Buildings facing the High Street, which had a return wing at the far end running north. Built in 1880–4, they were designed in a rich late-Gothic style by Bodley and Garner in close sympathy with Magdalen's medieval buildings. This was one of the very few modern Gothic works admired by William Morris (*not* the Oxford motor manufacturer) and Goodhart-Rendel considered that it had 'extraordinary merit'.[29] In 1928–30 Scott extended Garner's northern wing further to the north, then turned it towards Longwall Street, thus creating Longwall Quad (enclosed at the other end by the old schoolroom for Magdalen College School which Scott converted into a library).[30] And he did this with deferential subtlety, retaining the general style and massing of the earlier building and continuing its rhythm of gables and first-floor oriels, but simplifying the detail. Instead of Garner's elaborate treatment, Scott relied more on plain stone walls – more Cotswold than Oxford (although he must surely have looked at his father's self-effacing addition to St John's College of 1880–2) – but gave the new gateway through to the new quad different Gothic surrounds in the personal style he was evolving at Liverpool Cathedral.

This must have been a slightly poignant commission for Scott as he had known both G. F. Bodley and Thomas Garner and had owed his opportunity at Liverpool to the

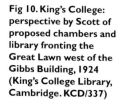

Fig 10. King's College: perspective by Scott of proposed chambers and library fronting the Great Lawn west of the Gibbs Building, 1924 (King's College Library, Cambridge. KCD/337)

Fig 11. Trinity Hall, Cambridge: the east end of North Court in 2012 (author)

former, although relations had become strained after they were made joint architects for the cathedral.[31] But Scott's continuation of their work was rather different internally as standards of accommodation had improved since the 1880s. After commenting that his treatment of the gateway 'shows that he is handling Gothic with his habitual taste and originality', the *Architect and Building News* noted that 'few dons alive now would venture to affirm that undergraduates do not require baths … there are bathrooms, w. c.'s, both luxuries beyond the pre-war dreams of even a fellow'.[32]

Scott adopted a very different style, or styles, for his next Oxford commission. In 1929 he was invited by Lynda Grier, Principal of Lady Margaret Hall, to design a chapel and other buildings for Oxford's oldest college for women. Scott was chosen because of his success with designing the new home of Whitelands College, the teacher training college for women which was then moving from central London to Putney. The Principal, Winifred Mercier, was a friend of Miss Grier, and she 'has told me much of your plans for Whitelands and all she has said has increased my eagerness to secure your assistance for Lady Margaret Hall'.[33] There was a problem with the commission, however, in that the college already had an architect in the shape of the redoubtable Sir Reginald Blomfield, who had recently prepared a scheme for a large extension.

With his usual courtesy and tact, Scott first approached Sir Reginald as 'I am of course unwilling to poach on anyone else's preserves'. The response of his occasional golfing companion was typically robust:

> My Dear Scott, I return Miss Grier's letter. The proper answer is to tell her and her Council to go to Hell – where no doubt in due course they will go. I don't mind about the job as I have other things to do, but I resent exceedingly the Council's superseding me after I have done all their other work under difficult conditions for the last 35 years… . However, this is no affair of yours, and as far as I am concerned you can go ahead, but don't alter my Library, you will spoil it if you do.

Scott nevertheless wrote back to the Principal asking the college to reconsider because 'a change of architects at the present stage would be a mistake, as the result would almost

Fig 12. Magdalen College, Oxford: extension to St Swithun's Buildings in 2000 (author)

Fig 13. Magdalen College, Oxford: entrance arch to Longwall Quad in 2013 (David Lewis)

inevitably be a break in the continuity of the general treatment of the work'. But the
Council of LMH had made up its mind; despite 'a due sense of gratitude to Sir Reginald
Blomfield for some very beautiful work', he was now too old, they felt, to see future
additions through to completion, and Grier emphasised 'how anxious we are to secure
you, rather than any other architect' in his place.[34]

Scott proposed a large detached block to the north of the existing buildings to
contain a new dining hall, offices, tutors' and undergraduate rooms. Blomfield's ranges
had begun in his Wrennaissance manner but the later wings were, he claimed, in a
'simple and modest Georgian'.[35] Scott continued the Georgian theme, in a less
stridently red brick, in what was to be called the Deneke Building, but gave the long
symmetrical elevation facing the gardens a simpler and more modernistic character,
similar to the style of Whitelands College, with horizontally-proportioned windows.
To the east and west, the terminating pavilions were given more conventional
Georgian elevations with a somewhat redundant pediment. The symmetry of the west
elevation was continued by single-storey corridors, one connecting it with Blomfield's
Toynbee Building of 1926, the other with the new chapel, a separate building which
Scott designed in a different style and which is by far the most impressive of his
additions to the college.

The Principal found it 'a surprise to see the Chapel put so far away from your other
proposed buildings, as we had rather expected it to be a centre-piece to them'.[36] As at
Whitelands, the chapel is detached and designed in the simplified Byzantine or Early
Christian style fashionable for church architecture at this time. It was this round-arched
manner that Scott had recently used for his church at Ashford, Middlesex, but here, as in
Putney, the plan was centralised. Externally, above the walls of special thin pale reddish-
brown 'multicoloured bricks', rises a central twelve-sided low dome, covered, like the
flanking roofs, in special small Lombardic tiles. Inside, the walls were of plain plaster
above a dado of Hornton Wood stone, while the oak of the stalls and the organ case was
limed. The attenuated baldacchino in the eastern apse, reminiscent of that in the church
in Bath which Scott had designed in the Early Christian style a few years earlier, was
delicately gilded. As Pevsner observed, the thin, elegant detailing of the fittings 'is in that
decorative fashion which came over from Östberg and the Paris Exhibition of 1925'.[37]

This, together with the simplified Byzantine style, the muted colouring and the generally
restrained treatment, make this exquisite chapel both a quintessential building of its time
and one of Scott's finest.

The chapel was consecrated (before the baldacchino with its painting by Burne-
Jones had been installed) at the beginning of 1933 by the aged Bishop Talbot, the leader
of those who had founded Lady Margaret Hall back in 1878. Although there were at first
problems with the acoustics (solved, on the advice of Hope Bagenal, by applying an
asbestos spray to the interior of the dome), the Principal was delighted with the building:
'Our gratitude to you is immense. The Chapel seems to me a thing of most satisfying
beauty. ... It is a joy to us to have a Chapel which draws visitors & evokes admiration
from all quarters'.[38] The *Architect and Building News* commented that, 'On viewing
another church by Sir Giles Gilbert Scott, as dissimilar from its predecessor as they are
from each other, one is led to wonder if there is any limit to his versatility. No two of his
churches are alike in form, yet each seems a completely logical, and even inspired,
fulfilment of the conditions of its problems, whether these conditions be of
accommodation, character or sites'.[39]

The admiration for Scott's work at LMH led him to be commissioned to design
buildings for another institution of education for women: the Society for Home Students.
Here, rather than brick, Scott used the squared random coursed rubble stone made
fashionable in Oxford by Sir Herbert Baker's Rhodes House and created an entirely
different style by having rounded corners, exotic sculptural detail and horizontal
proportions.[40] This was the manner discussed earlier which J. M. Richards described
in 1952 as 'whimsical-eclectic'. Later, Pevsner was less dismissive and rightly observed
that 'Scott was not a historicist, and he liked decorative details of a curly Baroque kind'.[41]
In fact, Scott's incomplete work at what became St Anne's College was an essay in the
modernistic style he was evolving at the same time for the New Bodleian Library.
This, Scott's largest and most prominent work in Oxford, was also his most
controversial and arguably the least successful, but it was a very difficult commission and
one which it is difficult to believe could have been handled better by any other architect
of his generation.

Oxford in the 1920s faced the same problem as Cambridge. In 1925, the Librarian at the Bodleian warned that, despite books being crammed into every available nearby basement, the library would run out of space in a decade. Financial assistance from the Rockefeller Foundation was secured the following year but it was not until 1934, when the threatened crisis was imminent, that Scott was appointed to design a new library building. This, however, was not to be an entirely new library on a new site but an extension to the existing Bodleian on the opposite side of Broad Street from Hawksmoor's Clarendon Building (which required the demolition of a great swathe of old and rather charming buildings – something that would not have been permitted later in the century).[42] And whereas at Cambridge the problem was to design a building to contain open access bookshelves, at Oxford what was required was a closed-access book store similar to those in several American university libraries, connected with the older Bodleian buildings by a tunnel. This store had to house five million books which, the University rather optimistically concluded, would solve the problem of space for two centuries.

'The appointment of Sir Giles Scott as the architect of this building, fresh from his completion of the library at Cambridge', reported the *Architect and Building News*, 'was one of the sensations of our unemotional architectural affairs in England'.[43] But, in truth, Scott had little scope to exercise his architectural skills for his task was, essentially, to give external architectural treatment to a large, half-buried rectangular steel book stack which could not rise higher than its three storey neighbours and which was to be designed and made by the Roneo company. This central stack was to be surrounded by corridors, with offices beyond, so there was no need for and no possibility of the grand axial route from entrance to reading room as at Cambridge. There was to be a reading room at the New Bodleian, but this was on an upper floor on the far, north side, and it was to be subsidiary to the principal reading rooms in the old Bodleian and, besides, was to be made convertible into an additional two-storey book stack if required.

Because of the constraints of the site, to achieve the maximum area for the book stack Scott could not align his building with the rectilinear geometry of the old library buildings, but a relationship was created by having a ceremonial entrance at the eastern

corner of the asymmetrical Broad Street front which terminated the long vista through
the Bodleian and the Clarendon Building. The main entrance to the New Bodleian was
in the centre of the eastern, Parks Road elevation, which was made symmetrical.
This entrance was given little emphasis as it gave access only to the encircling corridor.
Greater emphasis was given to the ceremonial entrance in Broad Street – an elaborate
neo-Baroque composition showing a 'Spanish influence' which incorporates a bust of
Sir Thomas Bodley – although, in the event, this door was never to be used.[44] The most
puzzling aspect of the design is the treatment of this long elevation. Because it runs
at an angle to the line of Broad Street, Scott brought a wing forward at the western
end (containing the staff canteen) but he rendered the intervening open space a dead,
unusable area by having a gratuitous raised plinth here which follows the irregular
curved old street line where a row of houses formerly stood.

Scott's main concern was with the style of architectural treatment of his large
interloper. Typically, he sought a compromise between tradition and modernity –
one guided by his conviction that a true modern style in architecture would come by
gradual evolution.

> There are those who would like to see the external walls of concrete, glass and
> steel, as representing the latest fashion in constructional expression; there are
> others who would consider this as dreadful as a jazz band in Westminster
> Abbey; again, there are those who would like to see a Tudor or Renaissance
> building, similar to the old buildings around the site. To my mind, the solution
> does not lie in any of these directions. I favour a modern building that does pay
> some respect to the traditions that produced the old buildings round about.
> Stone-faced walls seemed essential for this purpose. The general massing and
> the fenestration, however, might well be modern in character, the result being
> an entirely plain block, with a modern pattern of window openings.

Fig 19. New Bodleian
Library: ceremonial
entrance in 2010
(author)

Some might be content to leave it at this; personally I am not, for, apart from it
being out of harmony with its surroundings, I am not one of those who like to
think that buildings are machines and that ornament upon them should be
abandoned because ornament upon machinery is ridiculous. ... In this
Bodleian building I feel the right line of approach is to use traditional forms,
but only to use them where they help to emphasise the arrangement of
structural features, such as window openings. ... Ornament has, in fact, only
been used where it serves a definite aesthetic purpose, and not applied
indiscriminately merely to enrich the building.[45]

Hence the horizontal windows on the upper, recessed storey being separated by
ornamental flat piers rising above the lintel line, similar in character to those Scott
designed for Battersea Power Station. Ornamental cartouches, as much Baroque as
Deco, are placed above the ground floor piers. This abstracted classical order, whose
ashlar contrasts with the Bladon rubble stone, is perhaps the most impressive feature as
it articulates and unites the two elevations, and is also maintained in the treatment of the
separate ceremonial entrance. Other features, however, like the curved corners and
the curved or grooved treatment to the window jambs, seem arbitrarily modernistic.
The architectural treatment adopted may well seem more impressive when viewed up
close than as an overall composition and, as always with Scott, great attention was paid
to detail, to materials and to building craftsmanship.

The New Bodleian, unlike Scott's Cambridge Library, is not a building that has
inspired much affection. When the design was published, the *Architect and Building News*
found it 'disturbing to find projections and setbacks introduced which bear not the
slightest relation to the internal form or even to temporary partitions' (a radical
difference from Cambridge, where the internal arrangements governed the external

treatment). Considered generally, the building is representative of the characteristically English school which contrives to make the best of both worlds, functional and neo-classical.[46] And this has been the gist of all subsequent criticism, even though a compromise was precisely what Scott was aiming for.

Christopher Hobhouse, writing just before the Second World War, thought that 'in this work he has done himself something less than justice. He has banished proportion along with symmetry. The body of the building is huge and formless: its ground floor is ornamented like a draper's shop with a veneer of commercial classical stonework'.[47] Pevsner, needless to say, objected that it is 'Neither one thing nor the other, neither in an Oxford tradition nor modern for its date'. More recently, Geoffrey Tyack has written that 'the detailing – an odd mixture of classical and Art Deco motifs – does little to relieve the inert, shapeless mass of the wall surfaces, and the decision to use small blocks of rubble stone for so massive a building was visually unfortunate. …The New Bodleian exposes the limitations of the belief that large buildings of modern materials can be easily humanised by dressing them up in period details…'[48] although that is what Scott triumphantly succeeded in doing elsewhere. Perhaps, within the intimidating constraints imposed by the brief and by the character of Oxford, he tried too hard.

Work began on the New Bodleian in 1936 and the building was completed in 1940, after the outbreak of the Second World War. Only in 1946 was it formally opened by King George VI. On that occasion, when the King tried to put a ceremonial key into the lock of the ceremonial entrance door, it broke, allowing him to quip 'Britain Can Break It!' – a reference to the 'Britain Can Make It' exhibition mounted at the Victoria and Albert Museum that same year. Sixty years later, Oxford University found the problem of book storage as pressing as ever – the original planned life of the building having proved over optimistic (Scott himself had presciently wondered whether, two centuries hence, 'libraries as we know them, will by then have ceased to exist, and a central television station will wireless visions of books to readers' homes and they will turn the pages by pressing a button!').[49] In addition to finding storage for the Bodleian outside the city, Oxford University has, since 2011, embarked on altering and refurbishing the New Bodleian as a special collections library.[50] All of which surely confirms the wisdom of Cambridge's decision back in the 1920s to build a monumental new university library, capable of expansion, outside the city centre, thus allowing Giles Gilbert Scott to create one of the most successful, representative and imaginative institutional buildings of its time.

Acknowledgements: I am grateful for help from Otto Saumarez Smith, David Lewis and Elain Harwood, as well as to Richard Gilbert Scott over many years

1. J. M. Richards, 'Recent Building in Oxford and Cambridge', *Architectural Review*, vol.112, no.668, August 1952, p.77.

2. Sir Giles Gilbert Scott, 'Inaugural Address', *RIBA Journal*, vol.41, no.1, 11 November 1933, p.9.

3. H. C. Hughes, 'Recent Building in Cambridge' *Builder*, vol.144, 16 June 1933, p.958.

4. The central axial avenue in the old college from the entrance to the bridge across the Cam could not be continued directly through the memorial arch as King's College had declined to sell land to the south of the new building.

5. Scott to the Editor of the *Building News*, 16 April 1923, RIBA Drawings and Archives Collections.

6. That it was 'quiet and dignified and the work of a gentleman'; *Architect and Building News*, vol.136, 6 October 1933, p.9.

7. H. S. Goodhart-Rendel, *English Architecture since the Regency*, London, Constable, 1953, p.248; Nikolaus Pevsner, *The Buildings of England: Cambridgeshire*, Harmondsworth, Penguin, 1954, p.50.

8. Scott to W. J. Harrison, 24 June 1927, RIBA Drawings and Archives Collections.

9. This, the Forbes-Mellon Library designed by Philip Dowson, could have been built on the site of the Fellows' car park to the north, but this dubious amenity the dons were not prepared to sacrifice.

10. Quoted in Christopher Brooke, 'The University Library and its buildings' in Peter Fox, ed., *Cambridge University Library: The Great Collections*, Cambridge University Press, 1998, p.219. The architect of the sketch plans was possibly Arnold Mitchell, who had been responsible for the Agricultural Building in Cambridge (1910), or possibly the Cambridge architect W. C. Marshall, who had been responsible for the sensitive alterations made to the old University Library by C. R. Cockerell in 1904.

11. The device of leaving square piers between tall vertical windows behind which several floors run, so creating a classical composition for a multi-storey building, may be traced back in Britain via American libraries and commercial buildings to Burnet's Kodak building in Kingsway of 1911.

12. Scott draft for A. F. Scholfield, Librarian, n.d. (1924), RIBA Drawings and Archives Collections.

13. Scott to Scholfield 22 October 1924, ibid. King's Garden Hostel is by Geddes Hyslop from 1947–50.

14. Brooke, op. cit., p.223.

15. Scholfield to Scott 27 April 1927, quoted ibid., p.224.

16. Goodhart-Rendel, op. cit., p.252.

17. Scott to Scholfield, 3 December 1928, RIBA Drawings and Archives Collections.

18. Description by Scott in the *Cambridge University Reporter*, 14 May 1929, p.1040.

19. Scott to C. H. Reilly 14 November 1930; Scott to Scholfield 30 December 1930, RIBA Drawings and Archives Collections.

20. To Scott's distress, the contractor made the irreversible mistake of laying the foundations six feet off-centre, but he cleverly obscured this asymmetry in relation to Memorial Court by the careful design of the open metal gates and railings placed between screen walls marking its western boundary.

21. *The Times*, no.46892, 23 October 1934, p.9.

22. Quoted in T. E. B. Howarth, *Cambridge Between Two Wars*, London, Collins, 1978, p.168; Goodhart-Rendel, op. cit., p.248.

23. Olive Cook, *Cambridgeshire: Aspects of a County*, London, Blackie, 1953, p.39. The library had previously been housed in the superb building by Cockerell which is now the library of Gonville and Caius College.

24. Pevsner, op. cit., p.166.

25. Brooke, op. cit., p.225.

26. Scott's description in *Cambridge University Library 1400–1934 with a description of the New Building opened by His Majesty the King 22 October 1934…*, Cambridge, 1934, p.9.

27. Budden and Rowse envisaged three separate classical buildings in a row, the central one housing the library. In 1927, after the whole scheme was abandoned and the buildings by Wilkins spared, Kennedy and Nightingale – who had also been invited to submit a design – were asked to extend the library into the interior of the old Provost's Lodge and build a new lodge (classical, in red brick) behind in Webb's Court and, for access, replacing the ground floor of Wilkins's library with an open colonnade – an idea surely derived from Scott's unexecuted design. Kennedy and Nightingale also added the missing wing of Bodley's Court vaguely in the Bodley Tudor manner in 1927. For Scott's, and Stokes's, work at Downside, see Dom Aidan Bellenger, *Downside Abbey: An Architectural History* (London, Merrell, 2011).

28. Pevsner, op. cit., p.153.

29. Goodhart-Rendel, op. cit., p.178.

30. The old school hall was by J. C. Buckler, 1849–51; in 1930–31 Scott inserted a floor and designed bookshelves &c. but permission to remove all of this was granted in 2012.

31. Scott was already working on a continuation of Garner's choir at Downside Abbey and, back in 1905, had been asked to rebuild his chapel at a convent in Harrow following structural problems.

32. *Architect and Building News*, vol.124, 31 October, 1930, p.589.

33. Grier to Scott, 5 March 1929. Later, on 13 January 1930, Grier wrote that 'We were all immensely impressed by Whitelands'; RIBA Drawings and Archives Collections.

34. Blomfield to Scott, 8 March 1929; Scott to Grier, 11 March 1929; Grier to Scott 12 March 1929. Blomfield (1856–1942) was then aged 72; in a subsequent letter to Scott he wrote that 'I wish all our colleagues had such a sound sense of fair and honourable dealing.

35. Richard A. Fellows, *Sir Reginald Blomfield: An Edwardian Architect*, London, Zwemmer, 1985, p.87.

36. Grier to Scott, 8 October 1929, RIBA Drawings and Archives.

37. Jennifer Sherwood and Nikolaus Pevsner, Buildings of England: *Oxfordshire*, Harmondsworth, Penguin, 1974, p.232.

38. Grier to Scott, 19 January and 22 February 1933, RIBA Drawings and Archives Collections.

39. *Architect and Building News*, vol.133, 27 January 1933, p.129.

40. The combination of squared rubble stone walls with ashlar dressings was possibly pioneered by Leonard Stokes in his buildings for Emmanuel College, Cambridge, of 1909–14.

41. Sherwood and Pevsner, op. cit., p.237; Richards, op. cit., p.77.

42. The buildings demolished were Nos.35–47 Broad Street and Nos.2–4 Park Road plus two theological colleges in Park Road: St Stephen's House and Ripon Hall.

43. *Architect and Building News*, vol.146, 15 May 1936, p.179.

44. Richard Gilbert Scott, *Giles Gilbert Scott: His Son's View*, London, Lyndhurst Road Publications, 2011, p.16.

45. Sir Giles Gilbert Scott, 'The New Bodleian Building' *Oxford*, vol.3, Special Number, February 1937, pp.29–30.

46. *Architect and Building News*, vol.146, 15 May 1936, p.182.

47. Christopher Hobhouse, *Oxford*, London, Batsford, 1939, p.109.

48. Geoffrey Tyack, *Oxford: An Architectural Guide*, Oxford University Press, 1998, p.292.

49. Scott, 1937, *Oxford*, op. cit., pp.28–29.

50. After abandoning an irresponsible project to build a book store on a flood plain, Oxford has decided to store its books as far away as Swindon. The work to the New Bodleian, which involves opening out the ground floor colonnade, removing the raised plinth and restoring the reading room, is being carried out by Wilkinson Eyre architects.

2
Lutyens's Designs for Campion Hall, Oxford

David Frazer Lewis

Fig 1. The Chapel, facing east towards the High Altar (John East, 2012)

Roman Catholics were a recent presence at Oxford University in the first part of the twentieth century as the hierarchy had only lifted the ban on their attendance in 1896. Their number at first remained small, with only about sixty Roman Catholic students enrolled in 1908, compared with over five hundred non-conformist undergraduates.[1] Several Catholic institutions were quickly created, however, both to attend to the pastoral needs of students and to provide a place for those in monastic orders to study and teach. The Jesuits were the first order to establish a base amongst the colleges, with a modest institution known as Pope's Hall founded in 1896 in buildings belonging to St John's College immediately to the north of the Lamb and Flag public house on St Giles.[2] The primary pastoral care of Roman Catholic undergraduates was placed in the hands of a Roman Catholic chaplaincy the same year. In 1897, the Dominicans founded Blackfriars across the street from Pope's Hall. Oxford was still a staunchly Anglican university, and the establishment could be grudging in its acceptance of the new Roman Catholic presence, whose organisations consequently tended to keep a low profile.[3]

The first exception to this tendency came in the late 1920s, when a charismatic and socially well-connected Jesuit, Father Martin D'Arcy, began actively to seek converts within the University. This change came about not from any particular strengthening of the Catholic position in Oxford, but from the force of D'Arcy's personality. His strategy was to befriend potential converts and introduce them to a circle of engaging Catholic literati such as Evelyn Waugh and Eric Gill. D'Arcy particularly targeted men of genius and social influence, stating in an unpublished memoir that he had hoped to make Campion Hall into a place for 'the elite'.[4] These aggressive attempts to convert the leading lights of Oxford naturally rankled some within the university, including Hugh Trevor-Roper – who in his undergraduate days had been cultivated by D'Arcy and later wrote that he was, 'a pure Jesuit charlatan – who (so long as they are rich or fashionable) converts them all'.[5]

Fr D'Arcy was himself a graduate of Pope's Hall, which was renamed Campion Hall in 1918 after the Oxford scholar and Jesuit martyr Edmund Campion.[6] He had returned to Oxford in 1927 to teach and aimed to transform the institution by making Catholicism glamorous and intellectual: the inter-war period was to be the era of cocktails at Campion Hall. As part of his strategy for raising the Roman Catholic profile, D'Arcy was ready to build a grand permanent home for the Jesuits, which was to become unique in Oxford both for its program and its architect.

The Vatican had been urging Campion Hall to build a permanent home since at least 1921.[7] Around 1930, the then master, Father Ernest Vignaux, commissioned the Birmingham architect E. Bower Norris to make provisional plans for a new building on the site of their premises on St Giles, which he hoped to purchase from St John's College along with the Lamb and Flag public house.[8] Norris designed an L-shaped block in an

Fig 2. The main entrance on Brewer Street (Elain Harwood)

unremarkable collegiate Gothic style, its detailing surprisingly historicist but not of a quality comparable to Temple Moore's Anglo-Catholic Pusey House across the street.[9] The section drawing was inhabited by scale figures in vaguely medieval costume expounding canon law from podiums and kneeling in the shadowy chapel. Although Vignaux liked Norris, most of the other Jesuits took an instant dislike to him and were almost unanimously 'horrified by the banality of the plan'.[10] Norris produced a revised set of drawings, simplifying the detailing with some of the carved ornament removed, and a different artist rendered the perspectives in a cleaner, more streamlined style.[11] These were now peopled by scale figures in modern dress, giving the initial impression of a much-altered design although substantive changes were minimal. Norris's tall, narrow building, with five storeys of stacked accommodation, crowded the refectory, chapel, common room, and library into the St Giles frontage, with a slender spine of bedrooms extending from the back alongside a thin strip of garden. The fathers worried that such a plan would be highly inconvenient; the library, for instance, was three storeys above ground and there was only one cramped water closet per floor.

It was not clear whether Campion Hall could secure the land for Norris's building from St John's, and when a site near Holywell Mill became available for purchase from Merton College the Jesuit fathers, urged by their trustees in London, seized the opportunity to contact a new architect. Fr D'Arcy was eager to engage a fashionable architect more in keeping with his ambitious plans. To this end the Campion fathers hired Sir Giles Gilbert Scott, well known for his Catholic churches, to survey the site with an eye to selecting him to design a building.[12] However, the deal with Merton College fell through and references to Scott fade from the archives. The Bodleian was looking for a place to build its new extension (also by Scott, and a controversial design), while land in central Oxford was at even more of a premium than usual. Campion Hall returned to Norris's designs for St Giles.

However, it was by now 1933, and Campion had a new master in Fr D'Arcy himself. Norris's sole champion was gone, and the fathers were determined to have a more suitable design for their new home. D'Arcy showed the plans to the manager of Claridge's, who confirmed his suspicions that the provision and placement of lavatories was deficient.[13] It is not clear why D'Arcy did not return to Scott at this point. He was a Roman Catholic, with a long history of projects for the church, and he had experience of building for both Cambridge and Oxford, where his projects included the New Bodleian

Library and the chapel of Lady Margaret Hall. Perhaps D'Arcy wanted an architect whose building would not resemble any other in Oxford, or perhaps he felt Scott was too entwined with Oxford's Anglican establishment. Whatever the reason, Scott must not have been seriously considered because D'Arcy makes no mention of him in any of his memoirs.

Instead he turned to his network of social connections, and asked the opinion of his friend Lady Horner. She suggested that he show Norris's plans to Edwin Lutyens, who agreed they were no good. At D'Arcy's urging, Lutyens agreed to meet with Norris to offer suggestions for their improvement, but Norris refused, saying that his design was perfectly acceptable and that he resented the meddling of other architects. Lutyens meanwhile came up to Oxford to give his opinion on other potential sites for the building. Having seen the options, he urged D'Arcy to secure that on Brewer Street, a lane across St Aldates from Christ Church located to the south of Pembroke College Chapel. The site was conveniently close to the Catholic Chaplaincy on St Aldates, and would place Campion near the heart of the town and university.

At the end of the meeting, D'Arcy asked Lutyens if he could suggest a young architect to design new buildings on Brewer Street. 'Why don't you ask me?' Lutyens replied. 'Because you are far too expensive', responded D'Arcy.[14] Lutyens, sensing that this might be his only opportunity to design a complete collegiate institution, said that he would only charge minimal fees and promised to keep the costs in check.

Over the course of his career Lutyens had been consulted about a number of grand academic projects. He created designs for the University of London's Senate House and the Memorial Court at Clare College, Cambridge, but in both cases the designs were thought to be too expensive and another architect was appointed. His only executed building at Cambridge was a single range of student rooms for Magdalene College, a long brick 'Wrennaisance' block overlooking the Cam. Campion Hall, by contrast, was to be the university base of the Jesuit Order in England; although technically a Permanent Private Hall of the University, it was essentially a new college on the traditional Oxford model, complete with refectory, library, student accommodation, and chapel. The project was a prestigious and exciting one, even by Lutyens's standards.

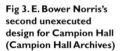

Fig 3. E. Bower Norris's second unexecuted design for Campion Hall (Campion Hall Archives)

Lutyens was exactly what D'Arcy was looking for. He returned to Campion Hall and convinced the Jesuits to accept the offer. The architect was not only highly skilled artistically, but undoubtedly more practical than Norris, and thus the famously extravagant Lutyens was hired for perhaps the only time in his career because he was 'the more practical architect'.

D'Arcy later wrote that he had chosen Lutyens for two reasons: firstly because of his role as designer of Liverpool's Metropolitan Cathedral, the greatest British Catholic project of the age; and secondly because he was a well-reputed genius, 'regarded as the greatest architect of the British Empire'.[15] He was just the sort of man that D'Arcy liked to cultivate. Though referred to only obliquely in his memoirs, D'Arcy aimed to win converts by portraying Catholicism as both excitingly novel and traditionally English. Lutyens fitted the bill perfectly – his architecture was novel yet traditional, clever, and even fashionable. Like D'Arcy himself, the design would at once respect the Oxford context and stand out from it, appealing to the sort of intellectuals that he invited to Campion.

The L-shaped block that Lutyens designed was intended as the first two sides of a complete quadrangle. D'Arcy dreamed of a Jesuit institute at Oxford modelled on the Institute for Advanced Studies at Princeton, where Jesuit scholars from around the world could take advantage of Oxford's bounteous academic resources. The architecturally defining features of Campion Hall were to be built in a second phase designed by Lutyens in 1942 after the first range was complete: a dining hall with arched windows and a Wren-like lantern, and a larger chapel with an octagonal lantern tower lighting the crossing.[16] Above basement level only five small windows adorned with carved stone crosses and a grand Delhi-order doorcase would interrupt the chapel's vast expanses of rubble-stone walling.

Until money could be raised for the expansion, however, the L-shaped building, which began construction in 1935 and was completed in 1936, would have to operate as a complete ensemble. A library, refectory, parlours and common room were fitted on to the ground floor overlooking an inner courtyard. The more public spaces – the parlours and dining room – were placed closer to the entry vestibule. A chapel was placed on the Brewer Street façade at the first storey level. Bedrooms were placed on the first and second storeys along a spinal corridor more liberally provided with lavatories and private basins than Norris's had been. Lutyens had originally hoped to design the rooms around staircases on the traditional Oxbridge model, but the Jesuits preferred corridors – a plan that since Butterfield's Keble College of 1868 had been considered more convenient for priests (and incidentally, a design that was much admired by Fr D'Arcy's favourite poet, Gerard Manley Hopkins).[17] An excessive number of staircases, which would have posed a substantial obstacle to elderly fathers, apparently had been one of the primary causes of objection to Norris's plans.

It is difficult to categorise the building in terms of architectural style. Lutyens, as usual, used his particular brand of ahistorical classicism while responding to the Gothic of the surrounding university in a way that gave Campion Hall a charming asymmetry and assertive massing. The day after the official opening by the Duke of Alba, *Country Life* rhapsodised that the new hall both respected tradition and showed great originality. Echoing the architectural concerns of the era, the article celebrated Lutyens's success at creating a structure 'free from irritating stylistic reminiscences ... at once a genuine expression of its architect's temperament and a practical solution to the problem presented'.[18] The author declared that Lutyens's architecture exhibited 'architectural good manners' and fused formal concerns with a functional plan. Not surprisingly, however, strict modernists criticised this approach. Nikolaus Pevsner later gave the hall one of the backhanded compliments he saved for Lutyens, writing that the architect had managed 'in terms of his, internationally speaking, retrograde style to make something interesting out of an unpromising frontage'.[19]

Fig 4. The garden façade (Elain Harwood, 2003)

That Lutyens managed to make an unpromising frontage successful is certainly true. It is all the more impressive considering that the narrowness of the lane means that the Brewer Street façade can never be viewed in its totality, but only at close range and at a sharp angle. The main feature announcing the hall to the street, therefore, is an arched doorway recessed deeply behind archivolts. The date of completion, the name Campion Hall and a Lutyens-designed crest are carved into the smooth ashlar surrounding the door. The whole ensemble is at once simple and strikingly sculptural, giving the building a presence on the street it would otherwise lack.

The care and cleverness of Lutyens's details are unmatched in inter-war Oxbridge. He abstracts the classical language and inverts expectations – where mouldings would normally protrude, they are instead recessed; where a full entablature would normally crown a column, there is only an architrave and cornice. In Oxford, the only buildings that approached Lutyens's inventiveness with classical detail were those by T. H. Hughes, designer of the 1932 Ashmolean Extension and Regent's Park College of 1938. Even so, his 'telescoped' cornices and careful alignment of recessed mouldings were devices pioneered by Lutyens. The best-known classical building of the period, Herbert Baker's Rhodes House, was conventional in its detailing; Baker's concern lay not with abstracting the classical language but with exploring narrative symbolism.

Lutyens nevertheless owed a debt to Baker. For the exterior walls of Campion Hall he chose a squared Bladon rubble stone trimmed with Clipsham ashlar, which had been first used at Rhodes House in 1926 and whose rough texture did not corrode as easily as Oxford's traditional but easily pockmarked and blackened Headington ashlar.[20] Bladon rubble stone became the material of choice for inter-war Oxford, appearing in Hubert Worthington's collegiate and university buildings as well as Sir Giles Scott's Bodleian Extension. Considering Lutyens's enmity with Baker at the time, it is a little surprising that he made this nod to his old friend and collaborator.

Part of the façade of Campion Hall, however, was rendered in stucco. That was because Micklem Hall, a seventeenth-century house on the site, was incorporated into

the new design. The building had been a boarding house for Christ Church and Fr D'Arcy believed that Edward VII may have lived there during his university days, another link with the highly romanticised view of British history that he cherished.[21] The Oxford Preservation Trust was keen that the building's significant features be altered as little as possible, and thus the chimney and Doric doorcase were left undisturbed, although Lutyens refaced half of the Brewer Street façade with rubble stone and capped it with a tile-hung gable to incorporate it into his larger composition. A panelled room became Campion Hall's new Senior Common Room, but much of the remaining interior was modified to accommodate the needs of its new owners.

The interiors of the new building exhibited typical Lutyens wit. A theme of bells – a reference to those that rule the hours of a canonical Jesuit day – appeared in decoration throughout the structure. Carved bells were used as finials on the newel posts of the staircases and provided an excuse to use the Delhi Order, which featured bells in the corners of its capitals. The refectory had a large plaster rose in the centre of the ceiling because Jesuits eat in silence and thus *sub rosa*. Somewhat ironically, the hall ultimately was not provided with a large bell turret as planned, because Christ Church feared that the noise would disturb the neighbouring Choir School. Instead small electric bells were fitted into each of the corridors.

Much of the furniture was custom-made, from ivory-knobbed reading desks in the library to special cabinets in the refectory that Lutyens designed to hold the Jesuits' napkins. The garden lobby was furnished with Lutyens's cobweb-back chairs, the andirons were all custom-designed, and a set of split library steps that resembled a Constructivist sculpture was fabricated so that the Jesuit fathers could reach the highest shelves of their new library. Fr D'Arcy recalled that 'even the fingers of the clocks were specially designed'.[22]

The palette of materials was typical of the 1930s – Rhodesian teak for the staircases and floors, unpainted English and Austrian oak for the library, and plain white plaster for many of the walls and ceilings. The doors were all custom-made and, strangely, featured doorknobs placed in the centre of the panels. Lutyens insisted on false ceilings in the refectory and library to maintain an appropriately domestic feel. He fought valiantly to keep the Jesuits from cluttering the simple spaces, forbidding picture rails and choosing the curtains and window fittings himself. 'I am rather fussy about curtain rods and hangings', he wrote.[23] At D'Arcy's request, his office even suggested a specific model of toilet brush that met Sir Edwin's aesthetic standards for the amply-provided lavatories.[24]

In keeping with his desire to make Campion Hall an engaging intellectual environment, Fr D'Arcy had amassed an impressive art collection, aided by his connections with Roman Catholic artists. It was part of Lutyens's duty to create a building where these *objets D'Arcy* could be displayed to advantage. Ever since the frescoing of St Jude's, Hampstead, against his wishes, Lutyens had been extremely sensitive about the placement of art in his buildings. At Liverpool, he had even taken it upon himself to reject some of the artwork that had been donated to the new cathedral.[25] D'Arcy was happy to give him authority over the approval and placement of works of art. Lutyens built a special octagonal pedestal on the stairs to the chapel to hold a copy of Michelangelo's Bruges Madonna that was given by Frank Brangwyn, and he fitted a carved plaque by Eric Gill nearby. He also arranged the donation of a seventeenth-century Iberian wood relief of Jesuit saints that was fitted into an alcove at the base of the stairs.[26] Augustus John's portrait of Father D'Arcy was hung in the refectory, and seventeenth and twentieth-century art was scattered around the corridors and parlours. By juxtaposing Michelangelo and Gill, Lutyens made clear that he was not concerned with the style of the art, but with the quality. Blending past and present was a hallmark of both D'Arcy and Lutyens's aesthetic taste.

This art was largely procured by donation. It gives some insight into the Oxford of the period that much of the money and support for the Campion Hall project came from

Roman Catholics outside the University, although an attempt by D'Arcy to raise funds in the United States was a failure.[27] Much of the money was provided by the Jesuit authorities, and art and money were sent by D'Arcy's pupils and converts.[28] Frank Brangwyn donated lithographs of the Stations of the Cross, which were fitted into the chapel panelling, and were published in a special edition as a fund-raiser with text by G. K. Chesterton. Even Evelyn Waugh contributed to the effort, writing a biography of Edmund Campion and donating all its profits to the building fund so that Campion Hall could be 'rebuilt on a site and in a manner more worthy of its distinction than its old home in St Giles's'.[29]

The chapel, though small, was the most significant ecclesiastical work of Lutyens's late career to be fully realised. It is a long, barrel-vaulted space rendered in plain plaster, entered through a door in a wooden screen that separates it from the antechapel. The nave is lined with oak panelling and paved in grey and white stone, its main axis terminated by the high altar set in an apse under a baldacchino. The windows are small, set high in the walls and filled with plate tracery of Lutyens's devising. To the right of the sanctuary is a smaller Lady Chapel, above which is a sick chapel with a window into the main space.

The simple interior is in keeping with thirties' taste, but the cheerful fittings and small size keep the chapel from the austerity that could result from such treatment. Sir Giles Scott's chapel at Lady Margaret Hall also features white plaster, oak panelling, pendant lights and a baldacchino in a semi-circular apse, yet the cool, severe, Byzantine feeling of that space contrasts greatly with Campion's Anglo-Italian warmth. These were the two most liturgically advanced spaces at Oxford, echoing trends in inter-war parish church design, their baldacchini, carefully orchestrated electric lighting, and forward-facing pews contrasting greatly with the uncanopied altars and inward-facing seats of traditional Oxford chapels.

Lutyens, however, was not merely responding to contemporary fashion. The use of plain surfaces and sublime scale had long been a part of his ecclesiastical design philosophy. His 1914 church at Knebworth features plain plaster walls, and his most elaborate church interior, that of St Jude's, Hampstead, originally had wide swathes of plain plaster as well. The use of simple materials did not impair the design, because for Lutyens it was the proportion and sculptural quality of the space and its fittings that were most important. When asked during a lecture at the Architectural Association, 'What is proportion?' Lutyens answered 'God'.[30] This may merely seem like a dramatic answer, but to some extent it hinted at the near-religious significance with which he infused his quest for ideal geometric and proportional relationships. He once wrote to his wife, 'Architecture is divine and spirit-making in the best sense'.[31] When asked why he bothered to continue reducing the width of bands of rustication on parts of the Midland Bank Headquarters that no one could see, he answered, 'God sees it'.[32]

Campion Hall is the most successful of Lutyens's late ecclesiastical designs not merely because of its materials and proportions – it is after all a relatively small space – but because of the quality and cleverness of its fittings. His electric light fittings with round glass reflectors and red tassels that resemble the shape of a galero, hung from the barrel vault in groups of three and later used in other commissions, perhaps allude to the cardinal's hat that appears on the crest of nearby Christ Church. And if the pendants were meant to be cardinals' hats, then the lights on the screen were certainly meant to be monstrances. The baldacchino over the High Altar is a relative of the guardhouses and canopies of New Delhi as well as the altar canopies that Lutyens had designed for Liverpool. The presence of this canopy alone sets the chapel apart from almost all other chapels at Oxford and Cambridge. Its arched roof is set on Delhi Order columns and carved with the descending dove of the Holy Spirit. Two praying angels kneel at the corners. Lutyens wanted a series of similar praying angels to line higher reaches of the transepts at Liverpool, creating a veritable heavenly host in the air above the

congregation, indicating how his taste in Christian symbolism tended toward the
universal, with crosses, doves, sunbeams, and angels featuring prominently in his
ecclesiastical designs.

Lutyens also preferred simple, universal designs for windows, using plain glass
with rectangular panes in most of his churches. When he deviated from this pattern,
visual interest came from variation of the shape of the leading, not from coloured glass.
At Campion, the leading either creates an interplay of geometric shapes or forms
Christian symbols like the cross and the chi-rho, thus avoiding the monotony of the
leaded pastel diamonds used by Scott at Lady Margaret Hall, while maintaining clarity
and simplicity. At Liverpool Metropolitan Cathedral, windows in the two large chapels
of the completed crypt feature radiant sunbursts, a rare use of coloured glass to his own
design found additionally only at the Herbert Memorial Chapel; in both spaces he used
a warm yellow glass to contrast with the clear glass elsewhere.[33] Lutyens summed up his
attitudes toward church glass in a 1932 address to the London Architectural Association
in which he described his Liverpool design:

> The [clerestory] glass generally I propose to keep clear, so that the passing
> clouds may be seen and give, by their movement, an impression of great
> stability to the vaults of the massive structure. The shrines and chapels in the
> thickness of the walls will cry aloud for glass whereby no outside movement
> may distract. In general, windows in their sequence should be the work of one
> mind and one community of craftsmen, endowed with one cadence of colour,
> and that restricted … I think perspective should be avoided, and no sense be
> given of a space beyond the picture plane common to the glass itself. The scale
> of figures should be kept small. Those large holy, haloed saints, bearded,
> and packed in grotesque stone crocketted niches, that bring outside in, should,
> in my opinion, be avoided.[34]

Lutyens's church designs are rich in symbolic geometries. At Campion, the candlesticks
and altar crosses have triangular and circular plans on three circular feet symbolizing the
Trinity and Eternity. In the highly creative plate tracery of the rose window, a central
cross is flanked by hearts (the Sacred Heart has particular significance to Jesuits) – a
geometric reminder of the Love of Christ set within the circle of Eternity. The symbolic
program of his Campion design is thus not merely applied surface decoration, but

Fig 9. The Sick Chapel (Elain Harwood, 2012)

integral to the three-dimensional conception of the chapel and its fittings.

The pews also are unusually designed, with a sill at the base painted bright red. When the fathers complained to Lutyens about the colour, he wrote that 'The red is my blood!' As part of the working relationship with their architect, the Campion fathers were bombarded with such jokes. The jokes were a famous part of Lutyens's personality, and he made no exception for the clergy, who for the most part seemed to enjoy them. His letters to Campion Hall are peppered with references to his own impending canonisation and puns on the Catholic liturgy. D'Arcy recalled that when asked the meaning of *Ave, Ave, Sancta,* Lutyens replied, 'two "aves" make one "holy"'.[35] One letter features a sketch of a cross-bearing Jesuit in a skirt with the caption: 'Do reverend fathers in Scotland wear black kilts?'[36]

Father Walker, superintendent of the building works, got into the spirit of things and wrote back with his own jokes, declaring that 'Father D'Arcy's knees are getting sore praying that you will have a bright idea re the old buildings' and once imagining Lutyens confessing to arguing with his clients and being set a penance of picking out chairs.[37] As far as the letters reveal, Lutyens only once overstepped the bounds of what the Jesuits found appropriate, and that was curiously with the reference to the pews being coloured with his own blood. An apology by letter followed a few days later.[38] There were occasional concerns about cost overruns, as was perhaps inevitable with Lutyens, but ultimately he kept roughly to the budget of £40,000 – the same amount of money, incidentally, that Norris's building would have cost.[39]

In the end, the relationship with Lutyens seems to have been a happy one, and for his part Father D'Arcy hoped to work with him again to complete the quadrangle.

Fig 10. Plan of Campion Hall

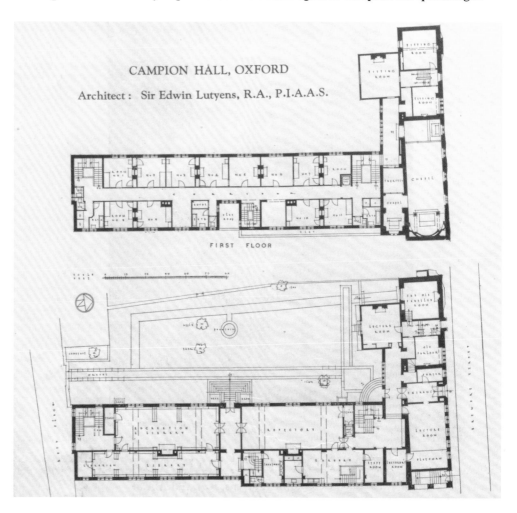

CAMPION HALL, OXFORD

Architect : Sir Edwin Lutyens, R.A., P.I.A.A.S.

FIRST FLOOR

After the first phase was completed, Lutyens would come up to Oxford to visit the Campion Fathers and attend chapel as frequently as once a term.[40] When he died in 1944, the regard that the Jesuits had for him was demonstrated by the installation of a memorial in the chapel, the only one in any of his churches. The stone tablet was designed by his office and mounted between the sanctuary and the Lady Chapel, bearing the inscription 'Architect and Friend of This House'.

There was one other tribute to Lutyens in the chapel. Not long before his death, the Campion Fathers had decided to have murals painted in the Lady Chapel by the artist Charles Mahoney. In a small vignette that was perhaps requested by the Jesuits (as it does not appear in Mahoney's preliminary sketches), Lutyens was depicted standing alongside some of the Campion Fathers at the bedside of St. Mary.[41]

When the pressures of growth finally led to Campion's expansion in 1958, the architect G. Armes created a sympathetic wing with tile-hung gables and Bladon rubble walls that, however, meant that Lutyens's plan for the complete quadrangle had been officially abandoned. Thus, in the post-war years, the grand Lutyens-designed institute envisioned by Father D'Arcy went the same way as his cathedral. Catholic commissions after the war paid little heed to the precedent set by Campion Hall. D'Arcy's programme for entrancing the English intellectual with a combination of novelty and nostalgia was felt to hold little relevance, and for his part, D'Arcy felt Campion Hall had squandered its earlier promise.[42] The hall also had little immediate influence on Oxford's architecture, although with the revival of Lutyens's reputation and the rise of Postmodernism in the 1980s, architects began to take an interest once again. Whether or not one considers Lutyens's architecture to have marked the end of an era, Campion Hall is a great monument and demonstrates the way one of England's greatest architectural minds responded to the context of an ancient university.

Fig 11. The memorial to Lutyens in the Chapel (David Lewis, 2007)

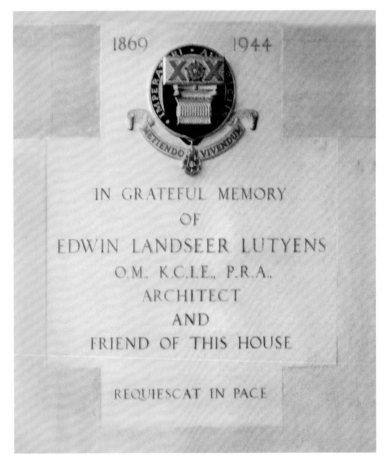

1. Peter Hinchliff, 'Religious Issues', in M. G. Brock and M. C. Curthoys, eds., *The History of the University of Oxford*, vol. 7, Oxford, OUP, 2000, p.104.

2. Geoffrey Tyack, 'Baker and Lutyens in Oxford', *Oxoniensia*, vol.62, 1997, p.297. Tyack's article traces the history of the buildings of Campion Hall in great detail.

3. Brian Harrison, ed., *The History of the University of* Oxford, vol.8, Oxford, OUP, 1994, p.299.

4. Fr D'Arcy, 'The New Campion Hall', manuscript, Cupbd 8, Campion Hall archives.

5. Richard Davenport-Hines, ed., *Letters from Oxford: Hugh Trevor-Roper to Bernard Berenson,* London, Phoenix, 2007, p.49.

6. Tyack, op. cit., p.297.

7. Letter, Vatican to Fr Keane, October 1921, Cupbd 8, Box 1, 6B, Campion Hall archives.

8. D'Arcy, op. cit.

9. Drawings Chest, Drawer 4, Campion Hall archives.

10. Letter, Fr Walker to Fr Keane, n.d., Cupbd 8, Box 14, 7A-G, Campion Hall archives; D'Arcy, op. cit.

11. Drawings Chest, Drawer 4, Campion Hall archives.

12. Letter, Fr Keane to Fr Walker, 7 June 1931, Cupbd 8, Box 14, 3O-3P, Campion Hall archives.

13. D'Arcy, op. cit. Jane Brown's *Lutyens and the Edwardians* (London, Viking, 1996) admirably traces in greater detail the network of Lutyens's Roman Catholic clients and their connection to the building of Campion Hall.

14. D'Arcy, ibid.

15. Fr Martin D'Arcy, *Laughter and the Love of Friends*, ed. William S. Abell, Westminster (Maryland), Christian Classics, 1991, pp.48–51.

16. DR40/7(1–3), RIBA Drawings and Archives Collections.

17. Letter, Fr Keane to Fr D'Arcy, n.d., Cupbd. 8, Box 3, 3B, Campion Hall archives; Geoffrey Tyack, *Oxford, An Architectural Guide,* Oxford, OUP, 1998, pp.231–2; Brown, op. cit., p.223.

18. 'Campion Hall, Oxford', *Country Life,* vol. 79, no.2058, 27 June 1936, p. 676.

19. Jennifer Sherwood and Nikolaus Pevsner, The Buildings of England: *Oxfordshire*, Harmondsworth, Penguin, 1974, p.224.

20. Tyack, 'Baker and Lutyens in Oxford', op. cit., p.293.

21. D'Arcy, The New Campion Hall, op. cit.

22. ibid.

23. Letter, Lutyens to Fr Walker, 14 June 1935, Cupbd 8, Box 5, 6A, Campion Hall archives.

24. Letter, Office Manager to Fr Walker, 20 February 1936, Cupbd 8, Box 5, 11A-B, Campion Hall archives.

25. Letter, Lutyens to Archbishop Downey, n.d. (c.1930), S2VA/120, Liverpool Metropolitan Cathedral archives.

26. Fr Gallagher, interviewed by the author, Campion Hall, March 2007.

27. Letter, Fr Walker to Lutyens, 21 March 1935, Cupbd 8, Box 5, 3A-B, Campion Hall archives.

28. Letter, Campion Hall to Fr Norris, 16 January 1935, Cupbd 8, Box 5, 2, Campion Hall archives.

29. Evelyn Waugh, *Edmund Campion*, Oxford, Oxford University Press, 1980, p.ix.

30. 1920 Address to the Architectural Association, quoted in Jane Ridley, *Edwin Lutyens,* London, Pimlico, 2002, p.296.

31. Letter to Lady Emily, 1911, quoted ibid., p.202.

32. ibid, p.318.

33. At the Hampstead churches, the stained glass was inserted by the parish to the design of other artists, and the coloured glass at Castle Drogo came from the client's previous chapel at Wadsworth House.

34. 1932 Address to the Architectural Association, quoted in Christopher Hussey, *The Life of Sir Edwin Lutyens,* London, Antique Collectors Club, 1985, p.545.

35. D'Arcy, *Laughter and the Love of Friends*, op. cit., p.53.

36. Letter, Lutyens to Fr Walker, 14 June 1935, Cupbd 8, Box 5, 6A, Campion Hall archives.

37. Letters, Fr Walker to Lutyens, 29 March 1935 and 14 August 1935, Cupbd 8, Box 5, 3A-B, Campion Hall archives.

38. Letters, Lutyens to Fr Walker, 20 and 24 January 1936, Cupbd 8, Box 5, 11A-B, Campion Hall archives.

39. Office of E. Bower Norris, Architect's Report on the Plans, typescript, n.d., Cupbd 8, Box 14, 1A-1E, Campion Hall archives.

40. D'Arcy, *Laughter and the Love of Friends*, op. cit., p.53.

41. Digitised studies, Liss Fine Art Gallery, http://www.charlesmahoney.com, accessed 20 August 2012.

42. D'Arcy, *Laughter and t*he Love of Friends, op. cit., p.57.

3
Conservative Attitudes: Walter Gropius in Cambridge and Maxwell Fry in Oxford
Alan Powers

Fig 1. E. Maxwell Fry, New Building for All Souls College, Oxford, 1938 (Courtesy The Warden and Fellows of All Souls College, Oxford)

Within a few weeks of his arrival in Britain in October 1934, Walter Gropius told his sister about his first visit to Cambridge. 'There is no doubt that this is a centre of culture with very old humus which could not easily be replaced', he wrote. 'Now I understand the conservative attitude of the Englishman, which makes it difficult for him to recognize anything new.'[1] Jack Pritchard, his host at the Lawn Road flats, introduced him to the County Education Officer, Henry Morris, who became his patron for Impington Village College (1936–39).

About a year later, one of the younger Fellows of Christ's College, the biologist Conrad Hal Waddington (1905–75), invited him to visit, in connection with a scheme for a new building at the College. Waddington met him at the station with the architect and planner (Margaret) Justin Blanco White (1911–2001), who in the following year became his second wife. She was a recent graduate of the Architectural Association, and had already met Gropius 'in connection with a book on housing'.[2]

The invitation was in the context of a decision in 1934 to use a special reserve fund for a new building at Christ's. The first architect engaged by the College was Oswald P. Milne (1881–1968), a pupil of Lutyens, designer of houses including Coleton Fishacre, Devon (1926) and buildings for Bedford School, Highgate School and for the Dartington estate, including the main school building, Foxhole, in 1934. Milne advised the College to choose the site for their new building to make a north side to Third Court, backing on to Hobson Street, where the only existing building was a tutor's house standing in the western corner. The brief was two fellows' sets and as many undergraduate sets as possible, with lock-up shops on the ground floor. The cost was not to exceed the £40,000 available in the fund.[3]

A new Master of Christ's, Charles Galton Darwin, a physicist and grandson of the pioneer of evolution, took up his position in 1936 and the building project developed with 'sketch plans' requested from Percy Morley Horder (1870–1944, one of whose best works, originally Cheshunt College, was built in Bateman Street in 1913) and Gropius & Fry, in addition to Milne.[4] Horder only sent a block plan, and was not considered as a competitor, while Milne's proposals were similar in style and typology to the 1934 St Michael's Court for Gonville and Caius by Easton and Robertson, traditional in their masonry elevations although slightly modern in their horizontal steel windows and ornamented with heraldry.[5]

Milne's project went up to the site boundary in Hobson Street with a return block joining on to the 1889 building by J. J. Stevenson and closing Third Court. Gropius by contrast aligned his main block at right angles to Stevenson's building, leaving a gap between them, and added a curved wing extending westwards to the boundary with additional shops. The effect was to add a triangle of land to the street by taking down the college's historic boundary wall. Some plane trees, then standing inside the wall, would

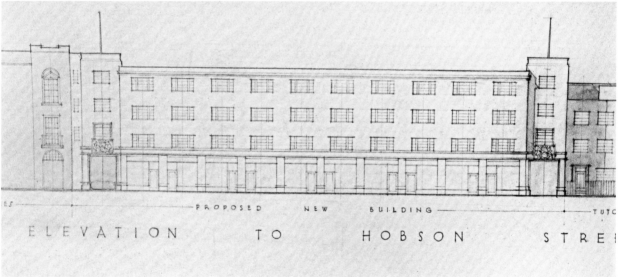

**Fig 2. Oswald P. Milne,
Proposed New Building
for Christ's College,
Cambridge, 1936.
Perspective. (Courtesy
Christ's College)**

**Fig 3. Oswald P. Milne,
Proposed New Building
for Christ's College,
Cambridge, 1936.
Elevation to Hobson
Street. (Courtesy
Christ's College)**

Fig 4. Walter Gropius and E. Maxwell Fry, Proposed New Building for Christ's College, Cambridge, 1936. *Architects' Journal*, **3 February, 1938. (Architectural Press Library/RIBA Robert Elwall Photographs Collection)**

thus become part of the public space in front of the shops, with a pedestrian entrance. Both schemes included a replacement for the existing tutor's house at the south end of the site in the form of a building attached to the main body of the scheme but more domestic in character and lower in height.

The two architects were offered £200 each to develop their schemes. Darwin was persuaded by the RIBA Secretary, Sir Ian MacAlister, that some professional opinion on the actual costs of the projects would prevent the Fellows from accepting an unrealistic proposal, and invited Milne and Gropius to chose someone. Charles Holden accepted their invitation, explaining that 'he would like to make a report which could be shown to the competitors' rather than picking one or the other.[6]

In his own report Milne explained his position between Modernism and historical styles. 'It is considered that the design of the new building should be of its date rather than a copy of the existing buildings, but a building self-conscious in its Modernism would be equally out of place. The design submitted is, therefore, modern in conception but in the English tradition, deriving its quality from good materials and dependent for effect on good massing and proportion rather than ornamental detail.'[7]

On his Hobson Street elevation, Milne tried to remain 'in keeping' with recent Neo-Georgian buildings adjoining, while giving his own building horizontal metal windows in a plain wall. The elevation is flanked by stair towers with gates beneath, over which carved coats of arms are shown, these being the only forms of ornament apart from plain cornice mouldings. A similar elevation treatment is shown on the College side of the building, composing the different blocks with masses of different height, indicating a flat roof on the tutor's house with a modern-looking terrace shelter.

In his report, Gropius explained that seven or eight alternatives had been considered, in line with his belief that design should proceed from researching all possible options. He justified the planning strategy in terms of the economic use of the site, with more sets, shops and parking spaces, and better conditions for shoppers. As he wrote, 'a line of trees is saved and an open space of some charm and dignity is formed to make a fitting boundary to the College and a welcome addition to the small open spaces of the town'. Putting the main block at an exact right angle to the Stevenson building would 'make a more suitable completion of the garden space', while by moving the bulk of the building inwards from the site boundary, it would effectively mask 'the unsightly illuminated dome of the cinema in Hobson Street', an unwelcome intrusion of Modernity.[8] The report notes that the beds in the undergraduate sets would be fitted, and 'pivoted at each end and counterweighted, in order to make it easy for an elderly person to make up', a gesture towards the legion of college 'bedmakers' who undertook this task together with cleaning the rooms.

The structural steel frame was based on equal bays corresponding to the grouping of sets, with hollow tile floors and roofs. The external walls would be faced in Ketton stone, matching that of St John's College, while the ground floor towards Third Court would be faced with glass block, behind which ran a service passage to the shops. The top storey of the main block contained two fellows' sets divided by a spine wall, sharing a sheltered roof terrace to the north. The tutor's house at the southern end of the block was slightly curved to meet an existing angled wall square on, and the continuous vertical glazing of the staircase was slightly bowed outwards.

The Christ's scheme has much in common with Gropius's design for the Ben Levy house at No. 66 Old Church Street, where the main rectangular body of the building has a number of picturesque appendages and curves to offset it and create more interesting spaces relating to the street and the garden. Some of these characteristics can also be found in the Impington design, shaped around existing trees with a curved adult wing also containing bow windows. Little consideration has been given to the question whether Gropius developed an 'English style', although Giulio Carlo Argan wrote in 1951 of the transformation that Gropius underwent in England, as:

> A way of returning to the sources of the very ideological tradition itself, of rediscovering confidence in the 'progress' which in Europe, after its first rich flowering, was so quickly corrupted by the aggressive egoism of the ruling classes. In this country, and during these years, faith in industry and in the educational mission retained their undeniable legitimacy. … It is probable that the collaboration with Maxwell Fry had helped Gropius to rediscover, in the few works of the English period, a simpler and more cordial accent, an easier and more spontaneous contact with the things of the world. There was no longer an ideal to defend to the death, but a programme to be developed.[9]

Gropius's English work has generally been undervalued in relation to the rest of his career, and a major building in Cambridge might have altered history's perception of it.

Early in 1937, Gropius accepted the invitation from Harvard to take up a professorship at the Graduate School of Design. A letter from Waddington prior to the College vote assumed that he would win the commission, which could be carried out by Fry in his absence, as happened with Impington. He added the warning that this circumstance might be used as 'an excuse for those people who do not want a modern design but do not see how they can get out of it', but added 'actually I am nearly certain that there are very few, if any, such people. All those with even partially open minds have been convinced by your designs, while others would never be convinced under any circumstances.' Waddington was hoping to get a majority for Gropius, although 'something may still depend on Holden, whose report is not yet in'.[10]

Holden prefaced his report of 15 January by stating 'I have not attempted to make any statement with regard to aesthetic considerations, except so far as these considerations had a definite bearing upon the convenience of the building in occupation and upon the life of the structure'. This evasion was perhaps predictable, and if Holden failed to win posterity's praise for recommending Gropius unconditionally, he did not reject him either. He was suspicious of steel-framed buildings, warning the College that it might last no more than 100 years, and pointing out that while Milne's design could be built with conventional load-bearing construction, it would be hard to adapt the one by Gropius.

Holden praised Milne's 'quiet outlook' and the ease of cleaning the 'windows of adequate size', and the usefulness of chimney flues, provided in addition to the requested central heating, for purposes of ventilation. He was more critical of the Gropius scheme, being unconvinced by his arguments about the economical use of the site. He called the addition of space towards Hobson Street 'an attractive feature and a real amenity as far as the town is concerned', although 'it would mean a corresponding loss to Third Court'. His attitude was generally pragmatic: how would the windows be cleaned? Would the down draught from the windows mean the writing desk would be moved away from them? Would the balconies in line above each other be used 'in rowdy escapades, especially where there are glass canopies over the shops?' He concluded by pointing out that no construction system other than a steel or reinforced concrete frame would permit such large windows, and any alternative would require 'entirely recasting the elevations'.[11] In fact, Holden had very little positive to say about the value of this particular example of Modernism.

On 23 February, the College sent Gropius and Fry a list of questions apparently based on a comparison between their design and Milne's. These indicate the suspicions among some of the Fellows, not only in stylistic terms but also in respect of the opening out of the College towards the town. In reply, Gropius showed how vital this planning move was to the whole concept, justifying the set-back in Hobson Street in terms of better sun and air, the retention of the trees, the reduction of noise from the street and the ability to add more undergraduate sets, because it would be possible for them to face either way from the central corridors. Gropius and Fry argued that

> The set-back plan ... substitutes spaciousness for narrowness, ... is more desirable aesthetically, and pleasanter to live in. In our opinion the courtyard is of greater benefit to the college, quite apart from any value due to the shops, than it is to the Town. It is likely nevertheless to be regarded by the Town as a public spirited work if planned.[12]

In addition, they had selected this scheme as providing more undergraduate sets than any of their alternatives. The dons apparently remained irked by the outward signs of Modernism, asking: 'To what extent and in what manner would you be willing to modify the façade of the building facing the Third Court?' The architects responded by citing

Fig 5. Walter Gropius and E. Maxwell Fry, Proposed New Building for Christ's College, Cambridge, 1936. *Architects' Journal,* 10 February, 1938. (Architectural Press Library/RIBA Robert Elwall Photographs Collection)

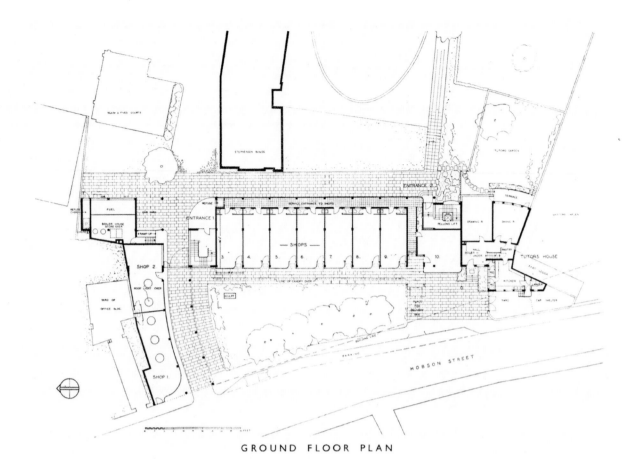

GROUND FLOOR PLAN

Fig 6. Walter Gropius and E. Maxwell Fry, Proposed New Building for Christ's College, Cambridge, 1936. Ground Floor Plan. *Architects' Journal,* **10 February, 1938. (Architectural Press Library/RIBA Robert Elwall Photographs Collection)**

evidence of the effectiveness of lighting low-ceilinged rooms from ribbon windows, going on to state: 'We feel that it would be wrong to put the very well tested technique of modern building to the service of imitation of whatsoever past style and we find that the sense of congruity which binds building of many different dates and styles in Cambridge is due not so much to affinity in point of style but in the material and scale.' They hoped that the stone cladding would put these anxieties to rest.

Gropius and Fry argued in favour of the proposed flat roof as less of a fire hazard than a timber roof and available for use as a roof terrace. Asked whether it would be possible to have all the rooms facing inwards towards the college, they replied that this would use the site less economically. Finally, they explained why they had not attempted to join on to the Stevenson Building, because any projection to the north of it would be cut off from Third Court and deprived of southern light, while the angle made with a building running on the line of Hobson Street (the angle that Milne's scheme incorporated without any disguise) 'is an acute one and for this reason unsatisfactory aesthetically in the general composition of Third Court as completed'.[13]

On 2 March 1937, ten days before leaving for the USA, Gropius made a presentation of his scheme at the College. This was followed by a motion to appoint him 'architect of the new building forthwith' which, contrary to Waddington's confident prediction, was defeated by 13 votes to eight. The identity of the eight is not officially recorded, but Waddington named two other Fellows, Wyatt and Saunders, as supporters, to whom may be added W. A. W. Rushton, for whom Justin Blanco White was designing a house, and the scientist and future novelist C. P. Snow.[14] The meeting then voted by 14 to five to make an approach to Sir Giles Gilbert Scott, but nothing was done about this and on 11 May the Governing Body decided to postpone the project and disband the buildings committee.[15]

The reasons for this choice must remain largely speculative. For a start, Milne's scheme was the cheaper, at £33,761 compared to £37,494 (later revised to £36,016) for Gropius. In rejecting Gropius, the College did not choose Milne. The immediate vote for Scott suggests some prior lobbying in his favour and given his continuing work for Clare College, he could have been seen as a safe option, although potentially expensive, for the Building Committee noted that Clare paid about £1200 per set, compared to £500 for the recent Fisher Building at Queens' by Norman Drinkwater.

It is impossible to say whether Gropius's imminent departure for the USA tipped the balance. He wrote to the Master to announce this on 13 January 1937, assuring him that the scheme was already well worked out and that Fry 'would be perfectly well able to make any modifications that might arise, and in many respects he is better qualified than I to supervise the building process'.[16] Fry suggested that had Gropius been successful, the partnership might have carried on, and they waited until November before formally announcing its demise. They seem to have hoped for a reversal of the decision and the drawings were published in the *Architects' Journal* in February 1938, although Gropius's name was omitted owing to an editorial error.[17]

Reporting to the Warden of All Souls, who was about to undergo a similar exercise, Darwin warned that:

> The whole college was torn into fragments with passionate hatred of one or both of the two architects. The result has been that a third name was brought up and thrust on our committee without any due consideration. We have managed to get the business into calm waters at last, but mainly by taking the line that building costs are rising rapidly so that it would be folly to start now since they should come down in two years or so when all the aerodromes have been built; meanwhile we need not continue our quarrels over a house that is not to be built.[18]

After the war, Christ's did build, with Sir Albert Richardson, by then an Honorary

Fig 7. Richardson and Houfe, Chancellor's Building, Christ's College, Cambridge, 1948–50. Perspective. (Courtesy Christ's College)

Fellow of the College, and his partner Eric Houfe. Richardson, Gropius's senior by only three years, spent much of the war in Cambridge with the evacuated Bartlett School of Architecture and strengthened his contacts in the university. In 1948–50 he built the Chancellor's Building on the east side of Third Court at a cost of £80,000, followed by its companion in a simplified style, the Memorial Building, more or less on the site of the 1937 projects, in 1952–3. The Senior Tutor's house was left in place with the new building passing its back and screening it from view. The tower at the west end of the Stevenson Building was capped by a new roof and square lantern, a move applauded by Pevsner as 'an asymmetrical and piquant accent'. He was surprisingly tolerant of the twin buildings, praising their plainness and fine stone facings, but regretted that they lacked the mouldings needed for a convincing Georgian design. With the temporary west wall of the Stevenson Building the space towards Hobson Street feels like a backyard. While the College has had the benefit of a car park, there were no shops to contribute what could have been over 70 years of rental income.

An anonymous contributor to the *Christ's College Magazine* in 1953 resurrected the story of the Gropius scheme, commending it as 'honest in the expression of its function and yet classically satisfying in its proportions, free and comfortable in its layout and yet the composition of masses and relation of surfaces studied with scrupulous care'.[19] Richardson was faintly praised, apart from his site planning: 'inside the College, notice how, just as a well-mannered youth will show respect to his elders, Gropius's block retires modestly behind the blind end of the Stevenson building, unlike Professor Richardson's block which ruins the view of a whole staircase'. In a later issue, another writer replied to defend Richardson's buildings which 'are and will be in a century, more satisfying than a monument of the transient phase, which the Gropius design so typified'.[20]

The project by Maxwell Fry for All Souls, Oxford, was developed in tandem with the Christ's scheme, lagging about a year behind. In a similar fashion, it represented the fulfilment of an earlier project, in this case first mooted in 1930. All Souls is a unique college, without undergraduates, its membership entirely composed of Fellows. Some were full-time academics at Oxford involved with lecturing and tutorials, but the younger Fellows, especially those awarded Prize Fellowships by examination, were encouraged to make links with a wider world.[21] Many qualified in the law, although not all practiced, finding other ways of serving the country in the church or the diplomatic service. Several had businesses, such as the publisher Sir Geoffrey Faber (1889–1961), founder of the eponymous imprint, elected a Prize Fellow in 1919 and Estates Bursar from 1923 to 1951. In this role, he directed extensive and profitable building development on the northern fringes of London.

A. S. G. Butler (1888–1965) was the College architect, best known for editing the Lutyens Memorial volumes published in 1950. Butler was connected to Faber by marriage, but whether that was coincidence is unclear. It meant, however, that he wrote more openly to Faber than might otherwise have been the case, discussing the finer points of Cotswold Manor and Tudor styles and the benefits of Georgian windows for better light in relation to his project for a new building flanking two sides of the Warden's garden in 1930, concluding, 'after all, it is not style that matters but proportion'.[22] The site was the only part of the College where there was much space to develop. It abuts The Queen's College, and the project was a response to their building plans. Queen's soon abandoned their scheme and All Souls postponed theirs, although Butler produced a further scheme in 1932. The following year the building idea was revived by the new Warden, William Adams (1874–1966), an academic in his early life but also much involved in public affairs as a member of Lloyd George's secretariat, founder and editor of the *Political Quarterly*, a practicing farmer and a strong believer in smallholdings.

Thus in 1936, a new brief for 'two common-rooms, increased service accommodation, Manciple's quarters, garage, and six or more sets of Fellows' rooms, [with] three spare rooms for visitors' was drawn up for the south-facing boundary of the

Fig 8. A.S.G. Butler,
All Souls College,
West Elevations of the
Warden's Quadrangle,
1930. (Courtesy the
Warden and Fellows of
All Souls College,
Oxford)

Warden's Garden, where a new building would separate this from the smaller Fellows' Garden to the north.[23] The chief motive for development was explained by the Sub-Warden, Sir (Ernest) Llewellyn Woodward:

> From the point of view of the College as a society, it is most desirable that its junior Fellows not engaged in academic work in Oxford should spend week-ends here. Unless we can provide them with reasonable accommodation, they will be disinclined to come here as regularly as they have come in the past. We cannot hope to provide, in a building no part of which is less than two hundred years old, and some parts of which are five hundred years old, all the amenities of a modern house, but we cannot expect busy people to come here for week-ends unless we can give them a reasonable degree of comfort. In the opinion of the Sub-Warden, this degree of comfort means at least a share in a sitting room.[24]

Style seems to have been a contentious issue in the Building Committee from early on, and the minutes of an early meeting record that 'a discussion of an aesthetic nature having sprung up the Warden adjourned the Committee'.[25] One of the members, the historian Richard Pares (1902–58) is identifiable as a leader of the Modernist faction, suggesting Gropius, 'Villarde' (presumably F. X. Velarde), and Holden as contenders some three weeks after this event.

Faber in turn lobbied the Warden to continue with Butler, as someone capable of dealing with the complexity of the problem, able to receive criticism and engage in dialogue, describing him as: 'A man who will take infinite pains; he is ingenious; and he is quick to respond to criticism. He has also what seems to me very desirable for this kind of work, a special sensitiveness for "period" and "atmosphere".' Faber warned that 'an architect of a different type risks putting an ambitious building into an inappropriate context' and 'a slap-dash solution of the "internal" problems – which are, after all, the primary problems'.[26]

Another set of recommendations was sent to the economist Sir Hubert Henderson, a later Warden, by his brother-in-law, Hope Bagenal, the Librarian of the Architectural Association, on 1 February 1937. He wrote brief descriptions of H. S. Goodhart-Rendel (Slade Professor at Oxford 1932 and at the time the Principal of the AA School),

John Murray Easton (in partnership with Howard Robertson and an AA stalwart), George L. Kennedy (active in Cambridge under the patronage of Maynard Keynes and architect for the conversion of Holywell Manor for Balliol in 1938) and J. C. Shepherd, in practise with Elisabeth Scott, a fellow student at the AA in the 1920s and one of the team of three architects who worked on the Shakespeare Memorial Theatre. Bagenal wrote, 'Shepherd is Miss Scott's partner, and an architect of great talent. In many ways he would be worth your while considering seriously. He is a thorough modernist in spirit yet with great appreciation of old work, and most careful to consider every aspect of a problem.' Bagenal clearly did not approve of the possibility of Gropius being selected, and wrote at the end of his letter, 'It is announced in the architectural papers that Gropius has been appointed Professor of Architecture at Harvard. You will probably understand that I would much prefer you to consider one of our own men, especially as there are a great many less well-known who have learned all there is to be learned from the modernists.' [27]

In March 1937 it was agreed that Butler's existing appointment be rescinded. Four architects were discussed: Gropius and Fry (which by then effectively meant Fry on his own), Scott, Shepherd & Breakwell (probably as a result of Bagenal's recommendation), Hubert Worthington (recently a Slade Professor in Oxford and designer of the Radcliffe Science Library, 1933–34), and finally A. S. G. Butler. C. H. Reilly, recently retired after 30 years as Professor of Architecture at Liverpool University, was suggested as an assessor, Holden having declined an invitation. Had Reilly been given this role, he would probably have supported Fry as an ex-pupil, but in fact the College did not make use of any professional help. The shortlist of architects must have been reviewed again, since Adams followed in Darwin's steps in seeking further advice from the RIBA on competition procedure and nominations. Sir Ian MacAlister produced a long list, writing, 'I have included A[myas] D. Connell, a brilliant young 'modernist' of the most extreme school. The others are all, I think, worthy of your consideration, although some of them are young and not very well known.'[28]

The Building Committee went on 8 June to look at photographs of works by various architects at the RIBA, and some of these were loaned for display in the College at the end of the year. At this point, the list included: A. S. G. Butler; W. G. Newton; Scott, Shepherd and Breakwell; Oswald Milne; Maxwell Fry; and Connell, Ward & Lucas. In October, the ones still in play were Connell, Milne, Newton and Shepherd. In an echo of Christ's shortlist, Woodward, the Sub-Warden, appears to have been lobbying for Morley Horder, although the committee refused to add his name.

Nearly a year then elapsed, during which the Building Sub-Committee membership was partly changed, including a new Prize Fellow, the philosopher Stuart Hampshire (1914–2004), a supporter of Modernism in architecture.[29] The shortlist had been reduced to Fry, Newton and Shepherd, who provided schemes seen by the Building Committee in October 1938.[30] The drawings by Newton have not survived, but the two other sets are complete, together with Scott & Shepherd's report. Newton was generally a traditionalist, although in 1932–3 he designed a remarkable generously glazed concrete science building for Marlborough College that was built right behind his Memorial Hall of 1921–5, a pure work of classicism. It seems likely that on this occasion, the schemes represented a gradation between Modernism and tradition with Scott & Shepherd in the middle, rather as Milne was expected to be in the anticipated three-horse race had it included Morley Horder in Cambridge.

They 'expressed their preference' in a report and the final decision was left for a College meeting on 26 November.[31] This preference was for Fry by a margin of five to two. The Fry faction (Faber, Pares, Jones, Routh and Hampshire), issued a lengthy document, and the Shepherd faction (Woodward and Craster) a 'Minority Report' raising questions about Fry's design from a detailed planning point of view.[32]

The arguments in favour of Fry were based mainly on planning, less in relation to

Fig 9. Scott, Shepherd and Breakwell, New Building for All Souls College, Oxford, 1938. Elevation to Warden's Garden and Section. (Courtesy the Warden and Fellows of All Souls College, Oxford)

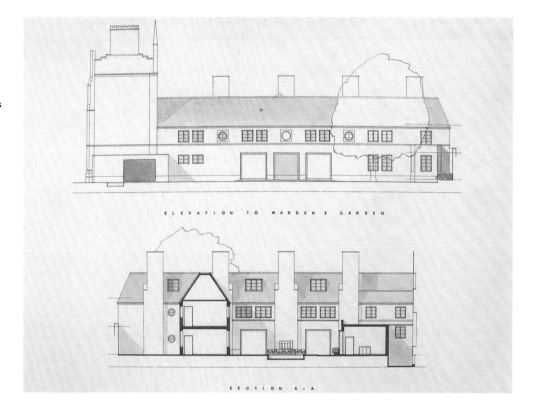

Fig 10. Scott, Shepherd and Breakwell, New Building for All Souls College, Oxford, 1938. Elevation to the Fellows' Garden west (Courtesy the Warden and Fellows of All Souls College, Oxford)

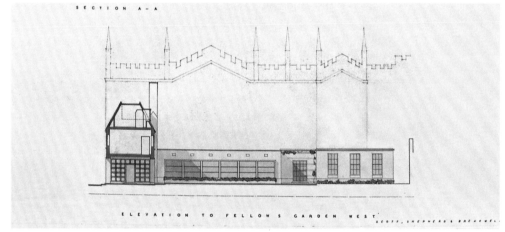

Fig 11. Scott, Shepherd and Breakwell, New Building for All Souls College, Oxford, 1938. Elevation to the Fellows' Garden east (Courtesy the Warden and Fellows of All Souls College, Oxford)

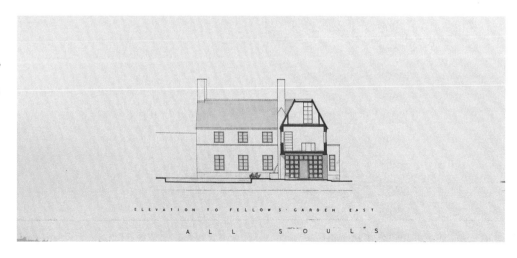

the scheme submitted but in respect of its possible further development, owing to his superior 'ability to plan a thing out in practical detail'.[33] Given Faber's support for Butler, it may seem odd to find him now supporting Fry, although his firm published Gropius's book, *The New Architecture and the Bauhaus* in 1935, and in the following year *Pioneers of the Modern Movement from William Morris to Walter Gropius*, by Nikolaus Pevsner.

An absolute majority of the Fellows was required, and Woodward wrote to warn the Warden, that it was 'possible that none of these plans will obtain a decisive majority at a College meeting, and that, even if there is a majority for one set of plans, a considerable minority of Fellows will feel most uneasy and disappointed over a choice made by the majority'.[34] He continued to make the case for Horder, writing to Faber that he wanted to strengthen the chances of Scott and Shepherd against Fry, believing that their scheme was already ahead of the two others.

Fry's report on his scheme is not in the College Archives, but he recalled that, 'My design was based on a reinforced concrete frame with a facing of Portland stone which fitted unobtrusively into its surroundings, but with the benefit of a garage in the basement, reached without touching the famous tree that punctuates the sweep of the High, and communicating by lift with a roof terrace commanding one of the loveliest prospects in Europe: prime examples, both, of putting the machine to good social use.'[35]

Fry's scheme was more varied and picturesque than the project at Christ's College. It was formed from two interlocking solid blocks in an L shape, making the most of its southern aspect with balconies at each level, the first floor being a continuous one with an open metal balustrade. A broad open passageway with columns joined the Fellows' Garden to the rear with the Warden's Garden in front. On the east side, the new lodging for the Manciple was to the north in the base of the short arm of the L, with a Fellow's set facing south. The lift for access to the roof terrace was in the eastern half of the ground floor, and for Fellows wishing to move on there after dinner a short breath of fresh air was gained as they crossed the pillared area in the centre. The pro-Fry report reflected that while:

> On the one hand it is a nuisance to have to climb upstairs or take a lift between two stages of a dinner party … we think the disadvantage is more than compensated by the light and the view, probably unrivalled in Oxford, which will be obtained from Fry's upper common-room and still more from his terrace outside it.[36]

Fry's recollection of Portland stone seems to be faulty, since the drawing suggests a yellower stone to match the existing buildings.[37] The upper levels were composed of solids and voids, with the Fellows' roof terrace partly beneath an overhanging canopy, of typically thin 1930s' profile, and, towards the centre, a cutaway section linked by a ribbon of concrete to the roofs on either side. In these compositional devices there are reminiscences of Fry's 1930s' house designs, as well as anticipations of post-war buildings such as Congress House and the Royal Festival Hall, all ultimately derived from Le Corbusier.

The 'Fry Five' grappled with the question of aesthetics at some length, but largely in secondary terms of its suitability in relation to the Hawksmoor block at right angles (to which Fry was planning to add a window on the south wall) and the fact that it was not 'ugly or bad in its kind'. They argued for taking a risk, asking, 'Fellows who disagree with us to make sure whether they object to Fry's style as bad, or only unfamiliar. If anything at all can be asserted about the future of taste in architecture, we think that future generations are more likely to accept this style than to condemn it: this seems to be a fair inference from the fact that, with certain exceptions, its supporters in the College are younger than its opponents.' Rather than pushing the difficult area of taste, however, they focused on practicality, arguing that, 'future generations of Fellows are

**Fig 12. E. Maxwell Fry,
New Building for All
Souls College, Oxford,
1938. Perspective
(Courtesy the Warden
and Fellows of All Souls
College, Oxford)**

more likely to thank us for two excellent common-rooms, nineteen other rooms with south light, and garage for eight to twelve cars, than for a building which, though more universally inoffensive to our own eyes, provides much less of these amenities.'[38]

Taking a contrary view, Grant Robertson wrote that the bulk of Fry's building was too great for the size of the Quadrangle, while the contrast in styles was 'so violent as to make that part of the College an architectural freak'.[39] A. H. Campbell, a Fellow whom A. L. Rowse remembered as a close friend of Auden and Isherwood who 'shared their frolics in rollicking Weimar Germany', wrote to the Warden from Birmingham:

> I cannot as yet make up my mind about the plans submitted to the College. I feel that, as a building is intended to last for centuries, it is better to be magnificent than mean. I have no objection to a new style as such; Oxford can digest anything so long as it is good in terms of itself. I like big windows and sunlight and I think the idea of a roof common-room and terrace is genius; no other College has got a place where one can enjoy in comfort the view of roofs and towers which is one of the best things in Oxford. Yet I don't somehow like the looks of his proposed building; it doesn't seem a very distinguished example of its style.[40]

The scheme by Scott, Shepherd and Breakwell, which the documents suggest was mainly designed by Shepherd, was unobtrusive, with a long pitched roof concealing a flat roof at its peak to allow a wider footprint. This was interrupted on the north elevation by three massive chimneys, with two passageways either side of the central stack framed by square openings. On the south elevation, the rhythm of paired windows is interspersed with round windows. The whole effect is like a simplified design by Lutyens and not unlike the Pfeiffer Tower at Newnham College, Cambridge of 1938 by the same firm. The Shepherd 'Minority Report' felt that Fry's work would 'date', while their preference would not. They felt that the massing of the more extended L shape of the design was more flattering to Hawksmoor and that 'the wholly southern aspect of Mr Fry's work is bought at too heavy a price', its height causing it to overlook and dominate the Warden's house.

As at Christ's, although there was a vocal group in favour of a modern design, the majority of Fellows rejected it. Fry wrote in his memoirs of his overnight visit to give a presentation: 'I led them up and down', he recalled, 'I expatiated on the practical benefits of the garage as on the celestial enjoyments of the roof terrace and all in vain, and as their politeness intensified itself I imagined a flight of steps opening in the floor and offering me a dignified exit, for the end, though as yet unannounced, was already predictable.'[41] He felt that this rejection was part of 'a blank wall of public prejudice' despite which the Modern Movement was 'gathering way'. Had Connell been among the contenders, he would surely have fared worse.

The administrative resolution was, as at Christ's, to defer the decision until June 1939, while seeking a further design from Morley Horder, at Woodward's urging, 'because I have been very much impressed by all the work – and particularly by the latest piece of work – which this architect has carried out at Somerville College, where the problem has been rather like our own – i.e. putting up buildings in a crowded and restricted site'.[42] A series of slightly farcical episodes ensued, involving Horder's failure to arrive at the meeting at which he was meant to present a scheme, blamed on a car breakdown. Although he did come a second time, on 22 June 1939, no record of his scheme remains; but it appears that the college held out the possibility of beginning it some time after June 1940. Horder died in 1944, and the new Committee was convened in June 1945. The Domestic Bursar reported that he had secured a supply of Clipsham stone. As at Christ's after the war, 'It was agreed that there should be no competition' and that 'the College should appoint an architect, furnish him with appropriate instructions and receive his drawings for consideration'.[43]

As Howard Colvin explained, 'by now the College had lost all enthusiasm for the "Modern Movement", and wanted a building "which would harmonize with the Warden's Lodgings and other adjacent buildings, perhaps of an "Annish" style."'[44] Their first choice of architect was C. H. James, who produced a very plain scheme, and in 1951, they went to Edward Maufe for a design. Both failed to receive building licences, and only recently the Manciple's house has been extended in this area to provide more rooms.

Colvin argued that, despite Fry's claim that the stylistic clash involved in his design was 'no more violent than the change from medieval to Georgian in the High Street front of the college', the amount of glass proposed 'would have belonged to a different technological and aesthetic world altogether'.[45] He concluded that 'Fry's building would have been an alien architectural presence within the walls of All Souls, and the failure to build it need hardly be regretted'. It is perhaps significant, given Colvin's influence in Oxford as a pioneer patron of post-war Modernism, that the genre for new buildings in historic college settings by then involved a solider and heavier use of stone, even where there was a frame structure to support it. Christ's repaid its debt to Modernism by commissioning Sir Denys Lasdun in 1968 for a terraced set of rooms on the northern boundary of the site.

The benefits that modern architecture might confer failed to impress enough of the voting members of the Colleges, whether in terms of cost and impermanence at Christ's or scale and appropriateness at All Souls. These schemes can be considered as part of the history of patronage in each of their universities, reflecting the difficulty of making effective decisions within an academic body. Each has a minor mythical status in the tale of Modernism's heroic passage from pre-war failure to post-war success among institutional patrons.

1. Walter Gropius to Manon Gropius Burchard, London 6 November 1934, quoted in Reginald Isaacs, *Gropius*, Boston, Little Brown, 1991, p.192.

2. Waddington to Gropius, 12 November 1935, 7/502, Bauhaus Archiv Berlin. In 1938, Justin Blanco White designed Shawms, a timber house in Conduit Head Road, Cambridge, for another Fellow of Christ's, Dr. W. A. W. Rushton. See Alan Powers, *Modern: the Modern Movement in Britain*, London, Merrell, 2005, pp.52–3.

3. Barry Supple, 'The Two World Wars', in David Reynolds, ed. *Christ's: A Cambridge College over Five Centuries*, Basingstoke, Macmillan, 2005, pp.170 *et seq.*

4. There is general agreement based on documents and oral history that schemes from the Gropius & Fry partnership were under the separate control of the two partners. Christ's was Gropius's project.

5. In 2011, the drawings by Milne, Gropius and a perspective of the post-war scheme by Albert Richardson, photographed by the author in 1985, could not be located.

6. ibid.

7. Oswald P. Milne, report to Master and Fellows, n.d., Christ's College archives.

8. Report by Walter Gropius, Christ's College archives.

9. G. C. Argan, *Walter Gropius e la Bauhaus*, Torino, Giulio Einaudi, 1951, translated by author from French translation by Elsa Bonan, *Walter Gropius et la Bauhaus*, Paris, Denoël/ Gonthier, 1979, p.153.

10. Waddington to Gropius, 14 January 1937, 9/358, Bauhaus-Archiv, Berlin.

11. Report by Charles Holden, 15 January 1937, Christ's College archives.

12. 'Reply of Messrs Gropius and Fry to Questions concerning Hobson Street Building', Christ's College archives.

13. ibid.

14. Waddington to Gropius, 14 January 1937; Maxwell Fry, *Autobiographical Sketches,* London, Elek, 1975, p.150.

15. Supple, op. cit., p.171.

16. Extract of letter from Dr Gropius to the Master, 13 January 1937, Christ's College Archive.

17. *Architects' Journal*, vol. 87, 3 February, 1938, pp.202–3 and 10 February, p.241.

18. Darwin to Adams, 29 April, 1937. All Souls archive.

19. 'The Gropius Building', *Christ's College Magazine*, Michaelmas Term, 1953, pp.8–12.

20. *Christ's College Magazine*, no.178, 1954, pp.8–9.

21. See S. Green and Peregrine Horden, *All Souls and the Wider World*, Oxford University Press, 2011, pp. 1–12.

22. A. S. G. Butler report, of 11 May 1930, All Souls archive

23. Building Committee, All Souls archive. The Manciple is the official in charge of catering and supplies.

24. Sir Ernest Llewellyn Woodward, to the Joint Committee on 28 June 1936, All Souls archive.

25. Minutes of Building Sub-Committee, 8 November 1936. The other members of the committee were The Warden (William Adams), the Sub-Warden, (E. L. Woodward), Estates Bursar (Geoffrey Faber), Sir Charles Grant Robertson (then serving as Vice-Chancellor of Birmingham University where he was involved in many building projects), Sir Edmund Craster of the Bodleian Library (responsible for commissioning Sir Giles Gilbert Scott's New Bodleian), Ian Bowen, A. M. H. Jones, Sir Hubert Henderson, and D. A. Routh.

26. Geoffrey Faber to Warden Adams, 11 November 1936, All Souls archive.

27. Hope Bagenal to 'Hubert', 1 February 1937, All Souls archive. On Bagenal, see Alan Powers, 'The Classical Theory of Hope Bagenal', in Frank Salmon, ed., *The Persistence of the Classical, Essays on Architecture presented to David Watkin,* London, Philip Wilson, 2008, pp.40–55.

28. Sir Ian MacAlister to Warden Adams, 28 May 1937, All Souls archive. The other names were: Scott, Shepherd and Breakwell; J. Hubert Worthington; A. S. G. Butler, A. E. Richardson, Amyas Connell, the Hon. Humphrey Pakington; W. G. Newton; R. Fielding Dodd; Edward Maufe; Verner O. Rees; Louis De Soissons; Anthony Minoprio; C. H. Holden; C. H. James; Maxwell Ayrton.

29. In *Unbuilt Oxford*, (London, Yale University Press, 1983, p.161) Howard Colvin lists Hampshire as a supporter of Fry's scheme for All Souls. According to the DNB, at Princeton in the 1960s 'he found its pastiche Gothic painful'. As Warden of Wadham College he oversaw extensions by Gillespie, Kidd & Coia in 1971–2.

30. Minutes of Building Committee, 30 October 1938, All Souls archive.

31. Recorded in summary of the building committee's activities, All Souls archive.

32. The Minority Report is not in the College archives, but is referred to in a letter from A. H. Campbell to the Warden, 15 November 1938.

33. 'Report of the five members of the Committee who prefer the design submitted by Mr E. Maxwell Fry', All Souls archive.

34. Woodward to Warden Adams, November 1930.

35. Fry, op. cit., p.153.

36. Report of the five members, loc. cit.

37. Portland stone was not used in Oxford before the work of Powell and Moya and the Architects' Co-Partnership in the late 1950s.

38. Report of the five members, loc. cit.

39. Robertson to Warden Adams, All Souls archive.

40. A. L. Rowse, *All Souls in My Time*, London, Duckworth, 1993, p.181; Campbell, loc. cit.

41. Fry, op. cit. p.154.

42. Woodward to Warden Adams, November 1938 (printed text of letter for circulation), All Souls archive.

43. Summary of Building Committee Minutes, All Souls archive.

44. Colvin, op. cit., p.166.

45. ibid., p.166.

4

Post-War Traditionalists in Oxford and Cambridge

William Fawcett

The pool of well-established architects in Britain after World War II was substantially the same as in the late 1930s. Their careers had been at a standstill during the war, so that an architect born much after 1905 was too young to have made a reputation in the 1930s and was still an unknown quantity; thus it is unsurprising that most Oxbridge building projects in the ten years after 1945 were put in the hands of architects who had been active before 1940, or those who inherited their practices. The modernist avant-garde had little success in Oxbridge in the 1930s and were no more successful in the decade after World War II, when architecture there was dominated – indeed, virtually monopolised – by traditionalists.

Then came a complete reversal of patronage. In the mid-1950s it was still adventurous to appoint a modernist architect, but by 1960 it was reactionary to appoint a traditionalist.[1] The change at Cambridge came when in 1956 students condemned designs by Stephen Dykes Bower for a new residential building at Queens' College, while at Oxford opposition to traditional schemes came from young Fellows. This was a time of change throughout British culture, symbolised by the 'angry young men', when established reputations were pushed aside by a radical younger generation.

The traditional architects working at Oxford and Cambridge after 1945 were generally older than those who adopted Modernism. The principal exception was Arne Jacobsen, an indication how modern architects abroad established reputations ahead of those in Britain, and also how those who did practice in Britain in the 1930s were being passed over by the 1950s. On the traditional side the youngest practitioner in this survey was Louis Osman who, as we will see, rather defies categorization. The major figures of the rising generation were born in the decade 1910–20 and trained as the Modern Movement gained ascendancy in the architectural schools during the 1930s; they were convinced modernists. As the younger architects took more and more commissions from the mid-1950s onwards, traditionalism became confined in Oxbridge to the smallest and most conservation-minded schemes, mainly by local architects, until its revival with Quinlan Terry's projects for Downing College, Cambridge, in the 1980s. But Terry was a generation younger again, born in 1937 and trained in the late 1950s when Modernism was no longer a utopian dream but prosaic reality.

A Forgotten Backwater

Is post-World War II traditionalist architecture in Oxbridge worth studying? In his epic book *Architecture: Nineteenth and Twentieth Centuries* of 1958, Henry-Russell Hitchcock included a chapter with the cumbersome title 'Architecture called traditional in the twentieth century'. He argued that it was a survival, 'sunk in inertia and conservatism, very different from the vitality of new developments'.[2] He claimed that after Lutyens's death in 1944, 'there has not been, either in England or elsewhere, any traditional or even semi-traditional building of consequence'. Although Hitchcock was writing at the short-lived zenith of the Modern Movement he realised that opinions could change, though he could contemplate no revival: 'however the future may evaluate the achievements of the traditional architects of the twentieth century, the chapter is now closed'.[3]

It is surely time for that re-evaluation. Revisiting buildings that were generally ignored or despised when they were built in the 1940s and 1950s may reveal overlooked treasures, as found elsewhere – notably with the anachronistic but exciting work in Ljubljana of the late-classicist Jože Plečnik (1872–1957), not mentioned by Hitchcock. Pevsner's comment on Victorian architecture could perhaps be applied here: '… the challenge of the unrecognized period, the period people laughed at and refused to know'.[4]

The traditionalists and modernists thought that much more was at stake than style, but their polemics are not very enlightening. The traditionalists' intense hostility to modern architecture seems to come down to practicality and taste: they thought that modern buildings were impractical and ugly. On practicality they were frequently right, but lapses in practicality are not enough to condemn an architectural style – witness Blenheim Palace. Equally dubious was the modernists' credo that social, economic and technical change called for a radically new aesthetic. Despite the unconvincing polemics, when it came to style the distinct positions were clear.

The Overhang

The decade after 1945 saw austerity as Britain struggled to recover from wartime exertions, damage and debts, with limited resources targeted at pubic housing, schools and industry. However, some building did take place in Oxbridge. Many of these schemes had been planned before the war and, though whether due to far-sightedness or force of habit is not always clear, they retained the familiar Oxbridge solidity and durability. It is sometimes hard to tell whether which schemes are pre-war and which post-date 1945.

Some schemes begun before the war were continued with few changes. At Clare College, Cambridge, Sir Giles Gilbert Scott (1880–1960) extended his Memorial Court

Traditionalists	Year of birth	Modernists	Year of birth
G G Scott	1880	A Jacobsen	1902
A E Richardson	1880	B Spence	1907
H Worthington	1886	L Martin	1908
A T Scott	1887	R Sheppard	1910
T Rayson	1888	H Casson	1910
M Sisson	1897	D Roberts	1911
R Erith	1904	L Brett	1913
R Hurd	1905	D Lasdun	1914
L Osman	1914	Architects' Co-Partnership	1915/16
Q Terry	1937	Chamberlin Powell & Bon	1919/20/21
		Powell & Moya	1921/20
		Howell Killick Partridge & Amis	1922/24
		C A St J Wilson	1922
		A & P Smithson	1928/23
		P Dowson (Arup Associates)	1924
		Stirling & Gowan	1926/1923

Fig 2. A.T. Scott at Downing College, Cambridge.
The centrepiece of Sir Herbert Baker's pre-war plan for the College was completed by Scott in 1952

buildings (the first phase had opened in 1922), faithfully reproducing the neo-Georgian pre-war appearance but with less generous interior layouts. In Oxford, his building of 1937 at St Anne's College was continued – an energetic design that is far removed from historic styles, although clearly not modernist. Gavin Stamp describes this further. After Scott, Clare turned to David Roberts and St Anne's to Gerald Banks and then Howell, Killick, Partridge and Amis.

At Downing College, Cambridge, the plan by Sir Herbert Baker (1862–1946) that had been started in the 1930s was heroically carried forward after the war by his partner A. T. Scott (1887–1962), no relation of Sir Giles.[5] The axial centrepiece with portico was completed in 1952, only slightly pared down from Baker's grand – even grandiose – concept. However, Kenny Court at Downing by A. T. Scott and Vernon Helbing, completed in 1962, is the dampest of squibs, with not only no ornamentation but no respite from banality in the regularity of its proportions. For their next buildings in the 1960s Downing also employed Howell, Killick, Partridge and Amis.

Living history – Sir Albert Richardson

Sir Albert Richardson (1880–1964) was the avuncular face of anti-Modernism in the 1940s and 1950s.[6] His architectural career stretched back as far as 1895 when he started as an articled pupil. He worked for various architects, including the late Gothic revivalist Leonard Stokes, before setting up the practice Richardson and Gill in 1908. Richardson enthusiastically joined the Edwardian classical revival, which was a fresh and exciting change from the excesses of Victorian Gothic and Edwardian Baroque styles. He published several books, including *Monumental Classical Architecture in Great Britain and Ireland in the XVIIIth and XIXth Centuries* (1914) which was a labour of love. In 1919 he became Professor of Architecture at the Bartlett School of Architecture in University College, London, where he was noted for ambidextrous sketching of symmetrical classical buildings on the lecture room blackboard.

Fig 3. Sir Albert
Richardson at Christ's
College, Cambridge.
Two residential
blocks were built in
1948 and 1952

Richardson and Gill's successful inter-war practice included neo-Georgian designs but also Arts and Crafts churches and commercial buildings that were modern, if not too modern. Richardson did not feel strictly bound by the architectural conventions of the past. At his home in Ampthill, on the other hand, he re-created a fantasy of the Georgian era, playing the part of a lovable English eccentric.

After the war, Richardson held a prominent place in the profession and the public eye. He was a member of the Royal Fine Art Commission, received the Royal Gold Medal in 1947, became president of the Royal Academy in 1954 and was knighted in 1956. He maintained a successful practice that included restoring bombed Wren churches as well as many new buildings. His masterpiece is Bracken House of 1954–9, built for the *Financial Times* in the City of London; in 1987 it was the first post-World War II building to be listed. Although traditional rather than modern, it has a Perret-like geometrical order and could not be considered neo-Georgian.

Richardson did not have any pre-war Oxbridge commissions, but when the Bartlett School was evacuated to Cambridge he lived in St Catharine's College. In the late 1940s he designed two new residential buildings for Christ's College, Cambridge (where Gropius and Fry had been rejected before the war). The four-storey front elevations that face each other across a court have a regular grid of double-hung sash windows. If they were twice as long they might acquire something of the no-nonsense grandeur of industrial revolution mills. There is a little more drama at the rear with bold staircase projections that have elongated windows. An elegant copper cupola was added to a neighbouring Victorian building.

In the same period Richardson added an infill building at Trinity Hall, Cambridge with a similar mix of old and new but not modern. The back elevation on to Garret Hostel Lane is an object lesson in how to design a blank two-storey wall. The centre of Cambridge was also lit by Richardson's 'candle' lamp posts, of which a handful survive. They are inefficient but demonstrate that Richardson could come up with new ideas in response to new problems.

In Oxford Richardson designed a number of buildings for St Hilda's College. Here an obviously neo-Georgian but inventive idiom predominates in the Principal's Lodgings of 1954–5 and Wolfson Building of 1960–1, somewhat in the spirit of Raymond Erith. With exceptions like Bracken House, many of Richardson's post-war designs have the feeling of quick sketch ideas that were built without receiving intense care in design development and detailing. This seems to apply at St Hilda's. The Cambridge buildings have more substance but they are only of moderate interest. In the 1960s Christ's College commissioned Denys Lasdun, Trinity Hall commissioned Arup Associates and Trevor Dannatt, while St Hilda's employed Alison and Peter Smithson.

The Traditionalist Convert – Marshall Sisson

Marshall Sisson (1897–1978) entered the Bartlett School of Architecture in 1920, where Albert Richardson was professor.[7] He was a star student who in 1924 won a scholarship to the British School in Rome, and in 1926 he travelled to the Middle East to study Roman buildings. He also travelled to the USA. After starting in practice in 1928 he designed several cubical modernist houses, some actually made of concrete. Two were in Cambridge, one a white cube and the other a more relaxed composition in brick.[8]
Then in 1935 Sisson won the competition for a new public library in Colchester with a neo-Georgian design. Why the change? Perhaps it was driven by expediency. Sisson had moved to Dedham, near Colchester, so the library was a big prize; Richardson was the competition assessor, and Sisson knew what would appeal to his old teacher. But the rejection of Modernism was permanent and thereafter Sisson never deviated from traditional styles. He joined the British Union of Fascists in 1935, so perhaps he was repelled by the un-British, even Bolshevik, associations of Modernism or what Reginald Blomfield termed *Modernismus*.[9]

Fig 4. Marshall Sisson at Pembroke College, Cambridge. The Orchard building was completed in 1957; exterior view

After World War II Sisson's new work was very traditional. He was active in conservation work, repairing bomb-damaged Wren churches in the City of London and Thomas Archer's St John's Smith Square, Westminster, which became a concert hall. With Albert Richardson he taught architecture in the Royal Academy Schools, where he struck Peter Smithson, who was a student in 1948, as a 'rabid classicist'.[10] He became an RA in 1963 and retired in 1970. His practice, based in Huntingdon, still continues and specialises in conservation.

Sisson built one new building in Oxbridge – the Orchard Building for Pembroke College, Cambridge. The project was initiated in 1951 and completed in 1957. Its layout and appearance are completely regular and orderly; Sisson's modernist houses also had rows of identical, evenly-spaced windows. From a distance the Orchard Building looks like the blandest of 1950s neo-Georgian, dropped into Pembroke with no regard for the architectural context (it is a Georgian-free college). But when viewed close-up the design's refinement is evident. It is beautifully detailed, from the granite course at ground level to the copper roof – satisfyingly earnest and thorough. The first floor windows look puzzlingly squat, as if Sisson felt obliged to use windows of exactly the same size for the student rooms on all the three floors. There is more fun in the staircases, with concrete cantilever treads and massive balustrading in attenuated Roman Doric columns.

Sisson used the same architectural language in a large country house refurbishment at Okeover in Staffordshire, for John Martin Robinson 'arguably the finest house built in England in the 1950s'.[11] Pevsner commented on Okeover, 'a remarkably good job it is, given that one accepts the necessity to add neo-Georgian to real Georgian (which one must be permitted to deny)'.[12] In Oxford Sisson was commissioned by The Queen's College to convert a group of existing buildings into a small residential quad, completed in the early 1970s. The new elements are in a low-key, traditional style.

Fig 5. Marshall Sisson at Pembroke College, Cambridge. Staircase

The Creative Traditionalist – Raymond Erith

Raymond Erith (1904–73) studied at the Architectural Association from 1921–4.[13] In 1928 he began his own practice with Bertram Hume, with whom he made modest progress in the 1930s, including success in an ideas competition for replanning in Stockholm. Erith's largest built work was a house for his wife's parents in Dedham, Essex, (1937–8), in a traditional style that had echoes of Sir John Soane. Erith moved to Dedham in 1936, becoming a near neighbour of Marshall Sisson, whose politics repelled him so much that he was prepared, in agreement with two Dedham neighbours, to shoot Sisson if the Germans invaded. With the outbreak of World War II the architectural practice was abandoned and Erith turned to farming in Essex.

Erith re-established his practice after the war, initially with small projects in Essex and Suffolk. He exhibited at the Royal Academy and gained a reputation in the profession despite turning his back on any form of Modernism, becoming an RA in 1964. In 1954 he was on the shortlist put forward by the RIBA for a new building at Exeter College, Oxford. He wrote, 'I know Oxford well (architecturally) and I think I could design a building that would be appropriate'.[14] Exeter chose Lionel Brett, but in 1955 Erith received commissions from two other Oxford colleges.

The first was for the Provost's Lodgings at The Queen's College, completed in 1959. It is a straightforward neo-Georgian house with rooms opening off a central corridor that connects to the college at one end and to the street, Queen's Lane, at the other. The main point of interest is the elevation to Queen's Lane, a back street that runs between blank walls – picturesque but austere. To suit this context while also giving the Provost's Lodgings some distinction Erith made his elevation practically blank but with elaborate rustication on the ground floor, using classical motifs in a highly non-standard way. Erith was playing with the language of classical architecture.

Fig 6. Raymond Erith at The Queen's College, Oxford. The north elevation of the Provost's Lodgings, completed in 1959

Erith then secured a series of commissions at Lady Margaret Hall, Oxford. His first building was a new library, in 1959–61. The ground floor was for bookstacks, with a first-floor reading room and second-floor galleries lit by high-level lunette windows. The elevations are idiosyncratic; Erith explained that they were generated by the building's function. The second building extended the library and provided four storeys of student rooms in 1963–6. The two buildings form one block but the arrangement of windows is jarringly different in the two parts. It is hard to decide whether Erith displayed casual indifference or confident assurance.

Erith's third building was at the entrance to the college (1963–6). It is joined to the library in an L-shape, but has quite a different character. The side facing the street has only a few small windows, and resembles a seventeenth-century stable block, or a barracks. The other side facing into the college has generous double-hung six-pane sash windows, unlike the casements in the adjacent library. This building exudes strength and permanence, although it is only just over forty years old, with none of the library's eccentricity. It is amazing to see such diversity in Erith's three adjacent buildings at Lady Margaret Hall, designed and built almost simultaneously. Erith himself claimed that he began by continuing the earlier tradition established by Sir Reginald Blomfield, but that later he turned in favour of greater simplicity and against so many windows; perhaps, too, he sought to create some synthetic history for a modern college.[15]

Robert Hurd at Emmanuel College, Cambridge

Robert Hurd (1905–63) studied English and History at Emmanuel College, Cambridge, in 1924–7, coming under the influence of the charismatic English don Mansfield Forbes – 'small, androgynous, homosexual … who enchanted most whom he met'.[16] Forbes promoted new ideas, especially in the visual arts. Putting his ideas into practice, he leased a Victorian house in Cambridge and with the architect Raymond McGrath converted it into 'Finella' – a manifesto of advanced taste. This was in 1928–9. Hurd returned to Emmanuel to study at the University's School of Architecture in 1929–30; it must have been a formative period.

Hurd then completed his architectural studies at the College of Art in Edinburgh and stayed in the city for the rest of his life. He set up in practice in 1932 with Norman

Neil (1899–1976). Neil left in 1950 and Ian Begg became Hurd's partner in 1952. Hurd quickly became involved in conservation issues, refurbishing and rebuilding houses in Canongate in Edinburgh in the 1950s. They are strongly contextual but Hurd opposed reproductions of historic buildings, arguing that 'buildings of twentieth century design and construction should be erected in the gaps where old property has been pulled down'.[17]

The commission from his old Cambridge college came in 1955. Several building projects were identified and the first to be taken forward was the replacement of the kitchens and provision of a new first-floor refectory in the north-west corner of the college's main site. It was built in 1957–9. The old east elevation to the interior of the college was retained, but the west and north elevations to St Andrew's Street and Emmanuel Road were newly designed by Hurd and Begg. These are important street elevations, more visible now than in the 1950s because a magnificent tree on the corner of the streets has been lost. The two-storey building is crisply detailed without ornamentation; the copper roof has tight eaves. There is a break between the stone-clad refectory and the rendered service areas (currently underplayed because the render's paint colour is a perfect match for the stone).

The new building's visual impact hardly lives up to its prominent setting (although it is not as feeble as Maufe's bicycle shed of 1938–9 for St John's College, Cambridge, on the corner of St John's Street and Bridge Street). It is pleasant and inoffensive and solid – but unadventurous. Hurd argued that a building in this location had to be secondary to the College's adjacent classical centerpiece, and that modern or pastiche-historical designs would both have been inappropriate.[18] He had decided, 'not to rely on any stylistic mediation, but to let the buildings simply reflect their functions, with varied surface treatment'.[19] There is one architectural gesture, a set of three tall, stripped-baronial windows to the first-floor refectory. The bays are slightly faceted on plan, but this is barely noticeable except when the sun catches them at just the right angle.

When it was finished in 1959 Hurd's building attracted a flurry of negative criticism from people who thought that it should have been bolder and more modern. Hurd and Begg developed ideas for other buildings at Emmanuel, but instead the College chose modern designs by Tom Hancock (1930–2006).

Fig 9. Robert Hurd at
Emmanuel College,
Cambridge. The new
kitchens and first floor
refectory completed
in 1959. This is the
west elevation facing
a busy street

Louis Osman at Newnham College, Cambridge

Louis Osman (1914–96) was the youngest of our group of post-war traditionalists.[20]
In 1931 he entered the Bartlett School of Architecture under Albert Richardson.
He made a start in architectural practice before World War II and served in the forces
from 1940–4. His practice was revived afterwards on a small scale; he never seems to
have had a partner nor any long-term architectural assistants. He had a wide range of
social contacts who provided a supply of work, much of it in domestic and refurbishment
projects. His were the original plans for the reconstruction of the bomb-damaged St
John's, Smith Square, London, as a concert hall that was carried out by Marshall Sisson.
Osman's interest in the integration of architecture with the arts was still more evident in
his restoration of Nos.11 and 14 Cavendish Square, Westminster, for the Covent of the
Holy Child Jesus, with Epstein's *Virgin and Child* set on the first-floor link that he
introduced between them.

In the mid-1950s Osman began designing metalwork and received many prestigious
commissions from the Goldsmiths Company of the City of London and other clients.
He designed, and his workshop made, the crown used for the investiture of the Prince
of Wales in 1969. His metalwork is highly individualistic and not at all imitative of
traditional styles. Yet although he achieved a higher profile as a metalworker, Osman did
not give up architectural practice. One of his most successful projects was a small gallery
in a side chapel at Lincoln Cathedral for the display of objects from the Cathedral
Treasury, realised in 1960.

The Principal's Lodge at Newnham College, Cambridge, of 1958–9 was one of
Osman's largest built projects. It is a two-storey brick villa built round a courtyard.
The entrance facade is on the north, built right up to the pavement edge. It is practically

windowless (like the entrance facade of the Provost's Lodgings at The Queen's College, Oxford), but enlivened by a shallow colonnade at ground floor and blank recesses on the first floor. Osman's house is attenuated and elegant, not echoing any historic style but suave without being wholly modern. It seems poised for the arrival of a couple in evening dress, stepping out of a sleek Armstrong-Siddeley car.

The Lodge's internal courtyard was surrounded by two-storey high sheets of glass – a technical *tour de force* that proved impractical. The glazing was removed and the courtyard roofed in during the 1990s. Some of the glass panels had sculptures fixed to them by Geoffrey Clarke, and these are now in the college's main corridor. The misdirected ambition seems characteristic of Osman, both as an architect and metalworker. His energy, persuasiveness and disregard for cost led to problems in several projects. Newnham's new buildings of the 1960s were designed by the local firm of Lyster and Grillet.

The last Traditionalist Building? Thomas Rayson at Mansfield College, Oxford

The prize for Oxbridge's last traditionalist building (of the 'survival' not the 'revival') would be difficult to award with certainty, but a strong contender must be the range at Mansfield College, Oxford, by Thomas Rayson (1888–1976).[21] Begun after Erith's work at Lady Margaret Hall but completed first, the foundation stone was laid in December 1960 and it was opened in 1962.

Rayson had been articled to a London architect and attended the Brixton School of Building before coming to Oxford in 1910. In 1919 he won a competition for housing in Witney and set up his own practice, specialising in domestic work in rural Oxfordshire and the Cotswolds.

The new building at Mansfield College is an L-shaped range of two storeys plus attics, in a super-restrained, chimneyless Cotswold cottage style. The contrast between Rayson's primness and Champneys's louche Gothic of the College's main buildings is almost comic. The new buildings are detailed with extreme care; in the framed entrance

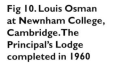

Fig 10. Louis Osman at Newnham College, Cambridge. The Principal's Lodge completed in 1960

doors, for example, the hinges align most beautifully with the transom rails. There is one semi-bold gesture – a staircase tower projecting towards the street. The buildings look durable; they are now fifty years old and have barely weathered. This is practical and commendable, but in terms of expression they suggest that there is really no need to change from familiar conventions. After the building was praised in the *Oxford Magazine* in 1963, Rayson responded with a letter about continuing the fight against architectural barbarism, but he was practically the last man on the ramparts.[22]

The Critical Heritage

Traditional buildings after the war attracted little critical attention in Oxbridge or anywhere else. The focus of discussion, whether for or against, was on modern architecture. The Cambridge classicist Hugh Plommer was a vociferous member of the 'anti' camp.[23] One might expect him to have welcomed new traditionalist buildings, but this was not the case. His words of praise were sparing: he greatly disliked Erith's mannerism and it is perhaps revealing that two buildings he commended, Scott and Helbing's Kenny Court at Downing College, Cambridge, and Rayson's addition at Mansfield College, Oxford, are notably anaemic. Plommer was much more exercised by what he saw as ignorant errors than excited by the spark of genius.

The mainstream view of the 1960s is usefully set out in *Cambridge New Architecture*. Non-modernist buildings and their clients were condemned, but some indulgence was shown to Richardson: 'Although the neo-Georgian style is not yet dead in England, Professor Richardson was probably the last architect to use it with integrity and finesse.'[24] There are, however, no Erith buildings in Cambridge.

In the *Buildings of England* volumes for Oxfordshire (1974) and Cambridgeshire (1970) Nikolaus Pevsner was on principle hostile to the continuation of pre-modern architectural styles, but made exceptions where he saw architectural merit. He even had kind words for the Dolphin Gate at Trinity College, Oxford, of 1947–8 by Sir Hubert Worthington: 'Quite a nice little piece, though of course twenty or twenty-five years out of date.'[25] Writing respectfully about Lady Margaret Hall, he described Erith's work as 'almost like a freak of nature'.[26]

Discussion and Conclusion

This has not been a comprehensive survey of post-war traditionalist buildings in Oxbridge, and has shied from the tricky dilemma of deciding whether to classify Easton and Robertson's science and engineering buildings in Cambridge as traditionalist or modern. The selection has emphasised college rather than university buildings, perhaps because the colleges were more individual and varied in their architectural projects.

It is interesting how strongly some of the traditionalist architects emphasised practicality, getting close to claiming functional determinism for their designs. Was this not supposed to be the distinguishing feature of Modernism, also known as functionalism?[27] But where the modernists stressed functionalism in their planning, the traditionalists often scored in terms of durability and ease of maintenance, and in this they have brought benefits to later college bursars. In reality architectural form is never determined by function but by the architects themselves, even when they are in denial, like Hurd at Emmanuel College, who claimed that he rejected all styles.

Few of the traditionalists were slavish imitators of past styles. Of this selection, Sisson at Pembroke, Cambridge, was definitely neo-Georgian, and Erith's Oxford projects have Georgian roots, more or less radically transformed. On the other hand, buildings by Sir Giles Scott, Richardson, Hurd and Osman, although self-evidently not modern, were not directly based on historic precedents.

Raymond Erith claimed to begin his additions to Lady Margaret Hall in a very contextual manner, but then rebelled. Indeed, most of the buildings discussed here were not contextual, and this may have increased the hostility of modernist critics such as Nicholas Taylor, versed in the *Architectural Review*'s 'townscape' campaign and that of the emerging Civic Trust. It is curious to note instead, how the softer modernists embraced that approach at Cambridge.

Has the study revealed any neglected masterpieces? No, but the buildings show the skill and commitment of architects whose careers personified an era that has a place in the history of British twentieth century architecture. There is a case for working in an uninventive way but with a good eye for proportion and mass, as seen perhaps in Sisson's work at Pembroke College, Cambridge. The most engaging buildings are by Raymond Erith. His work shows conclusively that inventiveness is independent of style, a combination of the formal and narrative that approaches a twentieth-century mannerism; he is the hero of the piece. It would be interesting to compare his mannerism with that of Powell and Moya at Brasenose and Corpus Christi in Oxford.

1. Louise Campbell, 'Building on the Backs: Basil Spence, Queens' College Cambridge and University Architecture at Mid-Century', *Architectural History*, vol.54, 2011, pp.383–405.

2. Henry-Russell Hitchcock, *Architecture: Nineteenth and Twentieth Centuries*, London, Pelican, 1958, p.392.

3. ibid., pp.408, 410.

4. Nikolaus Pevnser, 'The Anti-Pioneers', radio talk, 1966; reprinted in Stephen Games (ed.), *Pevsner on Art and Architecture*, London, Methuen, 2002, p.306.

5. Cinzia Maria Sicca, *Committed to Classicism: The Building of Downing College, Cambridge*, Cambridge, Downing College, 1987, pp.95–6.

6. Simon Houfe, *Sir Albert Richardson: the Professor,* Luton, White Cresset Press, 1980; Simon Houfe, Alan Powers & John Wilton-Ely (eds), *Sir Albert Richardson*, London, RIBA Heinz Gallery, 1999; John Summerson, 'Sir Albert Richardson', *Oxford Dictionary of National Biography* (http://www.oxforddnb.com/view/article/35737, accessed 10 Jan 2013).

7. James Bettley, 'Marshall Sisson 1897–1978', *Transactions of the RIBA,* vol.1, no.2, 1982, pp.93–100.

8. Alan Powers, *The Modern Movement in Britain*, London, Merrell, 2005, pp.214–15.

9. Reginald Blomfield, *Modernismus*, London, Macmillan, 1934.

10. Peter Smithson and Peter Carolin, 'Reflections on Hunstanton', *arq*, vol.2, no.4, Summer, 1997, pp.32–43 (p.34).

11. John Martin Robinson, *The Latest Country Houses*, London, Bodley Head, 1984, p.68.

12. Nikolaus Pevsner, *The Buildings of England: Staffordshire,* London, Penguin, 1974, p.215.

13. Lucy Archer, *Raymond Erith Architect*, Burford, Cygnet Press, 1985; Lucy Archer (ed.), *Raymond Erith Progressive Classicist*, London, Sir John Soane's Museum, 2004; John Summerson, 'Raymond Erith', *Oxford Dictionary of National Biography* (http://www.oxforddnb.com/view/article/31083, accessed 10 Jan 2013).

14. Letter from Raymond Erith to Exeter College, Oxford, 3 March 1954, 'Corner Site', Exeter College archives.

15. Archer, 1985, op. cit., p.146.

16. Dictionary of Scottish Architects, 'Robert Hurd', www.scottisharchitects.org.uk, accessed 15 October 2012; Elizabeth Darling, 'Finella, Mansfield Forbes, Raymond McGrath, and Modernist Architecture in Britain', *Journal of British Studies*, vol.50, no.1, 2011, pp.125–55 (p.131).

17. Robert Hurd, quoted in 'Edinburgh's Royal Mile', *Builder*, vol.182, no.5687, 15 February 1952, p.276; see also *Builder*, no.5705, 20 June 1952, p.912.

18. 'Architect's Statement' by Robert Hurd, February 1959, 'New Kitchen', Emmanuel College archives.

19. Robert Hurd, September 1957, ibid.

20. Jenny Moore, *Louis Osman*, Tiverton, Halsgrove, 2006.

21. A. Bruce, 'The Oxford War Memorial: Thomas Rayson and the Chester connection', *Oxoniensia*, vol.56, 1991, pp.155–68.

22. Hugh Plommer, 'New Buildings in Oxford', *Oxford Magazine*, vol.3, 21 February 1963, pp.196–8; Thomas Rayson, letter to the Editor, *Oxford Magazine,* 7 March 1963, p.234.

23. For example, Hugh Plommer, letter to the Editor, *Cambridge Review*, vol.79, no.1924, 8 February 1958, p.319; 'New Buildings in Oxford', ibid.

24. Nicholas Taylor, *Cambridge New Architecture*, Cambridge, published by the editors, 1964, p.16.

25. Nikolaus Pevsner and Jennifer Sherwood, *The Buildings of England: Oxfordshire*, London, Penguin, 1974, p.207; see also Nikolaus Pevsner, *The Buildings of England: Cambridgeshire*, London, Penguin, 1970.

26. Pevsner and Sherwood, ibid, p.232.

27. John Summerson, 'The Case for a Theory of Modern Architecture', *RIBA Journal*, vol.64, no.8, June 1957, pp.307–313; reprinted as 'The Case for a Theory of "Modern" Architecture', in Summerson, *The Unromantic Castle*, London, Thames & Hudson, 1990, pp.257–66.

5
The Richardson Candles, Cambridge
Simon Cornwell

Fig 1. Richardson Candle in Trumpington Street, 2013 (Sarah Duncan)

The listing of the Richardson Candles in Cambridge has finally recognised the twentieth-century street light as an item worth saving and preserving. Street lighting in the last century saw an extraordinary number of lighting designs which utilised many different building materials and often mirrored the architectural movements of the time. Unfortunately the vast majority have been lost and the Candles, a robustly elegant example of post-war rebuilding and civic pride, were also destined for the skip.

Like many cities after the Second World War, Cambridge's street lighting required urgent modernisation and the council decided to replace the antique gas installation with a modern electrical one. The historic city core required some sensitivity, and interested to gauge opinion and judge the diversity of options, the council allowed various manufacturers to trial street lights along King's Parade in the mid-1950s. It was obvious that neither the austere functional units nor the quaint 'heritage' offerings erected were in keeping with the architecture and were therefore unsuitable. So, probably aware of the successful remodelling of Parliament Square by Grey Wornum and his successful new street light for Westminster, the city's councillors commissioned architect Sir Albert Richardson to design a solution for Cambridge.

Richardson had gained some prominence, if not notoriety, in the street lighting field. He had advised on units in York, Skipton and Peterborough (amongst others), and had fought a bitter (and losing) battle against the standards installed in his home town of Amphill. 'Don't call them street lights, call them monstrosities', he bellowed. Yet the practicalities and economics of the lighting engineer clashed greatly with the artistic establishment of the 1950s as Britain started its post-war rebuilding efforts. As the lighting stock was gradually replenished, using the latest ideas in lighting technology, architects and critics were quick to condemn their efforts. Richardson was not alone; Betjeman and Nairn were similarly scathing as ungainly new street lights sprang up across the land.

It was the Festival of Britain which indirectly provided the solution for Cambridge's new lighting. The lighting engineers of Birmingham had teamed up with the REVO Electric Company of Tipton to design something new and fresh for their city's streets as part of the Festival celebrations. Their design was a mixture of the old and new: the fluted and decorated column harked back to a classical era, yet the use of the newly introduced fluorescent tube with a Perspex diffuser was completely contemporary. REVO's lighting engineers realised, however, that the unit had shortcomings, as the Perspex diffuser threw the majority of the light outwards, and so only included the 'Festival Lantern' in the 'Ornamental' section of their catalogue.

This combination of styles would have appealed to Richardson, whose Georgian affection was matched with a pragmatic dose of modernism. The Festival Lantern was close to his ideal of a street light, the only post-topped example erected along King's

Parade during the street lighting trial. Richardson smoothed the fussy capital detail and simplified the scalloped and grooved lantern caps, thus giving the unit a more refined silhouette. But, with a nod to his classical side and to the streets of Cambridge, he kept the fluting. He gave his reasons during a speech in Cambridge in 1957 when the 120 bespoke Richardson Candles were installed, explaining that 'The lighting in a city should be regulated by the city itself, by the condition and formation of the streets, by the buildings and houses, and certainly with regard for vistas and silhouettes.'

This statement underlined the diametrically opposed positions of the architect and lighting engineer. Richardson designed his Candles for their daylight appearance and their ability to both blend in and enhance the street scene, whilst the lighting engineer was primarily concerned with the adequate lighting of the street and its surroundings, and considered the daylight appearance as secondary. The result was minimally intrusive visually, yet gave little light. The Candles did not work in the confined city streets, where their indirect light wash was largely absorbed by the dark bricks of the buildings' frontages; and they certainly did not work within the wider streets where the majority of the light was cast away on the horizontal and not directed to the street below. But they looked majestic and unobtrusive during the day as Richardson had intended.

The Candles became an accepted and noticeable feature of Cambridge's street scene, much commented upon, and usually mentioned in guide books. While other architect-designed street lighting systems were gradually replaced, a small number clung on as the council deliberated between their inadequacy as street lights and increasing historical pedigree. Their final removal was agreed in 2010, faced by a Publicly Funded Initiative for Cambridgeshire and Northamptonshire which will see the replacement of all street lights in both counties. The listing of the Candles came just in time.

It is hoped that the listing of five groups of Richardson Candles in May 2011 will enable other schemes to be saved. It would be wonderful if the elegant concrete standards of Dublin or the last remaining REVO Festival lights in Birmingham could be similarly recognised and rescued. The twentieth-century street light is as much of our history as its earlier, more recognisable, gas forebear, and should not be allowed to disappear forever.

Fig 2. Richardson Candle outside the Fitzwilliam Museum (Author)

Fig 3. The festival Lantern (REVO)

Architectural Lighting Standards and Fittings

The FESTIVAL (right)

This elegant fluted column was originally designed in conjunction with the vertical fluorescent lantern as illustrated but can be supplied to accommodate other types of fittings if desired.

The fittings and columns themselves present a feature of architectural beauty, adding grace and dignity to the thoroughfare by day and providing most effective illumination by night.

The design is particularly suitable for Public Squares, Parks, Bridges, etc.

The standard is of cast iron, having a door opening measuring 24in. x 6$\frac{3}{4}$in. to house control gear accessories, time switch and cut-out.

The lantern shown is C13428 arranged for four 80 watt 5ft. fluorescent tubular lamps as described in catalogue section 6, page 37.

The column together with lantern gives a height of approximately 21ft. out of ground, and the normal finish is bronze paint.

The columns and lanterns illustrated were originally produced to designs by the City of Birmingham Public Lighting Department for installation in the principal streets of the city.

The FESTIVAL JUNIOR (left)

Height to top of column 12ft. 6in.
Door opening 14in. x 5$\frac{1}{4}$in.

The lantern shown is arranged for 40 watt 2ft. Fluorescent lamps

C14038	—	2 lights
C14040	—	4 lights

FESTIVAL JUNIOR

FESTIVAL

6
'The Ideal Campus': The Sidgwick Site, Cambridge
Alistair Fair

Fig 1. Sidgwick Site, detail of staircase, Raised Faculty Building (James O. Davies/English Heritage)

Writing in 1950, Nikolaus Pevsner welcomed the publication of Charles Holden and Myles Wright's proposals for the future development of Cambridge, praising especially their suggestion that the university might grow beyond the city core into the western suburbs.[1] There had previously been some incursions into this area by a scattering of college buildings and by Giles Gilbert Scott's University Library of 1932–5, but it remained largely a mixture of playing fields and large villas. Writing in the university's own *Cambridge Review*, Pevsner suggested that the new development could be 'an ideal campus'. The Backs – the open green area around the River Cam, behind the historic colleges – would be 'no longer backs but fronts'.[2] Moreover, he hoped that 'modern architecture of a high aesthetic standard ... could at last get a chance'.[3] The university had, in fact, already turned its attention in this direction, purchasing Corpus Christi College's cricket ground in Sidgwick Avenue and securing an option on several adjacent houses in West Road then owned by Gonville and Caius College.[4] The combined site

Fig 2. Robert Atkinson's scheme for the Sidgwick Site, plan (by permission of the Syndics of Cambridge University Library and Syborn & Atkinson)

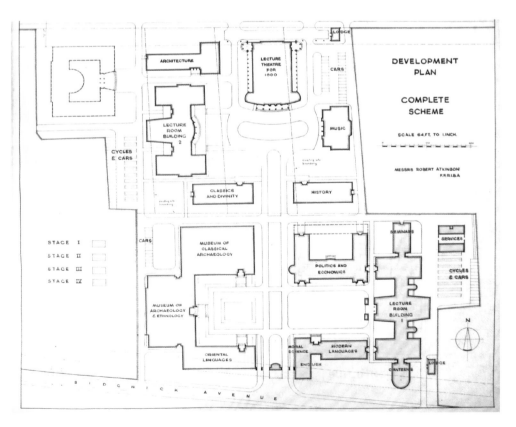

– some twelve acres – was developed from the late 1950s to accommodate many of the arts faculties, initially to a plan prepared by Hugh Casson and Neville Conder. Pevsner approved of their selection, romantically imagining his successors as Slade Professor enjoying the use of their buildings.[5]

As a major piece of 1950s planning and the earliest post-war attempt at a comprehensive university plan, it is surprising that the Sidgwick Site has not attracted more attention from historians.[6] However, as Louise Campbell has suggested, the design competition in 1958 for Churchill College casts a shadow over this period.[7] Along with the appointment of Leslie Martin as Professor of Architecture in 1956, Churchill has come to be seen as a decisive moment in the triumph of modern architecture (or at least a certain kind of modern architecture) in Cambridge, with earlier projects being dismissed as 'moderate' and 'conformist'.[8] Such assessments were perhaps given additional force by the lengthy gestation of the Casson/Conder scheme, its fundamentals devised in the first half of the 1950s. By the mid 1960s, their approach seemed rather old-fashioned to the rising avant-garde.

However, the design should not be seen simply through the lens of what followed. Both the development plan and the part of the site that was eventually completed by Casson and Conder reveal careful juxtapositions of scales and materials, controlled vistas and a delight in detailing, embodying the 'townscape' philosophy of the late-1940s *Architectural Review*. The design offered a compelling image of a new Cambridge in which the faculties were to be as much a focus of activity as the historic colleges, and of a 'modern' university. This last subject aroused particular discussion in the 1950s.[9] With the Barlow Report (1946) calling for universities to provide the scientists who could maintain Britain's place in an increasingly technological world, and Lord Robbins in 1963 presenting Higher Education as the forge in which to create 'cultivated men and women', the expanding universities had a front-line role in re-forming Britain. In this context, architecture could have symbolic as well as practical value, connoting progressive ideals whilst also providing the environments in which would be formed those who might lead the modern nation.[10]

'Each Faculty will be housed in a separate building'

The origins of the Sidgwick Site have as much to do with creating space for science as accommodating the expansion of the arts. The majority of the university's laboratories in the 1940s were located within the city centre on the New Museums and Downing sites, but neither location was the exclusive preserve of the sciences and both were cramped.[11] In June 1944, a syndicate was appointed by the University Senate to consider future needs.[12] It recommended in February 1945 that chemistry and metallurgy should be moved to Lensfield Road, thus releasing space for redevelopment. Not all welcomed this idea, however. Some criticised the bulk of Easton and Robertson's designs for the new Lensfield laboratories, feeling that a predominantly residential area was not the right place for a major university department. Various alternatives were discussed, including the Corpus Christi site in Sidgwick Avenue, but it was concluded that Chemistry laboratories would be yet more out of place there.[13] Others argued that the sciences should remain concentrated together; the removal instead of the Arts and Examination Schools from the New Museums Site would facilitate re-planning for science on more efficient lines.[14] Although there was also consideration of moving some scientific research to a greenfield location, today's 'West Cambridge' largely results from the Deer Report of 1966, which finally abandoned the ideal of a central science site.[15]

In parallel with these discussions, the Town and Country Planning Act of 1947 had prompted the university to form a Sites Committee to consider future development.[16] In September 1947 this body reported its initial thoughts.[17] It criticised the piecemeal nature of previous schemes and called for a framework by means of which future university buildings might be planned more systematically than hitherto. Among its recommendations were suggestions that the New Museums Site be rationalised and the arts be concentrated elsewhere. These ideas had been discussed at a meeting in June 1947 when George Salt, Fellow of King's College, had argued that future developments should not neglect the arts in improving the lot of the sciences. E. F. Weller, the Bursar of Gonville and Caius, and J. T. Saunders, the Secretary-General of the Faculties, accordingly proposed that the arts be centralised, ideally near the university library. A site on Mount Pleasant, close to the later New Hall, had a 'fine situation', but would have had to be cleared. The University Treasurer felt that the Corpus cricket ground in Sidgwick Avenue, considered in 1920 as a possible location for the university library, would be better. On 3 October 1947, it was resolved to recommend to the Council of the Senate that the university's Financial Board be asked to open negotiations for the purchase of the land.[18]

The Sites Committee suggested the construction on Sidgwick Avenue of general lecture theatres, arts faculty libraries, and faculty headquarters.[19] The organisation of the university as a series of faculties dated from the 1920s and the recommendations of the Asquith Committee, which had shifted the centre of gravity from the colleges.[20] The main requirement of the faculties was initially for library space. A 1935 report noted that:

> the growth of these [faculty] libraries in size and number is a feature of the recent development of the university and is the result of … the increased cost of books to the student, the inability of the University Library to supply every need, the larger part played by the university as compared with the colleges in teaching, new activities in research, and the new Departments and Institutions established, each needing a library upon the spot to provide the tools of study, teaching and research.[21]

In 1933, the opening of the university library presented the opportunity to concentrate within the old library buildings by the Senate House 'the scattered libraries of the literary faculties'.[22] By the 1950s, however, this accommodation was inadequate, and it was needed by the expanding central administration.[23] It had not been able to provide for all the faculties in any case. Oriental Studies' library, for example, was dispersed across ten lecture rooms.[24] Furthermore, the idea of faculty buildings as symbolic and functional entities was gathering momentum. The economics library was, for example, described in the 1930s as being the 'home' and 'unity' of its faculty, 'a means of bringing together [its] somewhat dispersed branches'.[25] The continuing growth in academic and administrative staff numbers was also important. In the late 1950s, it was joked that the History Faculty comprised a half-time typist in a city centre office, but matters were changing quickly.[26] Saunders suggested in 1949 that:

> We are moving towards a time when each faculty will be housed in a separate building or a separate part of a building with its library and staff common rooms. The older members of the university may not like this development but … it is bound to come, because the university will have to provide workrooms for many of its officers and will have to provide secretarial assistance and other aids to research and this cannot be done unless those facilities are centred in one building instead of scattered throughout the town in college rooms, private houses, and lodgings.[27]

No less significant was the question of the academic staff. The fate of University Teaching Officers (UTOs) who had no college fellowship taxed the university and colleges considerably.[28] Unlike Oxford, where faculty appointments were usually coupled with a college position, it was (and is) possible to be a Cambridge academic without a college. The problem had been noted in the 1930s, but as faculties expanded, an increasing number of academic staff found themselves in this position. In 1961–2, 45 per cent had no college.[29] The situation was especially acute in the newer disciplines.

Oriental Studies noted in 1963 that just eight of its thirty-five academic staff had an office.[30] Moral and Political Sciences complained that many of its UTOs were forced to see students in their own homes.[31]

An initial indication of the faculties that might move to Sidgwick Avenue was prepared by the Council of the Senate in 1949, and was refined by a special syndicate appointed in February of that year.[32] The list included Economics and Politics, Modern and Medieval Languages, English, Moral Science, History, Divinity, Architecture and Fine Arts, Music, and Archaeology and Anthropology, plus the Museum of Classical Archaeology and the university's society for non-collegiate students (soon to be transformed into Fitzwilliam College, but ultimately omitted from the site). Shared facilities would include a building for non-attached UTOs, plus lecture halls of varying sizes. Though apparently foreshadowing the centralised theatres constructed at such universities as Leeds during the 1960s, here the idea owed more to a longer tradition of halls gathered together in central Cambridge.

The Competition

Unfortunately, the university archives appear to be silent as to why Hugh Casson and Neville Conder's design was selected. To date no copy has been found of the long-list of practices that were considered, nor is there any record of the final decision. The relevant Casson papers in the RIBA Archives comprise drawings alone.[33] Elements of the following must, therefore, still be couched speculatively pending the discovery of more definite evidence.

A programme for the development of the Sidgwick Site was approved in March 1950 and a Standing Committee replaced the earlier syndicate.[34] Chaired by Henry Willink of Magdalene College, it initially included the historian Jack Plumb, Harold M. Taylor (University Treasurer and an authority on Anglo-Saxon architecture), the economist Austin Robinson, and H. C. Marshall. It was hoped that a development plan could be produced by October 1951; the deadline was later extended to October 1953. In its report to the university, the committee stressed the nature of the plan as a framework for long-term planning, not an immutable statement of intent. The aim was to avoid the 'variegated architecture' of earlier developments.[35] Only one building was to be designed in detail. Though a letter of July 1950 referred to three-storey buildings similar to Clare College's Memorial Court by Giles Gilbert Scott, in stripped-classical mode, or recent developments at King's by Paul Geddes Hyslop, the committee subsequently was 'anxious not to prejudge questions of architectural treatment, nor rigidly to bind the architects of thirty or forty years hence to a strongly marked style'.[36] These statements usefully remind us that 'master planning' as a discrete activity (and undertaken without any expectation that the planner would design buildings on the site) was a relatively new one.[37] As British university campuses were extended in the post-war decade and new universities were founded, it became increasingly important.

A long-list of architects was drawn up, of whom several were interviewed.[38] Who might this now-lost document have included? Perhaps Easton and Robertson, designers of the Lensfield Road Chemistry building, plus a major extension to the Department of Engineering and the new Addenbrooke's Hospital.[39] Were there university 'old hands', such as Lanchester and Lodge? Or perhaps some younger practices with experience of housing or industry? And who made the selections?

Two competitors proceeded to a second stage. The first, Robert Atkinson, had designed the Barber Institute of Fine Arts at Birmingham University (1935–9), had worked on the civic precinct at Norwich, and had been recently appointed in Cambridge for a residential development on Chaucer Road.[40] With his partner Alexander F. B. Anderson, he was developing designs for Croydon Art College. The second competing practice, Casson and Conder, reportedly made the long-list and then the short-list on the basis of Casson's work as coordinator of the Festival of Britain.[41] Under his guidance,

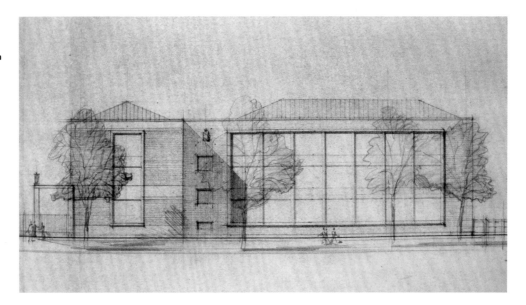

Fig 3. The Faculty of Architecture and Fine Arts as proposed by Atkinson (by permission of the Syndics of Cambridge University Library and Syborn & Atkinson)

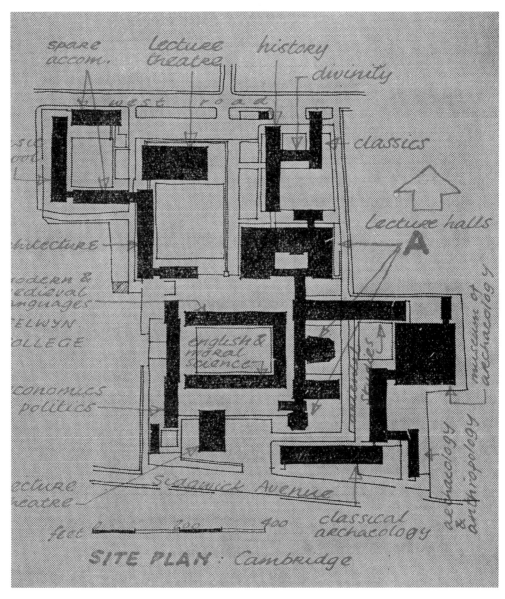

Fig 4. Casson and Conder's plan for the Sidgwick Site as illustrated by the *Architectural Review*

Fig 5. The courtyard at
the centre of the Raised
Faculty Building, looking
towards Economics and
Politics, as illustrated by
Casson (RIBA Drawings
and Archives
Collections, PA 342/2)

a diverse range of buildings had been brought together on the Festival site into a
coherent whole. Casson was in addition well connected, had written widely (not least in
the *Architectural Review*, alongside Pevsner), and had particular Cambridge links as a
graduate of St John's College. He was a former colleague of Christopher 'Kit' Nicholson,
who had taught in Cambridge until his death in 1948.

Although the short-listed architects were announced to the press only in May 1952,
they met university and city officials in late 1951, before submitting their schemes in the
autumn of 1952.[42] They had been given various instructions. In addition to the general
comments noted above, the presence nearby of college buildings was thought to
necessitate that the new Faculties have a domestic character 'whatever their style'.
The buildings were to be of modest height; 'the distribution of mass in groups of
buildings on the site' was emphasised. Atkinson's response to these stipulations was
very much in formal Beaux-Arts mode, with the site bisected by a broad thoroughfare.[43]
To the south were two three-sided quadrangles, while the northern area was
dominated by a thousand-seat lecture/concert hall. The buildings were in a similar
abstracted-classical style to the Barber Institute or Wallington Town Hall (1933–5),
though their elevational treatment varied. Flexibility was provided by leaving a site clear
for future requirements.

Casson and Conder's proposal was quite different. They stressed that 'the carefully
balanced combination in the layout of the formal and the picturesque, of the spacious
and of the intimate [will] be emphasised and enriched by the architectural character of
the buildings and in particular by the materials to be used'.[44] Casson had already
explored these 'townscape' ideas on the Festival site. Conder, meanwhile, had written in
1949 that modern architecture was characterised by contrasts between materials, shapes

Fig 6. Casson and Conder's initial design for the Lady Mitchell Hall (RIBA Drawings and Archives Collections)

and textures, and by informal relationships between buildings and landscape rather than 'approach avenues and laboured symmetry'.[45] His interest in the picturesque was fuelled by family connections to William Gilpin (1724–1804), one of the originators of the idea and whose books were on his shelves.[46] The architects had further explored the reconciliation of buildings and landscape in their work for the Cement and Concrete Association at Wexham Springs.[47]

At the heart of the Casson and Conder proposal for the Sidgwick Site was a loose series of quadrangles. Though recalling collegiate tradition, other precedents have been suggested.[48] For example, contemporaneous housing schemes were often formed by linear blocks arranged as loose courtyards, as in Tecton/Drake and Lasdun's Hallfield Estate at Paddington. Other influences could have included Eero Saarinen's General Motors Technical Centre, then under construction, which featured a water court similar to that suggested for the northern part of the site.

The design report made suggestions for each building of massing, materials and textures. Its centrepiece was the 'Raised Faculty Building', accommodating English plus Modern and Medieval Languages. This structure was conceived as an almost monumental anchor for the new part of Cambridge that was emerging. Casson, demonstrating his winning way with words, likened it to the 'High Table' of the Cambridge dining hall. It would be a foil for the other buildings that would gather around it, which could be more economically designed and less formal in character. Faced in stone, the ground floor was to be left open, nodding to the Corbusian idea of pilotis in its massive dark concrete columns but presented in terms of allowing vistas across the whole site. Indeed, views were emphasised throughout the document. However, they were not the axial prospects favoured by Atkinson. Casson highlighted,

Fig 7. Lady Mitchell Hall, as built (James O. Davies/ English Heritage)

Fig 8. Marshall Library, Faculty of Economics, interior (James O. Davies/ English Heritage)

(Overleaf) Fig 9. Raised Faculty Building from the south (James O. Davies/ English Heritage)

for example, the way in which the University Library tower would be seen at a slight angle, and much was made of the movement of the visitor's eye across buildings and through spaces. Also important was the treatment of the ground itself, which was to be 'modelled, textured and coloured as required to match the mood and function of the area concerned by a controlled variation of levels, ground patterns, and planting'. Thus, the area around the Raised Faculty Building is lifted above its surroundings to reinforce its importance (strengthening the 'High Table' metaphor). Surfaces including cobbles, bricks and slabs add to the variety of the lower level; aggregate-rich concrete bollards with integrated lamps and carefully handled bicycle stands make similarly important contributions.[49]

One wonders what debates might have taken place amongst the committee members. Was the selection of Casson and Conder difficult? Did anyone champion them? There are some clues as to their success. It was reported in January 1953 that the organisation of their scheme as a series of outward-looking quadrangles in sympathy with its setting was 'one feature of this plan … which my committee find particularly attractive'.[50] In this respect, the Atkinson scheme was rather more introverted, and its *beaux-arts* formality presented a greater contrast with its suburban surroundings. The loose framework of Casson and Conder's proposals was also stated to have counted in its favour,[51] and Conder later noted the value of having acknowledged 'the paradox that it was unlikely [all] to be built' such that 'it was less noticeable if a bit was missing'.[52] Atkinson's 'spare' site contrasted unfavourably with Casson and Conder's location of small departments that might easily relocate alongside other subjects likely to grow – an early exposition of the 'joker' principle later adopted by Chamberlin, Powell and Bon at Leeds. Casson and Conder's ages (they were born in 1910 and 1922 respectively) may have further helped. The Buildings Syndicate had in 1950 suggested the appointment of a young architect, given that the site would take many years to develop.[53] Atkinson, born in 1883, in fact died in 1952.

Although a letter of January 1953 implied that a decision had already been made, it was not until July that year that the winning scheme was submitted formally to the university authorities.[54] It was discussed by the Senate on 3 November.[55] Garth Moore, a lawyer, raised the sole dissenting voice. He questioned 'an atmosphere reminiscent of the Festival of Britain', suggesting that 'holiday camps and fun fairs are all very well but, after all, we are seldom in them for very long'. Moore asked whether the plan really was flexible: did it not imply that the site would be the preserve of modern architects? Robinson offered a robust response, suggesting that

> we need not look outside our own colleges to find examples … where the particular generation has not had the courage to trust the best architect of its own generation to do his best, and secured in consequence buildings which were not modernistic but were imitations of which the colleges themselves have learned subsequently to be ashamed.

His views carried the day; the scheme was approved on 5 February 1954.[56] Casson and Conder were invited in June 1955 to flesh out their proposals by designing the first buildings on the site; work was led by Conder with Michael Cain and Stuart Taylor.[57] Though Casson was clearly a key figure in getting work and liaising with clients, his numerous interior design commissions and his teaching both meant that, while he stopped by the office most days, in practice much was left to Conder and others, whose contribution should not be overlooked.[58]

The Raised Faculty Building was under construction by 1959.[59] The first block of shared lecture rooms was completed that year, in brown brick to contrast with the stone facings of the Raised Faculty Building. Economics and Politics (similarly in brown brick) completed the quadrangle in 1961 and also redefined the eastern edge of Selwyn College's garden, which was carried right up to the building.[60] By this date, the ideas

**Fig 10. The History
Faculty from the south
(James O. Davies/
English Heritage)**

**Fig 11. Interior of the
Seeley Historical
Library History Faculty
(James O. Davies/
English Heritage)**

espoused by Casson and Conder were becoming widely felt in university planning,
which was increasingly characterised by a shift from axial models to looser arrangements
in which buildings defined a variety of spaces between them.[61] Casson and Conder
themselves developed their ideas in several jobs for Birmingham University, including in
1958–62 a new University Square whose elevations and 'townscape' both recall the
Sidgwick Site.[62] In Cambridge, meanwhile, they were consulted by New Hall (now
Murray Edwards College) and Christ's College, though in neither case was a building
realised.[63] They were also invited to compete at Churchill College, submitting a scheme
featuring a gigantic obelisk.[64]

How should we interpret the Sidgwick buildings? The 1960s avant-garde viewed the
results critically: pedestrian; incoherent and mannered in their relationship of structure
and elevation; problematic in their evocation of the quadrangle (a college, not a Faculty
form); and somewhat windswept.[65] Clearly it is important to recognise the shifting
architectural debate, but it is also important to see the project on its own terms, in the
context of the early 1950s. In this respect, Robinson's response to Moore in the Senate,
noted above, presented the appointment of Casson and Conder as an opportunity for the
university to engage with contemporary architecture. The proposals certainly contrasted
with the more overtly traditional styling of some contemporaneous college projects,
such as Hyslop's nearby hostel for King's, perhaps one of the buildings that prompted
Robinson's view of much recent Cambridge architecture as 'imitations' of which the
colleges were now 'ashamed'.[66] We might now, following the example set by certain
recent historians, wish to accommodate such buildings within a broader definition of
architectural modernity, but there is no denying that, to the likes of Pevsner and
Robinson, they stood as evidence of inexcusable conservatism in university and college
patronage. In contrast, Casson and Conder's informal fusion of buildings and setting
generated a new and unique environment, making a particular statement of the place of
the arts in an evolving university. While this statement might have seemed 'old hat' by the
mid-1960s, in its own time it offered a prominent contribution to the increasingly

agitated debates about university architecture, its picturesque 'townscape' embodying what Pevsner would define in 1956 as a national style and reminding us of the significance that was attached to the role of the university in re-forming post-war Britain.[67]

Coda I: The Lady Mitchell Hall and a truncated site

Writing in 1962, Casson recorded a Cambridge taxi driver's warning: 'don't you build 'ere, Sir. They'll muck you about something terrible.'[68] Casson suggested that his experience had disproved this pessimistic observation, but, during the preceding three years, progress on the Sidgwick Site had in fact become significantly more difficult. In March 1959, A. E. L. ('Sandy') Parnis of the University Financial Board wrote to Casson, telling him that his proposals had come under sustained attack in the Senate.[69] The charge had been led by Hugh Plommer of the Faculty of Classics. Never a fan of modern architecture, Plommer's complaints included the non-axial layout and the elevations' 'disorder for the sake of disorder'.[70] The result, he said, was 'grimly utilitarian'. Parnis suggested that Casson should not worry, as Plommer seemed amiable enough.

However, in the summer of 1960, the Senate rejected the designs put before it for the Lady Mitchell Hall, a detached lecture theatre on the Sidgwick Avenue frontage.[71] Its remarkable ribbed concrete cladding (inspired by Maxwell Ayrton's Twickenham Bridge of 1933) and triangular rooflights anticipated Casson and Conder's later Elephant House at London Zoo; the design also hinted at the emerging 'New Brutalism' and Paul Rudolph's work at Yale.[72] For traditionalists, it was the 'nadir of the development to date'. Critics also questioned the architects' competence, pointing to functional problems with the earlier Sidgwick lecture halls and bewailing the lack of a lift.[73] Leslie Martin, Noel Annan and others replied by highlighting the dangers of revivalist architecture, but the vote was lost. Casson offered to resign, but stayed to make revised proposals.[74] The changes placated some, though Plommer and Moore remained unconvinced.[75] Nonetheless, the designs were approved, and the Lady Mitchell Hall and Little Hall (the latter with a 'candle-snuffer' rooflight not unlike the original Lady Mitchell design) were constructed on the Sidgwick Avenue frontage in 1961–4.

However, change was afoot, not least as the original master plan began to unravel. The intention had been to acquire from Gonville and Caius College the houses in West Road to the north of the former Corpus playing field. Caius, however, was not entirely happy with the way that matters were proceeding. In 1955, its Bursar complained that the College had not been consulted about the development plan (unlike Selwyn, on whose land it was not proposed to build) and that what was intended were not the 'domestic' structures originally implied.[76] In May 1959, an already difficult relationship was strained further. Caius – by now planning on the site of No. 3 West Road a new residence, Harvey Court, to designs by Leslie Martin and Colin St John Wilson – announced that it wished to retain No. 5 West Road, previously included in the Sidgwick development plan.[77] However, it would make Nos. 7 and 9 immediately available if it could acquire some of the former Corpus land to the south. After lengthy discussions, it was decided to secure the West Road frontage even if to do so meant the loss of ground on which it had been intended to build, and contracts were signed in March 1962.[78]

The removal of part of the intended development area forced the university to reconsider the planning of the Sidgwick Site. Faculty needs were re-examined, and, after much debate, it was decided to construct only 'general' buildings and not to provide for the more specialised needs of Architecture and Music.[79] The thousand-seat lecture/concert hall was removed, along with the 'water court'. Pevsner's tantalizing dream of 1953, in which the Slade Professor made his way from a packed gathering in the large hall to his office, passing through a rich townscape, now looked a long way away.

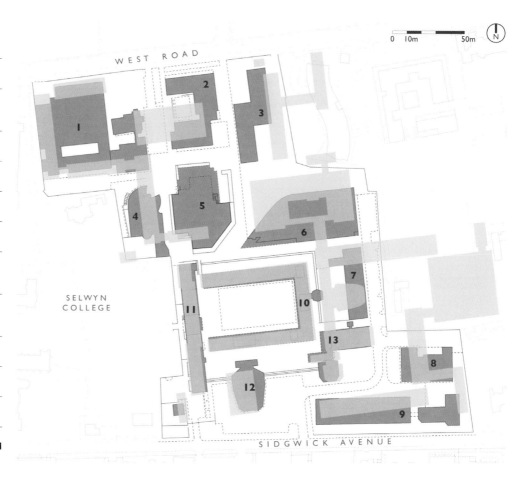

Fig 12. Comparison between Casson and Conder's original layout (in light grey) and (in dark grey) the site as developed by 2012 (Lefkos Kyriacou)

Coda II: A palm court?

Although Willink stressed that the University remained satisfied with Casson and Conder's work, even before the brouhaha of 1960 Parnis had suggested that the reduction in available area posed an opportunity to approach others, noting also that Leslie Martin, though silent on the matter, seemed unconvinced by what had been built thus far.[80] Indeed, the original intention had been that the development plan would accommodate a variety of designers. It was therefore decided that, while the southern area would remain the domain of Casson and Conder, elsewhere they were to act as consultants only.[81] A revised development plan was produced for the north of the site. Its focus was the History Faculty, ultimately designed by James Stirling.[82] It is worth concluding with a brief examination of this commission because it set a pattern for the subsequent development of the Sidgwick Site.

Stirling's appointment is, unlike that of Casson and Conder in 1953, well documented. Both Martin and Casson were invited in May 1962 to suggest possible architects. Martin was frequently asked for such advice in Cambridge and beyond. His three nominations all had Oxbridge experience. Howell, Killick, Partridge and Amis (HKPA) were engaged at St Anne's, Oxford, and had also worked at Birmingham. The Architects' Co-Partnership (ACP) had the 'Beehives' at St John's, Oxford, to their name, though Martin also cited St Paul's Cathedral School. Powell and Moya were working at Brasenose, Oxford. Also worth consideration, Martin suggested, were Denys Lasdun, Chamberlin Powell and Bon (CP&B), Philip Dowson, and James Stirling and James Gowan.[83] Of these names, Stirling and Gowan would have been particularly familiar with the Sidgwick Site, having earlier proposed a residential building for neighbouring Selwyn College.[84] Meanwhile, Casson echoed Martin in proposing ACP and Powell and Moya.[85] He also suggested H. T. Cadbury-Brown (his collaborator at the Royal College of Art), Leonard Manasseh, and, more exotically, Le Corbusier ('the greatest living architect'), Franco Albini and Aldo van Eyck. David Roberts, then teaching in the University and designing various college schemes, was added by the committee, along with several others with university experience including H. M. Fairhurst and Rolf Hellberg.[86]

Invitations to send images of their work went to HKPA, Powell and Moya, Roberts, Dowson, Cadbury-Brown, Fairhurst and Hellberg.[87] Powell and Moya declined, citing other commitments, while Hellberg was discounted, but visits to buildings by the rest took place in August 1962. However, no clear decision emerged. HKPA were popular, but it was felt that they were too inexperienced; their commission for an arts faculty building at Birmingham might have suggested otherwise.[88] There was some concern that David Roberts, the other frontrunner, was already stretched. However, a sense that Casson might return by default provoked a strong response, and further names entered the frame, including CP&B (busy at New Hall) and Arne Jacobsen (fresh from St Catherine's, Oxford).[89] Parnis, now at the University Grants Committee, made eclectic suggestions, ranging from modernists such as Trevor Dannatt to the traditionalist Raymond Erith.[90] J. S. Boys Smith, the Master of St John's, favoured Albini or Alvar Aalto.[91] Discussions with Ralph Erskine and Erik Sørensen added several possible 'Nordic architects', including Jørgen Bo and Sigurd Lewerentz.[92]

This distinguished list of names was cut down only gradually. Leslie Martin reiterated his belief in HKPA, Roberts, and ACP, but added that Stirling and Gowan should also be considered.[93] The committee added CP&B, Aalto, and Aldo van Eyck, plus Potter and Hare, a practice best known for church conservation.[94] Only on 1 November 1962, with Martin in attendance, was the final shortlist drawn up, featuring ACP, Roberts, and Stirling and Gowan.[95]

The rest of the story is well-known. Stirling and Gowan's design (essentially by Stirling, who split from Gowan in 1964) was favoured for its integrated planning, and because it alone could be built for the budget.[96] Described by Stirling as 'glittering, reflective and almost delicate', its expansive glazing and red brickwork echoed the earlier Engineering Building at Leicester University.[97] It offered a different image of the modern university to that of Casson and Conder. Plommer was no more impressed, however, likening it to an Edwardian hotel palm house, though one respondent thought this critique unusually mild and that the design might not, therefore, be too bad.[98] The basic concept survived to construction, though the refusal of the tenant of No. 11 West Road to give up part of her garden nearly derailed it. Willink, not a fan, hoped the dispute would mean the end of the scheme, but was dissuaded from sacking Stirling by Casson.[99] In the end, the design was rotated so that the library faces south-east, solving the land issue but exacerbating the problems of solar gain that were already implicit in the original south-westerly arrangement.[100]

Booth and Taylor suggested that the History Faculty and Harvey Court together presented 'true environments for today's academic community'.[101] Certainly these buildings' iconoclastic presence set a trend for individualism that has been followed by most subsequent construction on the Sidgwick Site. Perhaps unsurprisingly, given that many hands have been involved over many years, the northern area lacks the coherence of the southern part of the site.[102] The overall result is not quite the 'ideal campus' originally envisaged by Pevsner. Nonetheless, the site as a whole encapsulates in microcosm the terms in which Casson conceived Oxford and Cambridge, 'a panorama of architectural history from which hardly a famous name is missing'.[103] It offers an immersive encounter with key moments and ideas in the architectural history of the post-war British university.

Acknowledgements:
I have profited from discussions with David Adamson, Barnabas Calder, Elizabeth Darling, William Fawcett, Diane Haigh and Nicholas Ray. Nicholas Bullock, Elain Harwood and Alan Powers kindly commented on early drafts; further useful comments were made by the journal's anonymous referee. Lefkos Kyriacou produced the comparative site plan. James O. Davies kindly supplied present-day photographs. I would like to thank the Syndics of Cambridge University Library for permission to cite documents; the RIBA, *Architectural Review*, and Syborn and Atkinson allowed me to reproduce drawings. A grant from Wolfson College, Cambridge, helped with the cost of images

1. Nikolaus Pevsner, 'Visual aspects of the Cambridge Plan', *Cambridge Review*, no.71, 13 May 1950, pp.510–3; William Holford and H. Myles Wright, *Cambridge Planning Proposals*, Cambridge, Cambridge University Press, 1950, pp.59–60.

2. Quoted in Susie Harris, *Nikolaus Pevsner: The Life*, London, Chatto and Windus, 2011, p.454; See also Richard Gray, 'The Future of the Backs', *Town Planning Review*, vol.26, no.4, January 1956, pp.195–210.

3. Pevsner, op. cit., p.511.

4. *Cambridge University Reporter*, no.3598, 4 August 1948, p.1561, and no.3624, 2 February 1949, pp.764–6.

5. Pevsner, op. cit., p.511; Nikolaus Pevsner, 'The Sidgwick Avenue Site', *Cambridge Review*, no.75, 31 October 1953, pp.88–9.

6. 'Lecture Halls at Cambridge', *Architects' Journal*, vol.141, no.12, 24 March 1965, pp.707–17 (p.708).

7. Louise Campbell, 'Building on the Backs: Basil Spence, Queens' College, and University Architecture at Mid-Century', *Architectural History*, no.54, 2011, pp.383–405 (p.385).

8. Mark Goldie, *Corbusier Comes to Cambridge: Post-War Architecture and the Competition to Build Churchill College*, Cambridge, Churchill College, 2007, p.11; Philip Booth and Nicholas Taylor, *Cambridge New Architecture*, London, Leonard Hill Books, 3rd ed., 1970, p.42.

9. J. M. Richards, 'Recent building in Oxford and Cambridge', *Architectural Review*, vol.112, no.668, June 1952, pp.73–9; 'New University Buildings Improved in Style', *The Times*, no.53784, 8 March 1957, p.5; Lionel Brett, 'Universities Today', *Architectural Review*, vol.122, no.729, October 1957, pp.240–51.

10. Committee on Future Scientific Policy, 'Scientific Manpower', Cmd Paper 6824, London, HMSO, 1946; see also 'A "Churchill" College', *The Times*, no.54151, 15 May 1958, p.16; 'Britain's Research Effort Still Too Small', *The Times*, no.53986, 31 October 1957, p.7; Committee on Higher Education: 'Higher Education: Report of the Committee appointed by the Prime Minister under the Chairmanship of Lord Robbins', Cmnd 2154, London, HMSO, 1963, pp.6–7.

11. 'Sites committee of the Council: Report of the Secretary', September 1947, Min.VII.67 (1–50), Cambridge University archives.

12. *Reporter*, no.3429, 6 February 1945, pp.404–10.

13. *Reporter*, no.3598, 4 August 1948, pp.1555–9; Report of 3 June 1947, Min. VII.67 (1–50), Cambridge University archives.

14. *Reporter*, ibid.

15. 'Sites Committee of the Council: minutes', 23 July 1947, Min.VII.67 (1–50), Cambridge University archives; Christopher N. L. Brooke, *A History of the University of Cambridge*, vol.III, Cambridge University Press, 1994, p.547.

16. *Reporter*, no.3624, 2 February 1949, pp.764–6.

17. 'Sites Committee of the Council: Report of the Secretary', September 1947, Min.VII.67 (1–50), Cambridge University archives.

18. Brooke, op. cit., p.375; Report of 3 October 1947, Min.VII.67 (1–50), Cambridge University archives.

19. 'Sites Committee of the Council: Report of the Secretary', September 1947, Min.VII.67 (1–50), Cambridge University archives.

20. Brooke, op. cit., pp.352–7.

21. *Reporter*, no.3074, 2 June 1936, pp.1074–9.

22. *Reporter*, no.2955, 21 November 1933, pp.305–8.

23. 'Report of the Syndicate on the Sidgwick Avenue Site', 15 February 1950, FB780; Minutes of the General Board, 3 November 1948, GB32, Cambridge University archives.

24. Letter from E. B. Ceadal to W. J. Sartain, 10 June 1963, GB31, Cambridge University archives.

25. *Reporter*, no.2958, 13 December 1933, pp.403–11.

26. Brooke, op. cit., p.547.

27. Typescript memorandum, 1949, General Board box 30, Cambridge University archives.

28. For example the memo from Michael McCrum, 3 May 1961, OA4C, Leckhampton box 13, Corpus Christi College archives.

29. *Reporter*, no.2955, 21 November 1933, pp.305–8; Brooke, op. cit., p.574.

30. Letter from E. B. Ceadal to W. J. Sartain, 10 June 1963, GB31, Cambridge University archives.

31. Statement of Needs, 24 November 1955, FB 780/2, Cambridge University archives.

32. *Reporter*, no.3624, 2 February 1949, pp.764–6.

33. PA 342/1/1–18, PA 342/2/1–2, PA 342/3/1–2, RIBA Drawings Collection, London. Three drawings listed erroneously in the catalogue in January 2012 as PB 484/9/1–3 are missing.

34. *Reporter*, no.3865, 14 October 1953 pp.223–32.

35. Report of the Buildings Syndicate to the Council of the Senate, 23 May 1950, Min.IV.6, Cambridge University archives.

36. Letter from Noel Dean to W. L. Waide, 8 July 1950, file 26/2, Cambridge University Estates Management and Building Service archives; *Reporter*, no.3865, 14 October 1953, pp.223–32.

37. For broader parallels in the national planning system, see, for example, Mark Crinson and Jules Lubbock, *Architecture: Art or Profession? Three Hundred Years of Architectural Education in Britain*, Manchester University Press, 1994, p.124, which emphasises the 1947 Act as the provision of a framework in contrast to a rigid approach to civic design.

38. 'Report of the Committee for the Sidgwick Avenue Site', 20 April 1953, FB 780, Cambridge University archives.

39. Letters of 1945–7 relating to the appointment of Easton and Robertson, folder AP15, Addenbrooke's Hospital archive.

40. Paul Spencer-Longhurst, 'Robert Atkinson', *Oxford Dictionary of National Biography*; Annual Report of the Buildings Syndicate, October 1949 (and also minutes of the Syndicate, 22 November 1949), Min.IV.6, Cambridge University archives. Atkinson was also responsible for a small extension to the Fitzwilliam Museum.

41. José Manser, *Hugh Casson: A Biography*, London, Viking, 2000, p.163.

42. 'Plans invited for Cambridge site', *The Times*, no.52322, 27 May 1952, p.8; Record of meeting on 17 December 1951 with Atkinson, Casson and Conder, FB 780, Cambridge University archives; *Reporter*, no.3865, 14 October 1953 pp.223–32.

43. Sidgwick Avenue Site scheme by Robert Atkinson, report and drawings, 1952, P.XLIII, Cambridge University archives.

44. Copy of Casson and Conder's report, FB780/6, Cambridge University archives. The text was also reproduced in the *Architectural Record*, vol.115, no.4, April 1954, pp.149–55.

45. Neville Conder, *An Introduction to Modern Architecture*, London, Art and Technics, 1949, pp.17–18.

46. Alan Powers, personal communication, June 2012.

47. 'Structures Laboratory', *Architects' Journal*, vol.113, no.2936, 7 June 1951, pp. 739–41.

48. Allies and Morrison, 'Sidgwick Site Conservation Plan' (unpublished; copy loaned by Diane Haigh), p.8.

49. 'Lecture Halls at Cambridge', op. cit., p.715.

50. Letter from the committee to the Master of Selwyn College, January 1953, FB 780, Cambridge University archives.

51. *Reporter*, no. 3879, 20 January 1954, p.659.

52. Alan Powers, 'Neville Conder', *Oxford Dictionary of National Biography*.

53. Minutes of the University Buildings Syndicate, 9 May 1950, Min.IV.6, Cambridge University archives.

54. *Reporter*, no. 3865, 14 October 1953, pp.223–32.

55. *Reporter*, no. 3870, 11 November 1953, p.349.

56. *Reporter*, no. 3882, 10 February 1954, p.740.

57. Letter to Casson, 18 June 1955, FB 780/1, Cambridge University archives; 'Sidgwick Avenue Development', *Architect and Building News*, vol.228, no.39, 29 September 1965, pp.583–90.

58. Manser, op. cit., pp.160–3 and 212.

59. PA 342/1/1–18, RIBA Drawings and Archives Collections.

60. See, for example, letter from Austin Robinson to Henry Willink, 1 June 1956, (FB 780/3, Cambridge University archives) which invokes the way in which Clare College looks over King's. The direct connection has now been lost in favour of a more defensible boundary.

61. Diane Chablo, 'University Architecture in Britain, 1950–1975', D.Phil. thesis, University of Oxford, 1987, p.25.

62. Andy Foster, Pevsner City Guide, *Birmingham*, London, Yale University Press, 2007, pp.245, 253–4.

63. For the Christ's scheme, which is reminiscent of the Sidgwick Site, see PA340/3/1–2, RIBA Drawings and Archives Collections; For New Hall, see letter from Rosemary Murray to Casson, 22 July 1958, NHAR/1/1/1/6/1, Murray Edwards College archive, Cambridge.

64. Goldie, op. cit., p. 18–23; PA 340/4/1–6, RIBA Drawings and Archives Collections.

65. Booth and Taylor, op. cit., p.178; 'Sidgwick Avenue Development', op. cit., pp.583–90; 'Lecture Halls at Cambridge', op. cit., pp.708, 715.

66. Nicholas Ray, 'Cambridge composition', *arq*, vol.6, no.1, 2002, pp.33–48.

67. 'New University Buildings Improved In Style', op.cit.; Kenneth J. Robinson, 'Better buildings but bad neighbours', *Observer*, 2 July 1961, p.11; Nikolaus Pevsner, *The Englishness of English Art*, London, Architectural Press, 1956, and, for the original lectures, <http://www.bbc.co.uk/programmes/p00h9llv> (accessed 5 January 2012). For attempts to construct an 'English' Modernism, see William Whyte, 'The Englishness of English Architecture: Modern Architecture and the Making of a National International Style, 1927–57', *Journal of British Studies*, vol.48, no.2, April 2009, pp.441–65.

68. Hugh Casson, 'Bricks and Mortar Boards', *The Twentieth Century*, vol.172, no.1014, Summer 1962, pp.91–102 (p.91).

69. Letter from A. E. L. Parnis to Casson, 14 March 1959, FB 780/12, Cambridge University archives.

70. *Reporter*, no. 4137, 18 March 1959, p.1029–32.

71. *Reporter*, no. 4210, 12 August 1960, p.2036; 'Design for Hall Rejected', *The Times*, no.54838, 1 August 1960, p.8; For the design, see PA 342/3/1, RIBA Drawings and Archives Collections.

72. Booth and Taylor, op. cit., p.177. The link to Twickenham was pointed out by Conder to Elain Harwood.

73. *Reporter*, no. 4210, 12 August 1960, p.2040. A lift was subsequently added.

74. ibid., p. 2041; Minutes of the Sidgwick Avenue Site Committee, 8 August 1960, FB 780/16, Cambridge University archives.

75. *Reporter*, no.4249, 10 May 1961, pp.1660–4.

76. Letter from E. P. Weller to A. E. L. Parnis, 16 September 1955, FB 780/1, Cambridge University archives.

77. Letter from E. P. Weller to A. E. L. Parnis, 27 May 1959, FB 780/13, Cambridge University archives.

78. Financial Board minutes, 25 April 1962, FB 780/18, Cambridge University archives; See also extensive paperwork at the Estates Management and Building Service, filed as 26/26.

79. Letter from L. M. Harvey to C. K. Phillips, 12 December 1961, FB 780/18, Cambridge University archives; *Reporter*, no.4355, 22 May 1963, pp.1671–3.

80. *Reporter*, no.4358, 13 June 1963, p.1837; Letter from A. E. L. Parnis to Hugh Willink, 11 November 1959, FB 780/14, Cambridge University archives.

81. Architects' Lives: Neville Conder interviewed by Alan Powers, 1999, C467/42, British Library.

82. *Reporter*, no.4355, 22 May 1963, pp.1671–3; 'Model for Sidgwick Avenue Site', *The Times*, no.55708, 23 May 1963, p. 8; Conder, interviewed by Powers, ibid.: 'our block model of the site [showed a building of] that height, and that sort of bulk'.

83. Letter from Leslie Martin to C. K. Phillips, 3 May 1962, FB 780/19, Cambridge University archives.

84. Conder was first alerted to the Selwyn building in March 1959; see letter to A. E. L. Parnis of 31 March 1959, FB 780/12, Cambridge University archives. In November it was reported that the Master of Selwyn believed that it would not be built, not least as it seemed that he himself did not like the design; letter from Conder to Parnis, 9 November 1959, FB 780/14.

85. Letter from Casson to Willink, 17 May 1962, FB 780/19, Cambridge University archives.

86. Minutes of the Sidgwick Avenue Site committee, 8 May 1962; letter from Hugh Beaver to C. K. Phillips, 1 June 1962, FB 780/19, Cambridge University archives.

87. Minutes of the Sidgwick Avenue Site committee, 18 June 1962, FB 780/19, Cambridge University archives.

88. For example, letter from R. E. Macpherson to Willink, 14 August 1962, FB 780/20, Cambridge University archives.

89. Letter from R. E. Macpherson to A. E. L. Parnis, 17 August 1962, FB 780/20, Cambridge University archives.

90. Letter from A. E. L. Parnis to R. E. Macpherson, 4 September 1962, FB 780/20, Cambridge University archives.

91. Letter from J. S. Boys Smith to R. E. Macpherson, 22 September 1962, FB 780/20, Cambridge University archives. Aalto was later considered for Cripps Court at Boys Smith's college, St John's.

92. Letter from E. F. Mills to Leslie Martin 24 September 1962, FB 780/20, Cambridge University archives.

93. Letter from Leslie Martin to Willink, 25 September 1962 FB 780/20, Cambridge University archives.

94. Minutes of the Sidgwick Avenue Site committee, 27 October 1962, FB 780/20, Cambridge University archives.

95. A copy of Roberts's design report survives in file 26/10, Cambridge Estates Management and Building Service. It featured a slab block and stepped pyramid, with mullioned elevations to allow internal partitions to be rearranged.

96. Minutes of the Sidgwick Avenue Site committee, 16 April 1963, FB 780/21, Cambridge University archives.

97. Draft report, 10 May 1963, FB 780/21, Cambridge University archives.

98. *Reporter*, no.4358, 13 June 1963, pp.1838–9.

99. Conder, interviewed by Powers, op. cit.

100. William Fawcett, 'Understanding the History Faculty, Cambridge', in Alan Berman (ed.), *Jim Stirling and the Red Trilogy: Three Radical Buildings*, London, Frances Lincoln, 2010, pp.43–53 (p.48).

101. Booth and Taylor, op. cit. p.180.

102. A succession of development plans for this area was produced by Casson and Conder, and others; see Allies and Morrison, op. cit., pp.16–17.

103. Casson, op. cit., p.91.

7
Leslie Martin and
the St Cross Building, Oxford
Elain Harwood

Three very different Oxford faculties found in the late 1950s that by sharing a building they could gain better facilities than was possible individually within the cost constraints of the University Grants Committee. The result was also architecturally more assertive than could have been produced acting alone, even by the Faculty of Law whose greater ability to attract private funding partly subsidised the faculties of English Literature and Social Sciences, the latter responsible for the Institute of Statistics. Though the term 'Modernism' rarely appears in the minutes of Oxford's many building committees of the time, the St Cross Building (so-named in February 1964 after a suggestion it be called after President Kennedy was rejected) marked a new departure for the university at a time when the independently-funded colleges were beginning to turn away from traditional designs and to encourage a younger generation of architects.[1]

The architect of the new building was Sir Leslie Martin, who provided a link between Oxford and the more active Modern Movement underway in Cambridge. It is hard to define Martin's importance, for today his methods of working through younger assistants and omnipotent role in securing commissions for other architects are more discussed than his own work, particularly that as a teacher and theorist, first in the 1930s–40s and particularly in the 1960s. But for Martin the buildings he and his associates produced around 1960, mostly for universities, formed the core of his career, and he believed that 'the Manor Road library buildings occupy a kind of central position in our work'.[2] They exemplify the distinctive design features of his mature style, and the rich interiors deserve to be better known.

The Appointment of an Architect

The origins of the brief lay in the shortage of accommodation facing three arts-oriented faculties at a time when the university was building mainly for science. The Institute of Statistics occupied a house and several huts on the corner of Manor and St Cross roads, a site acquired from the Roman Catholic Church in 1946 with the Territorial Army as a sitting tenant, while English and Law were desperately short of space for their libraries in the Examination Schools. The Bodleian law collections had evolved piecemeal, and for many years were less comprehensive than those at the Codrington Library of All Souls and other college collections, but had grown quickly since 1945. An attempt to reorganise these holdings into a centralised law library had been stymied by the war but by 1955–6 the faculty found that it could not house the acquisitions pouring in under the national copyright agreement.

Law was a prestigious subject, and generous scholarships were being set up for international students as the British legal system was transmuted into those of the emerging Commonwealth nations. The Pakistan government contributed to the cost of the new building. Peter Shepheard, described by the Vice Chancellor, Alic Halford

Smith, as having 'sensitivity and experience', was invited in 1956 to join a faculty committee visiting new law libraries in the United States. Its report drew heavily on the experience of the Harvard Law School and other American institutions which had recently built or were proposing libraries for over 500,000 volumes, and not only defined the brief but identified the site in Manor Road. Shepheard's outline designs secured the promise of £150,000 from the Rockefeller Foundation, which became a useful weapon in ensuring its construction ahead of other projects.[3] He proposed an open stack and reading room set over a two-storey closed stack, behind a low block housing lecture theatres and seminar rooms.[4]

When in early 1957 the university's Building and Development Committee suggested that the Manor Road site be used for English and Statistics as well as Law, Shepheard was asked to make new proposals without the firm promise of an appointment. He produced designs for three separate, related buildings that filled most of the tight site, yet he could not provide the Institute of Statistics with all its required accommodation within the UGC budget. Mr B. Carter commented that 'the site was small and low-lying so that the placing on it of three low, straggling buildings was fundamentally wrong'.[5] The referral of Shepheard's scheme from Oxford's main executive body, the Hebdomadal Council, to the Building and Development Committee was described by the Registrar's assistant, Miss Colinette P. Good, as 'a King Charles' Head to the President of Magdalen [Thomas Boase], who heartily dislikes Shepheard's plan'.[6] More general doubts over Shepheard's abilities were voiced by the lively Committee on Elevations and the Choice of Architect, created in 1957 out of two older bodies. By October 1957 the Building Committee was considering whether the three faculties could share common facilities such as lecture theatres, seminar rooms and lavatories so that more money could be spent on their libraries. The notion of sharing lecture theatres had been agreed for the Sidgwick Site in Cambridge but had yet to be realised, and it was a novel collaboration at a time when law departments in other universities were commissioning independent buildings on a new-found scale.

Modernism had come late to Oxford. Only in late 1956 were the first young practices appointed to make additions to its colleges, led by Powell and Moya at Brasenose and the Architects' Co-Partnership at Corpus Christi and St John's. But the Committee on Elevations included several enthusiasts for Modernism, encouraged by the young economist David Henderson of Lincoln College and including Arthur (Thomas) Norrington, President of Trinity College, who was to commission Maguire and Murray in 1959. They asked to look at Shepheard's existing work, and were dismissive of his housing and schools for the London County Council, hall for Winchester school and two Oxford boat houses, mostly designed with Derek Bridgwater. They felt that the expansion of the brief to house three faculties gave an excuse to appoint a new architect, and agreed that the openness of the site away from the city centre made a modern design appropriate. In January 1958 the Committee on Elevations agreed not to appoint Shepheard.

A survey by the Committee on Elevations of new buildings at other universities showed how remarkably few modern buildings there were in 1957. Cambridge had appointed Casson and Conder to Sidgwick Avenue, but building had barely begun, and for its science and engineering buildings it was using Easton and Cusdin of Easton and Robertson, a safe choice by the 1950s. David Roberts had designed a health centre and additions to the colleges, while their correspondent, C. K. Philips of the Faculty of Medicine, drew attention to the university's Professor of Architecture, Leslie Martin, recently knighted and who had 'in the past eighteen months given the financial board the benefit of his highly practical and ingenious advice regarding the future development and redevelopment of university sites in the centre of Cambridge'.[7] Casson and Conder's success in Cambridge had led to a commission for a master plan at Birmingham, and Southampton had appointed Basil Spence on the hearty recommendation of Dr

Fig 2. Scheme by Peter Shepheard for the Faculty of Law, 1956. The octagonal lecture block is at the centre, with to the left the administrative and academic wing, behind which is the main library. Another department forms the east side of the courtyard plan

Hutcheson of Glasgow University.[8] Only Sheffield had ventured to hold an architectural competition, where the appointment by the RIBA of F. R. S. Yorke as an assessor had, its Registrar felt, pre-determined a modernist solution.[9]

Oxford, too, wondered whether to hold a competition, and queried whether Danish architects – specifically Jørn Utzon, Kaj Fisker, Carl Møller and Arne Jacobsen – could be invited to compete.[10] This was not possible under RIBA rules but could perhaps have been organised by the International Union of Architects. The suggestion is a reflection of the influence in Oxford, without a school of architecture, of Henderson, who had visited Copenhagen, and the University Surveyor Jack Lankester, whose passion for Danish architecture was informed by an ambition at the time to build a second career in furniture design.[11] Speaking on the Hebdomadal Council in March 1958, Alan Bullock asked that foreign architects be considered. The Committee on Elevations drew up a shortlist of architects for an invited competition, comprising Hugh Casson, Leslie Martin, Arne Jacobsen, Frederick Gibberd, Peter Shepheard, Powell and Moya and Chamberlin, Powell and Bon. This groundwork for the St Cross site was to inspire Bullock when that June he began to look for an architect for St Catherine's College and cast his eyes towards Denmark.

Like university bodies elsewhere, the Committee on Elevations eventually, if reluctantly, decided against a competition on the grounds of cost and because it would be required to accept a winner determined by an outside assessor. Its enthusiasm for Danish architects was not shared by the outside experts it then turned to, John Summerson and Robert Furneaux Jordan, although Summerson felt strongly that a modern idiom would be appropriate for the relatively open location. Instead, Henderson and Walter Oakeshott, Rector of Lincoln, visited Sir Leslie Martin, who was impressed with the site and 'the possibility that its development might mark a new phase in the university's way of dealing with architectural problems'. In other words, here was the opportunity for a modern building in central Oxford.[12]

Leslie Martin (1908–2000) had become head of architecture at Hull School of Art in 1934, whereupon he married and formed a practice with Sadie Speight. Following a wartime engaged in devising prototype stations and equipment as part of a research team at the London, Midland and Scottish Railway, he had secured his reputation as one of Britain's leading modern architects as Deputy Architect to the London County Council, with a leading hand in the Royal Festival Hall, and from 1953 as Architect to the Council. But in November 1955 he had a breakdown and thereafter worked largely from home, announcing his resignation when later that year he accepted the post of Professor of Architecture at Cambridge University for the following autumn.[13] He then based a small practice at his new home nearby in Great Shelford. Martin's training at Manchester provided a synthesis between the Arts and Crafts Movement and the Beaux Arts, shown in his fascination with Lethaby's ideas on the cube and square, and the more constructivist quirks of his pre-war buildings were steadily eliminated. Instead he explored a synthesis between Modernism and formal proportions in ad hoc collaborations with several younger architects and a formal 'association', not a partnership, with Colin St John Wilson. Patrick Hodgkinson was their first assistant. The use of an omnipotent grid came to inform his buildings and subsequently his urban planning schemes of the 1960s.

Having rushed to take on several major jobs following his decision to leave the LCC, by early 1958 Martin was only accepting jobs that offered 'an architectural challenge'. He reverted back to his prime interests in research, building up the school at Cambridge

Fig 3. Plan of the St Cross Building as built. The English Library is at the top left, with the missing columns, Statistics at the bottom and the Law Library to the right. (Mike Thrift, University of Oxford)

Fig 4. The English Library, St Cross. Note the absence of alternate columns on the lower floor (James O. Davies/ English Heritage)

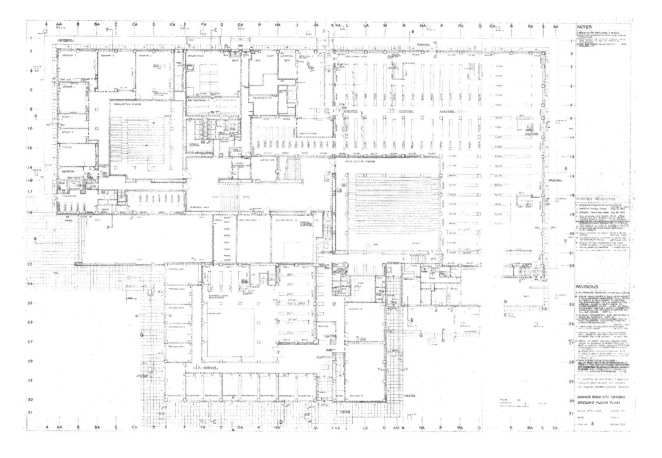

Fig 5. Upper terrace, entrance to the Law Library, St Cross Building (James O. Davies/English Heritage)

and offering advice to a string of academic clients, seeing his influence evolve through the work of others. Initially he offered to Oakeshott only that he prepare the plans, together with a statement regarding the appearance of the elevations, but in May offered to produce all the design drawings.[14] He was anxious not to expand his own practice, however, and suggested that the working drawings should be made by another firm, though later he agreed to prepare these too. Nevertheless the Committee was impressed, and Martin was appointed on 20 May 1958, although Shepheard was informed only in July – a disappointment he took with exemplary dignity, offering his successor 'every possible help'.[15]

The choice of Martin for the Manor Road libraries was overshadowed by Jacobsen's controversial appointment early the next year as architect of St Catherine's College. Martin may have been a Cambridge professor, but at least he was British, and subsequent press reports on St Cross's progress coincided with those regarding St Catherine's to demonstrate that the university's patronage was not all dispensed abroad. The irony of this was that north European sources were coming to dominate the work of Martin and his associates, and the library complex demonstrates their absorption of many elements of the work of Alvar Aalto, who had visited Cambridge in 1957.

The Development of the Design

Most Oxford academic staff had (and have) offices in their colleges, so the dominating features for the Faculties of Law and English were their extensive libraries, their contrasting demands making a challenging brief. Only the Institute of Statistics demanded a significant number of tutorial rooms (25). Proposals for a new library for the English Faculty were first made in 1949. The existing library was in the attic of the Examination Schools and when in 1955 staff declared that 'it would be dangerous to add more shelves', so overcrowded had it become, it was prioritised in the University Grants Committee's funding quinquennium of 1957–62.[16] In 1955 staff asked for a library holding 50,000 volumes, with desks for a hundred readers in a single, open, easily supervised space, together with a closed stack and a small room for its Old Icelandic collection. It was a brief on a different scale from the large, open stack requested by the Faculty of Law, which was anxious to have as many reports, journals and text books accessible as possible, believing that its discipline was exceptional in requiring quick access to a great many short references. English's additional brief for a large auditorium seating 250–300 people, smaller lecture theatres, seminar rooms holding up to thirty, and offices for visiting academics formed the basis for the shared accommodation with the other faculties. The difficulty, Lankester perceived, was to make Law the dominant element of the resulting composition to ensure the continued support of the Rockefeller Foundation.[17]

The first plans, produced in December 1958, followed a sequence of projects undertaken by Martin with Wilson and Hodgkinson mainly in Cambridge. Wilson recalled being 'very taken' at Cambridge by the courtyards of the colleges, 'a marvellous way for a college to expand incrementally and for non-residential elements to be introduced, as with Chapel Courts, Library Courts etc; it was the archetypal public, family space'.[18] Martin himself wrote how the design of university accommodation grew out of a form that had 'been known to work: the court'.[19] For a scheme at King's College Wilson added the stepped terrace, inspired by Jørn Utzon's studies of Mexican temple sites. Harvey Court, for Gonville and Caius College, Cambridge, based on a model by Patrick Hodgkinson from 1958, took the idea much further. Hodgkinson had worked for Alvar Aalto as a year-out student in 1954–5, shortly after the completion of the latter's Säynätsalo Town Hall with its raised plinth and external stairs, and Harvey Court comprised study bedrooms set over communal recreation facilities within a similar plinth, partly top-lit and with windows confined to one side.[20] The first layouts for St

Fig 6. Viipuri (now Vyborg) Library, lending library, photographed in 2003 (author)

Cross, in 1959, also set the three libraries and lecture facilities on each side of a square 'raised court' over Law's reserve stack, which thus got natural light from the sides and could therefore house carrels for researchers. In early 1959 the disposition of the four blocks was altered and the northern side given to the lecture theatres, the largest of which was to be sponsored by the Gulbenkian Foundation.[21]

Martin, and later Wilson, argued that if you studied the physical and operational requirements of a particular building type certain characteristics emerged that could be repeated and refined over subsequent commissions. In this they followed the lead of Aalto, who after his two square library halls at Viipuri evolved a plan for a series of modest public libraries that was long and low, and later also fan-shaped. Martin wrote that 'from 1933 the design of that library [Viipuri] has been transformed into the language of forms that Aalto developed and used throughout his lifetime', mentioning specifically 'the stepped levels and the carefully studied daylighting'.[22]

Though there was a debt to Aalto, Wilson described this first scheme for the St Cross Building as 'more inspired by Lou Kahn. Again the detailed design was by Hodgkinson. But librarians objected to the use of half levels and that there were too many columns'.[23] This design for the Law Library was based on pairs of tables for twelve readers set under a square rooflight, which formed a cube. This unit, separated by alleyways, was then extended as a grid to the stacks at the rear, with groups of four columns defining the structure and service ducts and an entrance on the diagonal. An added 'L'-shaped section permitted more stacks or small rooms within the library's secure area. The height of the building was constrained by that of the medieval church of St Cross nearby and there was little basement, a response to the poor ground conditions. Wilson recalled that 'the idea was that there would be a sort of hierarchy of spaces. So you get routes which would have a low ceiling and services, and clear spaces in the middle with rooflights that in themselves could be stepped through two storeys'.[24]

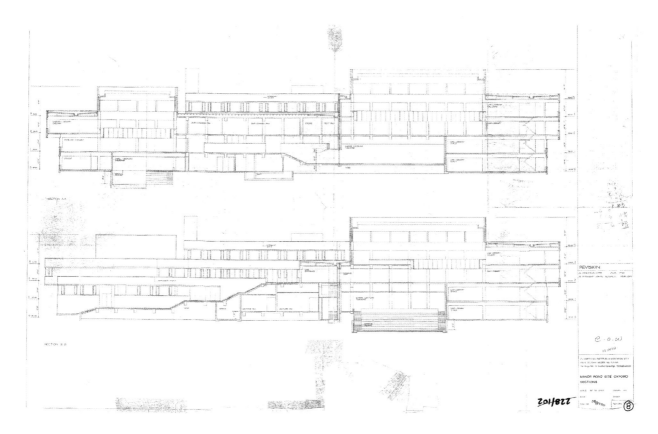

**Fig 8. Section of the
St Cross Building as
built (Mike Thrift,
University of Oxford)**

John Miller, who arrived in the office shortly afterwards, described it as 'ingenious, but too impractical', because of the many half levels, while the diagonal entrance made it difficult to fit the smaller libraries around it.[25] Designs for these were less developed. An L-shaped space housing the catalogue and control area occupied an intermediate level between the entrance and the main part of the English Library, a plan deemed too small and awkward.[26]

Lankester conceded that a design with so many groups of columns might be possible in the Law Library but was not appropriate in the English Library, smaller and with a brief requiring openness.[27] Martin insisted on going to a meeting on his own, and gave away the tartan grid, to Wilson's lasting regret. 'I believe that was the moment when I knew that I would soon have to move on and become my own master', he reflected.[28] Miller recalled that 'Leslie came down into the office with some sketches in red chalk, very rough. Patrick Hodgkinson was very good at interpreting Leslie's ideas, though he was sniffy because they were so different from his own – less complex and looser, more Aaltoesque, ironically, since *he* had worked for Aalto.'[29] This revised scheme adopted a simpler grid, with single columns and a simplified section for the smaller rooms and service accommodation. Nevertheless the hierarchy of spaces and L-shaped galleries remained.

The Norrington Report in 1959 recommended improving faculty libraries, rather than those in colleges, to meet the growth in undergraduate studies. The Faculty of English demanded space for more books and 150 readers. Although it had the poorest funding of the three faculties, and their design had to be simplified, the Faculty – led by Helen Gardner of St Hilda's College and an authority on T. S. Eliot – stuck out for the largest building possible. Lankester had to call another meeting of the three faculties in December 1959 when a third design was accepted, in which the clearest hand was Martin's own. The courtyard gave way to a broad outdoor stair set over the seminar rooms as the centrepiece of the design, from which the three departments were set off landings – English at the bottom, Statistics and the lecture halls in the middle and Law at the top.

Although Martin eliminated the diagonal axis, each library is entered from a corner containing the control desk set under a mezzanine housing smaller related accommodation. By rolling out a similar pattern across all three libraries the development gained a great homogeneity – difficult to achieve as the briefs for were so at variance. English remains the most open. The details, including desks and stack widths, were all related to the proportions of the structural system. A change in November 1959 switched the position of the lavatories and seminar rooms under the outside stairs, but otherwise this was largely the scheme that was realised.

English nevertheless remained unhappy even with the clean grid of single columns offered in late 1959. Caught between his role as designer and that of the adroit committee man, Martin conceded the removal of eight of the sixteen columns supporting the English Library's gallery, so that only those in the corners and the centre of each side were installed. Most published drawings show the full grid, but in February 1961 he was unsuccessful in securing the columns' reinstatement against the wishes of the faculty building committee and Gardner in particular. She reported in March to Hugh Keen at the University Chest that Martin 'very much … urged us very strongly on aesthetic grounds to allow him to go back to the original design with sixteen pillars'.[30] In March Gardner and Margaret Wheeler (an authority on Jonathan Swift) wrote to Martin asserting that 'we all think that the overriding considerations are convenience and flexibility in what is, after all, rather a small room. We have always made it clear that it was undesirable in a library of this kind to have too rigid a definition of space.'[31] Martin backed down, and the final result is a less principled but more free-flowing space.

Economies had to be made as costs rose with inflation to £644,558 in 1961, and the university accepted a fluctuating tender. A pale sand-faced Leicestershire brick and windows of black anodised aluminium – reflecting those of Säynätsalo – were approved in July 1960 by the Curators of the University Chest. The paving of the courts and steps was of brick like the walls. Internally the floors were of rubber and cork, while in the reading rooms the columns were of concrete 'with a very fine finish similar to marble'

Fig 9. Gulbenkian Lecture Theatre (James O. Davies/ English Heritage)

Fig 10. Foyer and internal staircase (James O. Davies/ English Heritage)

and the lecture rooms were lined in teak. In the entrance halls and common rooms the brickwork was exposed, but the seminar rooms were plastered.[32]

Construction proceeded slowly, beginning in late 1961 and completed only in 1964. The University Grants Committee gave £120,000 towards the fixed furniture, and Martin designed special tables in conjunction with Gordon Russell, reflecting an interest in furniture design first seen when in 1937 he published a 'unit' system and constructed with built-in light fittings, made of brass in the Law Library and steel in English.[33] They are all still in use today.

Assessment of the Scheme

The Institute of Statistics has been entirely remodelled, but the other two libraries have changed relatively little, and their faculties are to be congratulated on the respect they have shown the building – a tribute to their forbears who fought so keenly to get what they wanted. The Law Library has the greater rigour, with its full grid of columns and a more aggressive balcony that cuts into the square to give the L-shaped form, but the simpler plan and more extensive natural side light makes the English Library a particularly pleasurable space in which to work. The height of the roofs holding the skylights give a cool, white light, while the clever section and underlying sense of order imposed by the grid create a sense of great calm. This control and logic, and good materials, extends to the broad internal stair, a space of unexpected scale and sophistication, warm after the cool light and finishes of the libraries. The low ceilings here, again a contrast to the height of the libraries, make the sense of interlocking spaces more intense. The *Architectural Review* believed that 'this multi-faculty complex epitomizes some of the most intellectualized concepts current in British university design today' for evolving the idea of shared accommodation and its 'spiral hierarchy of growth', a reference to the similar layouts adopted by the different libraries.[34]

Though the building was still under construction, Wilson was convinced that the St Cross libraries led to his and Martin's appointment to build a new library for the British Museum in 1962. A plan made up of a series of L-shaped layers appeared in their first scheme for this, with an L-shaped catalogue hall linking a public reference room and six specialised facilities over a square general reading room. A still tighter, stepped composition based around a square was produced by Wilson in 1972 on a reduced site.[35] Variants can be seen at James Stirling's History Faculty building in Cambridge, where the square plan evolved into a fan shape, and very clearly in the humanities libraries that Wilson eventually realised at St Pancras.

The question of authorship was early raised, when Martin asked that he and Wilson be jointly credited in a press statement released by the university in September 1960, and Lankester refused. The incoming Registrar, Folliott Sandford, allowed Wilson to be acknowledged only as giving assistance or working in association.[36] The snub was not quickly forgotten, and Hodgkinson, too, was anxious to receive recognition for his contribution to the early schemes. In fact the complex of libraries as finally realised seems to have been one of Leslie Martin's most personal buildings, in which his signature features of a defining grid, a common building typology and broad staircases are all evident.

The pattern of gridded work spaces linked by galleries evolved on to an urban scale with Martin's plan for Whitehall, exemplifying the 'relationship between pattern of use, pattern of form, and technique'. This formed the bulk of the theoretical work in which he became enmeshed after 1965, when he extended the grid to encompass whole cities in a rejection of Camillo Sitte's picturesque plans and Christopher Alexander's structures for organic growth.[37] Wilson complained that Martin's grid studies had become 'rigid and cold' by the early 1970s when he used the grid as a solution for all problems.[38] At St Cross, however, the concept was still young, fresh and vigorous, and the structural control genuinely enhances the logic of the very three-dimensional and tightly controlled spaces, from the libraries themselves to the lecture theatres and the linking spaces, without feeling forced.

Colin Amery in 1983 argued that 'Sir Leslie's particular gifts have been to identify the characteristics of a certain building type and then to explore and develop these characteristics so that structural, formal and organisational development can take place. Their coolness and abstraction are, I suspect, simply that they are the products of their time – they will remain some of the best products we are likely to see.'[39] The St Cross Building is a particularly good example, Richard MacCormac highlighting it as 'a tour de force compositionally' for its 'supremely controlled complexity'.[40] It exemplifies Martin at his best for, as described by Peter Carolin, 'he challenged both history and common assumptions and he did so with clarity and modesty – always striving for quality and searching for "the great idea"'.[41] If Martin's later career disappoints, and it remains tantalising to wonder what happened to his innovative talents in the 1960s, then St Cross exists as a reminder of what might have been. It was the perfect solution to a difficult brief, and the building has not lost its force through repetition elsewhere.

Acknowledgements:
I would like to thank Malcolm Airs, John Miller, Mike Thrift of the University Estates Directorate, and Sue Usher, Librarian to the Faculty of English, for their exceptional help in giving access to archives and helping me understand the phases of the design. I am grateful to Mike Thrift for supplying plans and James O. Davies for the photographs

1. Reports, 2 December 1963 and 25 February 1964, in UR6/S/28/ file 4, Oxford University archives.

2. *RIBA Journal*, vol.82, no.8, August 1973, p.386.

3. Letter from Miss C. Good, Registry, to Jack Lankester, Surveyor to the University, 17 December 1957, in Committee on Elevations and the Choice of Architect, UR6/BPPA/1, file 1, Oxford University archives.

4. University of Oxford, Law Library Committee, *Oxford University Law Library*, Oxford University Press, 1956.

5. Reported to the Building and Development Committee, 14 November 1957, UR6/S/28/1, file 1, Oxford University archives.

6. Letter from Miss C. Good to Jack Lankester, 31 10 1957, UR6/S/28/1, ibid.

7. Report, January 1958, in UR6/S/28/1, ibid.

8. Report, 31 October 1957, in UR6/S/28/1, ibid.

9. Note from Douglas Veale to Miss C. Good, January 1958, UR6/BPPA/1, file 1, op. cit.

10. Report, 18 January 1958, in UR6/S/28/1, ibid.

11. Jack Lankester in conversation with Brian Harrison, 28 June 1989, C608/33, British Library Sound Archive, Harrison tapes.

12. Report, 29 March 1958, in UR6/S/28/1, op. cit.

13. Norman Engleback to the author, 16 March 2002.

14. Report of meeting between Martin and the Committee on Elevations, 17 May 1958, in UR6/S/28/1, op. cit.

15. Letter from Peter Shepheard to P. H. Sandford, Registrar, in UR6/S/28/1, ibid.

16. Report, 30 May 1955, in 'The New Library, file A', file held at the English Faculty Library, University of Oxford (by kind permission of Sue Usher).

17. Report October 1958 by Jack Lankester, in ibid.

18. Colin St John Wilson in conversation, 1 May 2002.

19. Leslie Martin, *Buildings and Ideas 1933–83 from the Studio of Leslie Martin*, Cambridge University Press, 1983, p.16.

20. Patrick Hodgkinson on Leslie Martin, *arq*, vol.5, no.4, 2001, p.297.

21. Reports 22 October 1958, 20 April 1959, Buildings and Works Committee, in 'The New Library, file A', op. cit.

22. Martin, '*Buildings and Ideas*', op. cit., p.11.

23. Wilson in conversation, 1 May 2002.

24. ibid. See also Wilson, 'Architecture – Public Good and Private Necessity', *RIBA Journal*, vol.86, no.3, March 1979, p.110.

25. John Miller in conversation, 24 September 2012.

26. Notes of meeting with the English Faculty, 20 April 1959, in 'The New Library, file A', op. cit.

27. Meeting, 2 May 1959, reported ibid.

28. Sarah Menin and Stephen Kite, *An Architecture of Invitation: Colin St John Wilson*, Aldershot, Ashgate, 2005, p.93.

29. Miller, 24 September 2012.

30. Letter, 16 March 1961, Margaret Gardner to Hugh Keen, Secretary of the University Chest, in 'The New Library, file A', op. cit.

31. Letter, 3 March 1961, ibid.

32. Jack Lankester, 11 July 1960 (after report 7 July), in UR6/BPPA/1, file 3, Oxford University archives.

33. Note of meeting with Leslie Martin, Douglas Lanham and P. Martin, 17 November 1961, in 'The New Library, file A', op. cit.

34. *Architectural Review*, vol.134, no.800, October 1963, p.280.

35. Colin St John Wilson, *The Design and Construction of the British Library*, London, British Library, 1998, pp.10–12.

36. Memo 22 September 1960, in UR6/S/28/1, file 2, Oxford University archives.

37. Leslie Martin, 'Architects' Approach to Architecture', *RIBA Journal*, vol.74, no.5, May 1967, p.194; Leslie Martin, 'The Grid as Generator', in Martin and Lionel March, eds., *Urban Spaces and Structures*, Cambridge University Press, 1972, pp.6–27.

38. Menin and Kite, op. cit., p.234.

39. Colin Amery, *Financial Times*, no.29165, 7 Nov 1983, p.13.

40. Richard MacCormac, 'Buildings, Ideas and the Aesthetic Sense', *arq*, vol.4, no.4, 2000, pp.300–2.

41. Peter Carolin, oration, 2000, in Biography File, RIBA British Architectural Library.

8

Choosing an Architect: Arne Jacobsen and St Catherine's College, Oxford

Geoffrey Tyack

Fig 1. A preliminary drawing of the courtyard at St Catherine's with the bell tower between the lecture room and library blocks

St Catherine's is architecturally the most important twentieth-century collegiate building in Oxford, comparable in its coherent singleness of vision to Keble in the nineteenth century and New College – that epitome of medieval collegiate planning – in the fourteenth. Its character derives from its uncompromising Modernism: the antithesis of the cosy informality that is often supposed to characterise Oxford's architecture. The College grew out of Oxford University's Delegacy for Non-Collegiate Students, later renamed St Catherine's Society and housed since 1936 in a building by Hubert Worthington (now the University's Faculty of Music) in St. Aldate's, south of Christ Church Meadow. In 1956 the University agreed to create a new residential college preserving the old name, to be housed on land purchased from Merton College in Holywell Great Meadow, to the north-east of the ancient city centre.[1] The style of the new building was chosen by the small group of men responsible for the selection of an architect, and it was their decision to eschew local talent in favour of Arne Jacobsen that ensured that Oxford acquired a major building by one of the leading modernist architects in Europe.

Before the mid-1950s, Oxford University was notoriously resistant to modernist architecture. Most college and university buildings were designed either in a version of the neo-Georgian style or in an Arts and Crafts-influenced Tudor-Gothic. The latter style was chosen, against the original wishes of its architect, by Lord Nuffield for the new post-graduate college begun in 1949 that bears his name, but when the fellows of St John's

Fig 2. An air view of the college taken shortly after completion. The two residential blocks are to the right and left. The lecture rooms, library and dining hall occupy the three blocks within the courtyard, and the common room block is adjoined to the dining hall at the bottom

came to build a new block of rooms in their North Quadrangle in 1958–60 they rejected the neo-Tudor designs of their architect, Sir Edward Maufe, in favour of an uncompromisingly modernist building – The Beehive – by the radical Architects' Co-Partnership.[2] Other colleges followed their lead, and it was in this changed climate that the key decisions about the design of St Catherine's were made.

Architectural choices in Oxford colleges are usually made by committees of academics, few if any of whom are experts in architecture. This sometimes leads to chronic indecision, but at St Catherine's this fate was avoided, mainly because the informal committee responsible for choosing the architect shared a common vision of the kind of building they wanted. That vision was clearly articulated by Alan Bullock in an unpublished typescript headed 'On being a Client'.[3] Oxford, he wrote, had reached a point where 'playing safe was much more likely to arouse criticism than striking out in a new direction'. An increasingly prosperous age, freed from post-war austerity and energised by science and technology, seemed to demand a new style of architecture, even in tradition-bound Oxford. Where better then to demonstrate the virtues of the new architecture than in a new college on a large virgin site away from the city centre?

Bullock was no expert on architecture. But in 1957, not long after the proposals for a new college were formally adopted, he made two visits to the United States, one to the East and the other to the West Coast, partly in order to familiarise himself with recent developments there.[4] A year later, in 1958, formal discussions on the choice of an architect began. St Catherine's was technically still a department of Oxford University, and the deliberations were entrusted to a Sub-Committee of the University's 'Committee on Elevations and Choice of Architects', a body established in 1956 with an implicitly modernist agenda.[5] Bullock, as Censor of what was still St Catherine's Society, was a member, as was Jack Lankester, the University Surveyor and 'technical advisor to the committee'.[6] There were also two heads of houses: Maurice Bowra, Warden of Wadham (Bullock's undergraduate college), former vice-chancellor and one of the most colourful Oxford figures of the day, and Roger Norrington, President of Trinity, a future vice-chancellor best known now as the man who devised the 'Norrington Table' for ranking Oxford colleges according to their undergraduates' success in the final examinations. Bowra and Norrington were both classicists by training but were broadly sympathetic to the Modern Movement in architecture, and Bullock (a historian) and Lankester (an architect) embraced it with genuine enthusiasm, seeing in St Catherine's an opportunity to give practical expression to their vision of a future liberated from hide-bound tradition.

But who was to give that vision tangible form? The architects for most large-scale architectural projects in post-war Britain, at least outside the public sector, were chosen by open or limited competition: a method widely employed for at least a hundred years and recommended by the profession's governing body, the Royal Institute of British Architects. Bullock, however, was opposed to the idea of a competition, believing that it would prevent a fruitful creative collaboration between architect and client. Both he and his colleagues on the sub-committee preferred the older method, deeply rooted in Oxford, of informal patronage, and in September 1958, as a first stage in the process, Lankester supplied photographs of the work of some of the leading members of the new British architectural establishment. They included Richard Sheppard and Partners, best-known for their schools and later for Churchill College, Cambridge; Powell and Moya, soon to be celebrated for a block of new buildings at Brasenose College and later to work at Christ Church and Wolfson College; Yorke, Rosenberg and Mardall, architects of Gatwick Airport; and the Architects' Co-Partnership, whose 'Beehive' at St John's was already under construction.[7] There were also pictures of work by younger exponents of the 'New Brutalism' which was to make such a heavy imprint on Britain's towns and university campuses in the 1960s: Chamberlin, Powell and Bon, later to design the Barbican housing development in London; Denys Lasdun, architect of the National Theatre; and William Howell, whose slab-like blocks of flats on the Alton West housing estate on the edge of Richmond Park in London had aroused much enthusiasm among the international avant-garde.[8]

Yet more names were suggested by Robin Darwin, Principal of the Royal College of Art, among them Basil Spence, architect of Coventry Cathedral and later of the University of Sussex, and Leslie Martin, 'a most sensitive designer and able committee man' who had been one of the team responsible for the Royal Festival Hall in London and who was currently engaged in the preliminary stages of the St Cross Building for the faculties of English, Law and Economics, built at the same time as St Catherine's.

Fig 4. Perspective drawing from Jacobsen's office showing the west or entrance side of St Catherine's College, with the Master's House in the distance

But in pressing their claims Darwin expressed the hope that:

> In their eagerness to revolt from the timidity of Cotswold Tudor [the committee] will not go too far and want the new college to look like a research lab. The present mood of some of the younger dons I have met is almost neurotically glass mad.[9]

The committee now began visiting a selection of recent buildings by the recommended British architects, starting with the Architects' Co-Partnership's famous rubber factory at Brynmawr in Wales and two blocks by Richard Sheppard at the Pershore College of Horticulture. Then, at the end of October, they made a whistle-stop tour of London buildings: Powell and Moya's Churchill Gardens estate; Bousfield Primary school, Kensington, by Chamberlin, Powell and Bon; Lasdun's Hallfield School, Paddington; a boys' club at Stepney by Yorke, Rosenberg and Mardall; a terrace at Hampstead by Howell and Amis; and a block of flats by the young *enfant terrible* James Stirling and his partner James Gowan at Ham Common. Though much touted in the architectural press, none of these buildings made an overwhelming impression on Bullock or the rest of the committee. As Bullock later wrote:

> [The] great burst of university building which marked the 1960s in Britain had not yet begun and I felt no conviction in looking at the buildings we visited that a British architect would have the self-confidence to stand up to the pressures of tradition in a place like Oxford and striking a balance between creating something which would be so out of keeping with the rest that it would never be accepted as an Oxford college and producing an imitation which would fail to establish a distinctive identity of its own. We were, in fact, searching for an architect who could grasp and express that identity for us, before it had yet taken clear shape in our minds.[10]

Fig 5. Munkegård School, Denmark, houses for the inspector and caretaker (RIBA Robert Elwall Photographs Collection)

Jack Lankester had meanwhile been urging the committee to look abroad for an architect. Trained as an architect himself, he had visited Scandinavia and was convinced

that Danish architecture and design was the best in Europe.[11] Denmark had embraced the Modern Movement earlier than Britain, embarking on innovative social housing schemes during the 1930s.[12] More important, Scandinavia had, as Lankester later asserted:

> escaped the industrial revolution, not having any resources of raw materials, coal, iron and so on, so the craft conditions continued right through the period of the industrial revolution in England. There was a strong tradition of properly designed artefacts, you see it everywhere, … the man in the street recognises and appreciates the difference between a properly designed object and one that is not, and is prepared to pay for it.[13]

Through the Danish-raised engineer Ove Arup, who had worked in England since 1926, Lankester was now put in touch with the Danish Building Centre in Copenhagen.[14] They provided him with a list of buildings by leading Danish architects, and on 7 November, fresh from their rather disappointing visit to London, the committee flew off to Denmark itself, where they saw work by Vilhelm Wohlert, notably the Louisiana Museum just outside Copenhagen; Jørn Utzon (already chosen as architect of the Sydney Opera House); and C.F. Møller, whose best-known work was the University of Aarhus, completed in 1946. Utzon's work struck the committee as 'rather alarmingly original', and Lankester later wondered whether Møller's work would export well. But what most impressed them was the work of Arne Jacobsen, above all the town hall at Rodovre (1954–6) and, even more, a school at Munkegård in Vanevre (1949–57), a little to the north of Copenhagen, the qualities of which stood out even in the grey skies and

Fig 8. One of the student study-bedrooms, with its Jacobsen-designed furniture

driving rain of a Scandinavian November.[15] For Lankester, these buildings 'had the stamp of mastery. This man never seems to put a foot wrong … He seemed to equal or excel everybody else in all departments'.[16] Bullock now felt that it was possible:

> to answer a question which photographs had failed to settle, whether the austerity of Jacobsen's style – the unbroken straight lines, the absence of any ornament or relief, the simple geometrical proportions – produced an impression of impersonality and coldness or humanity and warmth. One look at Munkegaard [sic] school was enough to satisfy me: I have never seen a school more perfectly fitted – in its scale, its colour, and in the planting of its courtyards – to make a child feel at home in it. From the moment I walked into Munkegaard School, I felt convinced that after nearly two years of looking we had found the architect we wanted.[17]

The contrast with some of the much-lauded but sometimes depressingly factory-like English schools of the 1950s must have been striking.

Arne Jacobsen was 58 years old in 1958. He had trained in Denmark in the 1920s, the decade of the Bauhaus, whose ideas about the unity of modernist architecture and design he enthusiastically espoused. He later wrote that the style he and his fellow students were searching for was 'at least theoretically, timeless', its underlying idea 'hidden in the rules of basic architecture', best exemplified in modern times by the work of Mies van der Rohe, especially after he moved to the United States in 1938:

> I have always defended pure functionalism, and I have to say that I consider Mies … to be the most important living architect, and for us architects who work in the ordinary way he provides an excellent example of how to achieve an architecture that is clear, sane and readily comprehensible, without modish additions.[18]

Jacobsen had a small office and was well-known for not undertaking more than one major

Fig 9. The college under construction, showing one of the concrete beams being put into place

work at a time. Bullock had already expressed scepticism about the size of the large British architectural firms, and the resulting lack of close personal involvement by the nominal architect:

> If the Architect is going to become no more than a business manager or organiser who cannot reasonably be asked to produce a work of beauty, surely people will say that they can manage without one ... I suppose everyone who builds a building wants it to be a masterpiece – and is a fool to want this. But, if people hadn't in the past we should never have got any.[19]

In 1958 Jacobsen's most prominent work, the Royal Hotel in Copenhagen (1956–61), was under construction, and he was engaged in the design of its cutlery, lamps and furniture, all of which have become icons of late twentieth-century design. In commissioning Jacobsen, St Catherine's would have the opportunity of realising that elusive goal: a building which would exhibit the union of the arts for which architects, artists and designers had striven for centuries.

On returning to Oxford, Lankester reported to the Committee on Elevations and Choice of Architects on the sub-committee's investigations. The work of the larger British firms was, he said, vitiated by 'the inability of one man to supervise and completely control the design of all the work attributed to him', while the smaller and younger firms did not have 'any very large or intricate work to show'. The work of the Danish architects was, by contrast, 'of a higher standard than anything the British architects ... have to offer', and that of Jacobsen was 'quite outstanding'. He was at the height of his powers, and insisted on controlling every aspect of the design himself. He was also 'versatile to a degree, his interests covering the design of furniture, wallpaper, lighting fittings, and landscape gardening'.[20] He was therefore unanimously recommended as architect, though the sub-committee recognised the possible opposition that might arise through the appointment of a foreign architect and was prepared to look for a British architect who might work in partnership with him: a suggestion that was later backed by Basil Spence, then President of the RIBA.

Before formally being offered the commission, Jacobsen – who had been in Paris when Bullock and his colleagues went to Denmark – was invited to Oxford, the visit fortuitously coinciding with an exhibition of his work at the RIBA in February 1959. He was duly wined and dined, and, along with his assistant Knud Holscher (who, unlike him, spoke English), took the opportunity, in Lankester's words, to 'look round the various colleges to find out how the colleges worked'. He also examined the site, entered into discussions about the design, promising to produce sketch plans within the next six months and undertook to design most of the furniture and landscaping.[21] He confirmed that the design work on the Copenhagen Royal Hotel was almost finished and that he was prepared to work within a tight budget.

Bullock later wrote:

'When we finally got Jacobsen to visit Oxford, it soon became clear that the question was, not whether we should appoint him, but whether he would accept the appointment if we offered it to him. He would undertake no commission, however attractive, unless he was convinced that he could produce a solution which would satisfy him. This may have been one of the reasons for his reputation as a "difficult" man to work with, but it was not a pose and I soon came to see Jacobsen's difficult side as an expression of the personal quality I most admired in him – his integrity, which in practice meant a refusal to accept second-best solutions or to compromise with his own high standards'.[22]

Jacobsen was chosen as architect on 26 February 1959, subject to the appointment of a British co-architect, who he insisted should be in a subordinate capacity; he suggested Philip Dowson from the Arup firm, but in the event Dowson decided that an associate architect was no longer needed, and resigned the commission, no doubt to Jacobsen's relief, in September.[23] Lankester meanwhile undertook to provide support from the University Surveyor's office, managing the contract, chairing the site meetings, issuing instructions to the contractors, and maintaining 'intermittent but decisive' contact with Jacobsen.[24] He later claimed 'a major part in persuading the University to appoint him, on the basis that my office could supply the necessary support. Looking back, I do not think that any other arrangement would have worked.'[25]

The announcement of Jacobsen's appointment led to predictable expressions of outrage from the British press, but in Oxford the reaction was generally favourable. The site of the new college was some distance away from the city centre, and the buildings would not impinge on cherished historic structures. By 1959 the stylistic battle between Modernism and 'Cotswold Tudor' had been won, modernist buildings were being commissioned by several of the colleges, and several were already going up in the Science Area. So when Jacobsen's designs were finally revealed in 1960 public opinion was prepared. Whether it was able to accept Jacobsen's severe, strictly controlled, minimalist architecture was a question which had to await the completion of the buildings in 1964.[26] When Jacobsen was given the commission no-one yet knew what they would look like, or how they would be planned. Bullock and his colleagues had put their faith in a foreign architect who had supplied no plans or elevations, who had never designed a building outside his own country and who had never visited Oxford before being offered the commission. But, looking back from a perspective of fifty years, who can say that their confidence was misplaced?

Acknowledgments: This is a slightly amended version of a chapter that appeared in R. Ainsworth and C. Howell (eds), *St Catherine's, Oxford: A Pen Portrait* (London, St Catherine's College and Third Millenium Publishing, 2012). I am very grateful to Roger Ainsworth – the current Master of St Catherine's – and to the publishers for allowing me to reproduce the text; to the College Archivist for giving me access to relevant unpublished material; and to Nathan Jones, the College's communications officer, for supplying images

1. For the early history of the college, see Margaret and Derek Davies, *Creating St Catherine's College* Oxford, St Catherine's College, 1997, pp. 1–58, and R. Ainsworth and C. Howell (eds), *St Catherine's, Oxford: A Pen Portrait* London, St Catherine's College and Third Millennium Publishing, 2012, pp. 11–27.

2. Geoffrey Tyack, *Modern Architecture in an Oxford College*, Oxford, Oxford University Press, 2005, pp. 19–41.

3. St Catherine's College archives, correspondence files on Choice of Architect. Bullock had been head (Censor) of St Catherine's Society since 1952.

4. He failed to attract funding from the Rockefeller Foundation, but succeeded in raising a substantial sum of money from private individuals and companies. Funds also came from the University Grants Committee.

5. R. Trotman & E.J.K. Jarrett, *The Non-Collegiate Students and St Catherine's Society* (Oxford, Oxford University Press, 1962, pp. 55–6. See also B. Harrison (ed.), *History of the University of Oxford*, vol. 8, Oxford, Oxford University Press, 1994, p. 701.

6. Interview in *How to be Modern: Arne Jacobsen in the 21st Century*, Oxford, Museum of Modern Art, exhibition catalogue, 2002, p. 24.

7. Minutes of St Catherine's Sub-Committee, 22 September 1958. Other architects considered at this stage were Stirrat Johnson-Marshall, Frederick Gibberd, and Casson and Conder.

8. He was a founder member of the Howell, Killick, Partridge and Amis partnership, which later carried out work at St Anne's and St Antony's Colleges.

9. Darwin to Bullock, 1 October 1958, files on Choice of Architect, St Catherine's archives.

10. 'Working with Arne Jacobsen', quoted in Ainsworth and Howell, *op. cit.*, p. 56, and quoted in P.E. Skriver, *Arne Jacobsen: A Danish Architect*, Copenhagen, Ministry of Foreign Affairs, 1971, p. 52.

11. Davies, op. cit., pp. 60–61.

12. M. C. Donnelly, *Architecture in the Scandinavian Countries*, Cambridge, Mass, MIT, 1992, pp. 315–6.

13. Lankester, op. cit., p. 28.

14. Arup to Lankester, 2 July 1958, files on Choice of Architect, St Catherine's archives.

15. Interview with Lankester in *How to be Modern*, p. 34; St Catherine's archives, 'On being a Client'. For Munkegård School, see Tobias Faber, *Arne Jacobsen*, London, Alec Tiranti, 1964, pp. 60–73.

16. Draft memorandum from Lankester to the Committee on Elevations and Choice of Architects, 15 January 1959, St Catherine's archives.

17. Ainsworth and Howell, *op. cit.*, pp. 56–7; Skriver, *op. cit*, p. 52.

18. Quoted in Arne Jacobsen and Astrid Bowron *Arne Jacobsen: how to be modern in the 21st Century*, Oxford, Modern Art Oxford, 2002, pp. 16–17.

19. Bullock to Colin Boyne (editor of the *Architects' Journal*), 12 June 1958, St Catherine's archives.

20. Memorandum by Jack Lankester, 14 November 1958, St Catherine's archives.

21. Davies, op. cit., p. 64. Holscher became project architect for St Catherine's, moving temporarily to Oxford to supervise the work in 1962: Ainsworth and Howell, op cit., p. 59.

22. Quoted Ainsworth and Howell, *op. cit.*, pp. 58–9

23. Dowson subsequently designed several buildings in Oxford, including the Nuclear Physics building at the corner of Banbury Road and Keble Road, and the Sir Thomas White building at St John's College.

24. *How to be Modern*, p. 25.

25. Lankester to Derek Davies, 30 August 1995, St Catherine's archives.

26. See, *inter alia*, *Architects' Journal* Vol. 140, no.6, 5 August 1964, pp. 323–42; *Architectural Review*, vol. 136, no. 811, September 1964, pp. 174–95, Nikolaus Pevsner called St Catherine's 'a perfect piece of architecture': *The Buildings of England: Oxfordshire* Harmondsworth, Penguin, 1974, p. 240.

9

A Strange Brutalist 'Primitive Hut': Howell, Killick, Partridge and Amis's Senior Combination Room at Downing College, Cambridge

Otto Saumarez Smith

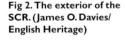

Fig 1. The SCR seen beyond the portico of Wilkins's Hall. (Myke Clifford, 2013)

The architectural character of Downing College is defined by its first architect, William Wilkins, whose Greek revival buildings (constructed from 1807) form a large three-sided court, the spaciousness of which feels closer to an American campus like the University of Virginia than to the tight enclosure of a traditional Oxbridge college. Wilkins's buildings are an academically classical, restrained and dignified set piece.

This article focuses on the addition to this singular and significant site by Bill Howell of the firm Howell, Killick, Partridge and Amis, with a kitchen block, renovation of the hall, and new senior combination room (SCR).[1] This is particularly intriguing for its subtle suggestions of a classical structure within what remains a modernist project. Its form of a semi-detached pavilion on a podium of steps, visually separated from the adjacent Ionic portico of Wilkins's hall by a blank stone wall, has palpable echoes of a pedimented temple. It is a gem of a building, designed on a 1' to 1½' grid, its composition from pre-cast concrete elements belied by the carefulness of the detailing and expense of finishing. The concrete columns and lintels, cast with Portland stone aggregate, were ordered several inches too large, so they could be sanded down and further smoothed by the application of an acid-etched finish.[2] The building has two axes, presenting two front façades at right angles. The third visible side is defined by a rustic looking chimney flue that makes a sharp contrast with the Adamesque chimney piece inside.

Although it is not strictly historicist, the SCR suggests an intriguing and, for its date, a highly unusual attempt at making a modern building that synthesises with its context,

Fig 2. The exterior of the SCR. (James O. Davies/ English Heritage)

Fig 3. Rear elevation of the SCR, showing rustic chimney flue. (Elain Harwood)

through a suggestion, or reinterpretation, of historical forms. There is no direct statement about the intention behind the use of classical forms, and there is no comparable approach in the architect's *oeuvre*. Andy MacMillan of Gillespie, Kidd and Coia suggested at the time to Howell that the SCR was influenced by Soane, and was told to 'fuck off'.[3] Howell's partner John Partridge is also reticent about discussing this aspect of the project.[4] Although there is no direct testament it is possible, nevertheless, to explain the form the building takes by the way it relates to the structural philosophy of its architect, and also by the stimulus towards compromise provided by the Fellowship (many of whom would have preferred a more traditional building) through looking at the gestation of the project in the college's archives.

Wilkins's plan was only ever partly realised, with more buildings intended to the south. The assorted additions to the college by later architects show a variety of approaches to contextualism. By placing Howell's project within this larger narrative of extensions to Wilkin's scheme, it is possible to demonstrate how attitudes to contextualism in a Cambridge college have changed during the twentieth century, and how the project is in many respects unique.

The Genesis of the Project
The first extension to Downing was in 1873, by Edward Middleton Barry. He scrupulously followed Wilkins's Greek vocabulary to the point that his additions are most easily distinguished by the use of a slightly pinker variant of Ketton stone.[5] Barry's buildings are an unusually faithful continuation of an earlier scheme for any age, but especially for the mid-Victorian period, where there was little theoretical vocabulary with which to talk about context. It is in stark contrast to Alfred Waterhouse's contemporaneous work at Pembroke, which has no discernible relation whatsoever to the earlier character of the college. It also contrasts with Arthur Blomfield's addition of a cumbersome Byzantine chapel to another Wilkins set piece in 1876, at the East India Company College, Hertfordshire.

Sir Herbert Baker, employed from 1929, was the next architect to make his mark on the college, in his own words having 'the honour of adding buildings which consorted with [Wilkins's] classic dignity'.[6] Pevsner commented that: 'With the astonishing self-assurance which this architect possessed and which appears so naïvely in his memoirs, he abandoned Wilkins's design just enough to irritate.'[7] At the time, though, it was seen by the Cambridge architect H. C. Hughes, of Hughes and Bicknell, as a careful job:

> For a long while both lack of money and also the fear that any modern building would spoil the old had prevented the authorities of Downing from completing the serene wings of Wilkins' neo-Greek building. The new building most wisely accepts that the grand scale of 1820 is gone for ever.... . Accepting a relationship in material and height, the architect has produced a range of a more useful and habitable scale. To do so, he has reopened the old vein of the Ketton quarries ...[8]

Baker died in 1946, but it was only after Howell's appointment in 1964 that his successor, Vernon Hellbing, ceased to be the college's architect; the last building by Baker's firm, Kenny Court, was completed in 1963. There were those amongst the fellowship who wanted the firm to have the SCR project.

In the wake of the Robbins Report of 1963 many colleges were enlarged to meet the targeted expansion of higher education in Britain. In early 1964 the fellowship decided to expand the college by building 'housing for sixty further graduates within the domus, the reconstruction of the College kitchens, extension of the Hall and the reconstruction of a new combination room'.[9] The extra graduates would in the end be housed off site, with extra on-site accommodation only provided with Quinlan Terry's residential range in Howard Court of 1992–4. At the time the SCR was located at the end of the hall below a chapel, so a new SCR would have the added benefit of creating more space in the hall for increasing numbers of students.

At a meeting on 17 January 1964 it 'was agreed that a further building in the Style of Kenny B should not be erected', by a margin of 21 votes to three.[10] Fellows were asked to submit names of possible architects for the project, who were then asked to submit photographs of recent projects, to be shown in an exhibition. The list of architects arrived at by this method show that the fellowship was divided as to what kind of architect to choose for the project, with names including both radical and more established modernists as well as a number of traditionalists.

The architects put forward were Hellbing of Baker and Scott; Brett and Pollen; Casson, Condor and Partners; James Stirling; Denis Clarke Hall; Fello Atkinson of James Cubitt and Partners; A. B. Davies; Raymond Erith; Robert Matthew and Johnson Marshall; the Oxford Architects Partnership; Wallace Hunt; Leach, Rhodes and Walker; and Howell, Killick, Partridge and Amis. Denys Lasdun and also Powell and Moya told the college that they were too busy to take the job. C. H. Aslin had also been proposed, but he had been dead since 1959.

HKPA were put forward by three separate fellows. The Master, the classical scholar W. K. C. Guthrie, had come into contact with Howell through the planning of the proposed University Centre. 'I have no suggestion that I want to press, but I find the model of the proposed University Centre quite attractive and I have also had some contact with its architect Howells [sic] over the planning of it and found him a very reasonable and pleasant person to deal with', he explained.[11] Despite the non-dogmatic tone, Guthrie appears to have been an important proponent of the move towards an unabashedly modernist scheme at the college. The architect Peter Bicknell, who had taught Howell at the Cambridge architecture school, was a fellow of the college. Though he originally put forward RMJM and Fello Atkinson for the project, John Partridge remembers him being a significant supporter of HPKA.[12]

Fig 8. Houses for Visiting Mathematicians, University of Warwick, 1967–70 (Elain Harwood)

Fig 9 (overleaf). Main elevation of the SCR (James O. Davies/ English Heritage)

Fig 10. Bill Howell as a Tommy, from *Popular Arts of the First World War* 1972

comparing it with Robert Venturi's mother's house – which also suggests a split pediment. It is an intriguing suggestion, but it is not particularly convincing that Howell was engaged in an analogous enterprise. Howell's death, in a car crash in 1974, means that it is impossible to speculate how far this project was a premonition of later architectural developments, or even a post-modern turn. But its dissimilarity becomes very obvious when comparing the SCR to Venturi's own attempt to fit in with a scheme by William Wilkins at the National Gallery extension (1986). Venturi quotes elements of Wilkins's scheme, such as copying the form of Wilkins's order, but then redeploys them in an intercolumnation he describes as a jazz rhythm; in contrast Howell's SCR tries to link the buildings through formal resonances rather than quotation.[30]

Howell, who had flown with the RAF in the Second World War, collected First World War memorabilia and published a book on the subject with Barbara Jones in 1972.[31] In the flyleaf there is a photograph of him, with his bushy moustache, in full fancy dress as a Tommy. Such eccentricity is a long way from the common image of the dogmatic modernist architect. He had written in 1957 that 'maybe we should get more vulgarity (I should prefer this to the anaemic official good taste) … we should also get some splendid eccentricities, a department in which we used as a nation, to excel'.[32]

In this respect, Howell's mathematician's houses at the University of Warwick (1967–70) are perhaps the closest parallel with the SCR within the architect's oeuvre. There is no similar playing with historical style as at the SCR; they are a group of globular, bunker-like cottages, arranged in a circle around a tree, suggesting a kind of village green. However there is a similarly playful respect towards the foibles of an academic community. Each family house is connected to a smaller volume at the back, containing a sparsely furnished room with a blackboard spanning the curving walls.[33]

Even if the SCR has a certain eccentric wit, it is also highly serious, even solemn, and should not therefore be seen as an early manifestation of jokey Postmodernism. Such an idea does not fit with the architect's *oeuvre* as a whole. As with many of their contemporaries, HPKA's work was heavily indebted to Le Corbusier. Peter Smithson described their blocks at Roehampton, which are clearly modelled on the Unité d'Habitation in Marseilles as 'an act of homage to Le Corbusier', John Partridge adding that 'we are happy to embrace this description'.[34] The SCR is not a disavowal of this modernist heritage, but is an attempt to situate the modernist ideal of structural integrity within a broader historical lineage, made necessary by the sensitive context at Downing.

Writing about his approach towards architecture, Howell described it as being

located in the 'most respectable ancestry' of 'architecture in which the interior volume is defined and articulated by actual, visible structure'.[35] Whilst stressing the undogmatic nature of such a list ('I like lots of architecture, old and new'), Howell placed himself within a lineage which stretched back to Stonehenge, taking in the Gothic cathedrals, Renaissance classicism, Japanese timber-framed houses, Victorian cast-iron building, and the Hertfordshire schools of the 1940s.

Although making the structure visible was a foundational desire of Modernism, according to Howell: 'In the early days of the Modern Movement, there was a lot of talk about "structural honesty" and "expressing the structure", but curiously enough this seldom took place in the interior.'[36] The structural system of the SCR, devised with the engineer David Powell of Redlich, Powell and Partners, features paired columns, to create an outer and inner square of columns supporting cantilever brackets that hold up a pre-cast central lantern, weighing seven tons, in the centre of the room.[37] John Partridge reports that the architects were thinking of the Octagon at Ely Cathedral in this element of the design, but it is difficult not to see it rather as a reinterpretation of a Roman *compluvium* (a central opening in the roof of an atrium letting in air and light).[38]

This system was born out of the 'desire not to lose the columns, either within the room or from the outside ...' in the same way the adjacent hall has its exterior portico and pilastered interior.[39] The system also creates a space defined by columns within its interior space, a kind of cube within a cube, which for Howell also carried historical resonances:

> We have always had a sneaking regard for columns set within the space (i.e., inside the enclosing skin), provided this can be done without sterilising useful space, because if the intention is to create an architecture whose form consists of structural enclosures, these become even more apparent and communicative if you are living with your support system; they create that room within a room effect, of which John Soane was the past master.[40]

Howell takes from classicism a suggestion of it as a structural system, enclosing space. By stripping away the detailing of classicism, and presenting columns, lintel and pediment in a purely structural way, it could be seen to comment upon the supposed structural genesis of classicism in the primitive hut as presented by Laugier and others.

It learns from classicism that structure ought to be apparent both inside and outside. It is this element of the classical system that Howell writes about admiringly:

> Interior renaissance architecture, at any scale other than the small domestic, consisted of space articulated by structural forms. They were, very often, fictive structural forms: i.e., the column, the pilaster and the entablature were used as a set of images to define the enclosure of space, but were not always – indeed not often – its actual structural system.[41]

Howell's interpretation of classicism at Downing is particularly appropriate considering the Greek revival context, which was a style that emphasised simplicity, functionalism and austerity, where the 'use of classical orders was strictly regulated by Laugier's doctrine of 'apparent utility'.[42]

As already mentioned, the SCR was built in tandem with a project to enlarge and refurbish the hall. The approach to this aspect of the project gives a further insight into the way that Howell engaged with Wilkins. The language used by the architect is the sixties concept of 'rehabilitation' rather than the contemporary ideal of 'conservation'. The ambition was to make 'the best of [the hall's] great architectural possibilities in a really imaginative way and which would be in the spirit of the original Wilkins scheme.'[43] Howell sought the advice of the architectural historian Sir John Summerson about the redecoration, whose suggestion that they work with Colefax Fowler was taken up.[44]

Fig 12. Perspective drawing of proposed interior redecoration of the Hall

Howell had initially presumed that the scagliola finish on the columns had been introduced by Barry, 'partly because as a member of the Reform Club I did not need any convincing of connection between the Barry family and the use of scagliola.'[45] On seeing that a marble finish was included in an original engraving it was retained. The colour scheme 'consists of two basic colours – a wall colour, which picks up the burnt orange tones from the scagliola, and a lighter stone-colour, used in a variety of tones for the main architectural elements...'[46] Three chandeliers were 'based on the Regency shape of the ones in the Travellers' Club.[47] A more dubious decision was to alter some of the original Wilkins plaster mouldings, which Howell complained were 'indeterminate, slightly chinoiserie'.[48] Howell's historical awareness and sensitivity to context were progressive for the period in which he was working. However, the approach to conservation at Downing is more ambiguous, especially when judged by contemporary standards. Nevertheless, John Partridge argued that the modernisation made the hall 'more consistent with the Neo-Greek of its exterior'.[49]

Debates about the suitability of the approach at Downing continued on its reception. Walter Segal wrote in the *Architects' Journal* that the 'combination room does prove, however, that reinterpretation can offer greater pleasure than reproduction, and that while nobody can fully appreciate the scale of the past, it is possible to adjust it to our level by using its canons in different contexts'.[50] J. M. Richards ignored the question of style when writing about Downing in the early 1980s, seeing it rather as an exemplar of sensitive modernism, writing that the 'additions to Downing College are a model of intelligent grafting of new on to old and a demonstration that in doing so harmony of scale and materials are more important than similarity of style'.[51]

Marcus Binney's letter, following a complimentary write up in *Country Life*, was much more critical of its success:

> The architects are no doubt congratulating themselves (and to be fair, being congratulated) on the skilful way in which they have integrated old and new; but in my mind there is no doubt that Wilkins, the original architect of the College, would be turning in his grave could he see this travesty of a design. While it is obvious to all that the new building copies most of the essential features in a simplified way – columns, pediment and podium of steps – in almost every other respect it turns its back on the spirit of the original ... Wilkins was a neo-classical architect of considerable refinement, and his style very simple and restrained, and for this reason special attention must be paid to his spacing, proportion and detail. Yet the crowning feature of the new design is a broken pediment, a baroque element that would have been anathema in Wilkins' day ... go and see it in all its pristine ugliness.[52]

The next time Downing came to build a sub-committee was appointed to choose an architect. They were 'in favour of choosing an architect specialising in the classical style'. They recommended that Quinlan Terry be invited to prepare a scheme.[53] Other names suggested included Dennis Lennon, Roderick Gradidge and Terry Farrell.[54] Quinlan Terry remembers that it was Cinzia Maria Sicca, an architectural historian then engaged in writing a history of the buildings at Downing, who was the initial driving force behind the appointment.[55]

The stated intention of Terry's new lecture theatre block, the Howard Building, was that 'Stylistically and architecturally it perpetuates the restrained classicism that is characteristic of Downing College .... It was felt appropriate that the general lines, proportions, materials and construction of the adjoining building should be maintained.'[56] However, as built it is in a much more playfully Baroque spirit. Terry defended the use of 'a more Baroque and theatrical version of the Orders, and the use of a giant Roman Corinthian order with a modillion cornice and a small pediment with finials' as 'appropriate', to 'emphasise the theatrical side of its nature.'[57]

Fig 13. Perspective drawing of the Howard Building by Quinlan Terry

David Watkin has also pointed out that Wilkins himself had intended the chapel to have a Roman Corinthian order.[58] Seeing the Howard Building in the context of Terry's career, the use of Baroque and Renaissance elements might well be seen as a move away from the restrained Soanian classicism of his mentor and partner Raymond Erith.

The building elicited what Martin Pawley described as 'an utterly dispassionate demolition job' by Gavin Stamp, in which he felt that Terry had 'indulged in his affection for Renaissance precedents and has ostentatiously ignored the neo-classical character of the buildings.'[59] One of the main causes for Stamp's concern was that 'what unifies all the buildings of Downing College, whether they are by Wilkins, Barry, Baker, Scott or even by W. G. Howell (designer of the strange Brutalist "primitive hut" senior combination room behind Wilkins' dining hall) is that they all rise from the same plinth level or stylobate. The Howard Building does not, however.' Terry's approach was defended by Leon Krier and, surprisingly, Sir John Summerson.

In 1994 the Royal Fine Art Commission, then made up of many established modernists of the period including Philip Dowson, Michael Hopkins and Philip Powell, published *What Makes a Good Building*. It was written by Sherban Cantacuzino, who also wrote the introduction to the 1981 monograph on Howell Killick Partridge and Amis. In the section on context, Downing is used as an exemplar of what to do and what not to do in a reaffirmation of modernist ideals. Ideas about context had come full circle, with the Terry building denigrated and HPKA's celebrated: 'Quinlan Terry's Howard Building at Downing College in Cambridge, even if not an actual copy, is a repetition of what has been, whereas W. G. Howell, in his Senior Combination Room at the same college, has transformed an heirloom and made it bear fruit.'[60]

These then remain live debates. Quinlan Terry completed another major project for Downing with a library that discards the Baroque exuberance of the Howard Building for a monumental Greek Doric portico, with shades of Ledoux, perhaps responding to criticism by creating something more in keeping with the dominating Greek classicism of Downing.[61] The library gives a much-needed monumental accent to the rather underwhelming approach to Downing, although it raises questions as to how suitable such strict classical forms are to a building that will need to adapt to future needs. The modern world of science and technology is jokily referred to by an image of a radio-telescope in the frieze. Lately, in refurbishing the hall and the SCR, the college have looked to the firm Caruso St John, a practice whose 'buildings do not look like buildings of the past, but they are infused with their lessons'.[62]

In looking at the more recent history of additions to Cambridge colleges, one can discern a multiplicity of approaches, from strict traditionalism to the privately eccentric vocabularies of Edward Cullinan or Richard MacCormac. However the majority of architects have practised a politely retiring and historically literate modern approach. The SCR is remarkable, both in its own time and in ours, for its unusual combination of the bristling confidence and audacity which is characteristic of much Sixties architecture, whilst simultaneously presenting an intelligent and witty dialogue with its classical neighbour.

Acknowledgments: Thanks are due to Kate Thompson for guiding my research at Downing College archives and Elain Harwood for carefully editing the piece. I also received valuable suggestions and advice at various stages from John Partridge, Quinlan Terry, Andy MacMillan, Diane Haigh, James Sutherland, Tim Collett, Alan Powers, Alistair Fair, Nicholas Bullock, Gavin Stamp, Frank Salmon, David Pratt, Richard Butler, Aaron Helfand, Max Bryant and Lucian Robinson. The work was made possible by the Kemp Scholarship at St John's College, Cambridge

1. I have referred throughout to Howell as the architect of the SCR, which is not meant to negate the collaborative contribution of other members of the firm. However, Howell was the college's primary contact, as well as the author of the key drawings.

2. John Partridge, interviewed 27 January 2012.

3. Andy MacMillan, interviewed 18 February 2012.

4. John Partridge, interviewed 27 January 2012.

5. Cinzia Maria Sicca, *Committed to Classicism: The Building of Downing College Cambridge*, Cambridge, Downing College, 1987, p.78–9.

6. Sir Herbert Baker, *Architecture and Personalities*, London, Country Life, 1944, p.138.

7. Nikolaus Pevsner, *The Buildings of England: Cambridgeshire*, London, Penguin, 1970, p.68.

8. H. C. Hughes 'Recent Building in Cambridge', *Listener*, vol.7, no.167, 23 March 1932, p.407.

9. The Bursar, letter to Robert Matthew Johnson Marshall and Partners, 23 March 1964, Downing College Archives. 'Domus', the Latin word for a house, was used to denote colleges during their early history, and survives in such current uses as the domus bursar; see Joseph Kilner, *The Account of Pythagoras's school in Cambridge as in Mr Grose's Antiquaries of England and Wales, and other Notices*, Oxford, 1790, p.112.

10. Downing Minutes, DCGB/M/1/12, 17 January 1964.

11. W. K. C. Guthrie, letter, 26 February 1964, Downing College archives, DCAR/1/2/4/1/13.

12. John Partridge, interviewed 27 January 2012.

13. 'Notes on practices', unsigned, 5 May 1964, Downing College archives, DCAR/1/2/4/1/13.

14. *The Times*, no.61479, 12 March 1983, p.10.

15. Hugh Plommer, *The Line of Duty*, Cambridge, Burlington Press, 1982, p.6.

16. Report, 20 May 1963, of the Council of the Senate on the planning of a University Centre, reproduced ibid., p.26.

17. Downing Minutes, 27 November 1964, DCGB/M/1/10.

18. Howell to Dr Fisher, letter 8 March 1965, Downing College archives, DCAR/1/2/4/1/47.

19. Report on an informal meeting of the Governing Body, 10 January 1966, Downing College archives, DCAR/1/2/4/1/47.

20. W. K. C. Guthrie, Letter, 21 April 1966, Downing College archives, DCAR/1/2/4/1/47.

21. Governing Body Minutes, 6 May 1966, DCGB/M/1/10.

22. Governing Body Minutes, 8 July 1966, DCGB/M/1/10.

23. Thomas Sharp, *Town and Townscape*, London, John Murray, 1968, p.22–3.

24. Nikolaus Pevsner, *The Englishness of English Art*, London, Penguin, 1964, p.181.

25. Nikolas Pevsner, Visual Planning and the Picturesque, Los Angeles, Getty Trust, 2010, p.193.

26. Quoted in Colin Ward, 'Is Conservation More than Nostalgia', *Talking Green*, Nottingham, Five Leaves Press, 2012, p.133.

27. Quoted in What Makes a Good Building? An Inquiry by the Royal Fine Art Commission, London, Royal Fine Art Commission, 1994, p.34.

28. Louise Campbell, 'Building on the Backs: Basil Spence, Queen's College Cambridge, and University Architecture at Mid-Century', Architectural History, vol.54, 2011, p.390.

29. Lionel Brett, Our Selves Unknown: An Autobiography, London, Gollancz, 1985, pp.159–60.

30. Robert Venturi, interviewed 28 June 2010.

31. Barbara Jones and Bill Howell, Popular Arts of the First World War, London, Studio Vista, 1972.

32. W. G. Howell, 'Freedom to Build', The Times, no.53960, 1 October 1957, p.2.

33. See Sherban Cantacuzino, Howell, Killick, Partridge and Amis: Architecture, London, Lund Humphries, 1981, p.92.

34. 'Attitudes to Architecture: Howell, Killick, Partridge and Amis', Arena, vol.82, no.906, November 1966, p.101.

35. W. G. Howell, 'Vertebrate buildings: the architecture of structured space', Architect's Approach to Architecture, RIBA Journal, vol.77, no.3, March 1970, pp.100–8.

36. ibid.

37. 'Precast pavilion', Concrete Quaterly, no.86, July/September 1970, pp.2–6.

38. John Partridge, interviewed 27 January 2012.

39. Concrete Quarterly, op. cit., p.5.

40. ibid, p.3.

41. W. G. Howell, RIBA Journal, op. cit., p.101.

42. J. Mordaunt Crook, The Greek Revival, London, RIBA 1968, p. 33.

43. 'Downing College – The Redecoration of the Hall', 12 July 1968, Downing College archives, DCAR/1/2/8/1/63.

44. ibid.

45. ibid.

46. 'The Hall', 29 April 1969, Downing College archives, DCAR/1/2/8/1/63.

47. ibid.

48. ibid.

49. Sherban Cantacuzino, Howell, Killick, Partridge and Amis: Architecture, London, Lund Humphries, 1981, p.82.

50. Walter Segal, 'Cambridge Manners', Architects' Journal, vol.150, no.10, 10 October 1969, pp.1516–18.

51. J. M. Richards, Times Literary Supplement, no.4090, 21 August 1981, p.960.

52. Marcus Binney, 'New Building in a Cambridge College', Country Life, vol.150, no.3872, 26 August, 1971, p.50.

53. Minutes of meeting of the New Buildings Committee, 26 February 1983, Downing College archives, DCGB/M/1/12.

54. ibid.

55. Quinlan Terry, interviewed 26 January 2012.

56. Quinlan Terry, letter 23 October 1984, Downing College archives, DCAR/1/2/4/1/35.

57. ibid; Quinlan Terry, letter 6 July 1983, Downing College archives, DCAR/1/2/4/1/35.

58. David Watkin, Radical Classicism: the Architecture of Quinlan Terry, New York, Rizzoli, 2006, p.222.

59. Martin Pawley, 'The Strange Death of Architectural Criticism', Architects' Journal, vol.208, no.1, 2 July 1998, p.24; Gavin Stamp, Architects' Journal, vol.187, no.11, 16 March 1988. p.36.

60. What Makes a Good Building? An Inquiry by the Royal Fine Art Commission, London, Royal Fine Art Commission, 1994, p.69.

61. See John Melvin, 'Entrance Orders: Quinlan Terry at Downing College', Architecture Today, no.46, March 1994, pp.26–31. The project took some time to get through planning regulations: 'Terry fails in classic test case', Architects' Journal, vol.191, no.10, 7 March 1990, p.9.

62. Giles Worsley, 'The Odd Couple', New Statesman and Society, vol. 18(ii), 24 October 2005, pp. 42–4. For the project see, Tom Emerson 'Revision and revival: Caruso St John's intervention at Downing College Cambridge,' Architecture Today, no.207, April 2010, pp.44–51.

10
Representing Science: the Architecture of the New Museums Site, Cambridge, 1952–71
Barnabas Calder

Fig 1. The New Museums Site, Zoology and Metallurgy building, Arup Associates (author)

After the triumph of radar and nuclear weapons in the Second World War it was clear that the Cold War would be fought in large part through science and technology. Demobilisation from 1945 was succeeded from 1950 onwards by rearmament for a new, high-technology war based in competitive physics and engineering.[1] Anxiety about Soviet progress, particularly in nuclear and missiles technology, led Churchill to argue in a 1955 speech for a huge expansion of technological research and education. A 1956 White Paper led to the founding of new Colleges of Advanced Technology; and the national memorial to Churchill, as the hero of the Second World War, was the foundation in 1958 in Cambridge of Churchill College. The new college, built on a higher budget than its contemporaries, was to have a minimum of 70% science and engineering undergraduates.[2]

Cambridge was the obvious place for this scientific flagship: in the twentieth century it had proved itself as a world centre for physics in particular. Some of the greatest discoveries of this spectacular scientific boom occurred in the New Museums Site Science area. Once the Botanic Gardens, this city-centre site had later housed some of the university's earliest purpose-built scientific facilities and museums. In 1964 it was crowded with shabby buildings ranging in date from 1865 to 1959, the small courts between them cluttered with improvised sheds; the New Museums Site was (and, despite the upheavals outlined below, largely remains) an architectural low-point in Cambridge.[3] Yet these humdrum or makeshift buildings, 'overcrowded and often far from robust as to internal walls and floors', housed the discoveries in 1897 of the electron and in 1932 of the neutron, the splitting of the atom (also in 1932), the understanding of the mechanism of nervous conduction through the 1930s and 1940s, and in 1953 the working-out of the structure of DNA.[4] Two of the world's few computers were on the site, and the eventual architect for part of the scheme, Philip Dowson, recalls being shown to a 'dark basement', where he was told that 'two Nobel Prizes were won in here'.[5] This article explores the attempts of the 1950s and above all the 1960s to re-plan and redevelop this large, irregular city block into a science area which would allow substantial departmental expansion.

The contemporary debates on these schemes were largely framed in terms either of practicalities (traffic planning, maximisation of space etc.) or of aesthetic impact on the context. Yet underlying these discussions, this article proposes, lay an unspoken clash over attitudes to the rise of the sciences in Cambridge. These clashes crystallised in particular around the unbuilt high-rise proposals of Denys Lasdun and Partners from 1960–64, provoking his eventual resignation from the job. The same issues arose to a proportionately lesser extent in the considerably smaller project designed and executed on part of the site by Arup Associates in 1964–71.

Cambridge University in the 1950s and 1960s was decentralising from warrens of town-centre departmental buildings into purpose-built teaching and research facilities on open sites in the suburbs or outskirts. It was the decision in 1952 to move Chemistry from the New Museums Site which initiated discussions of how to reallocate their space. A particular pressure for redevelopment was the poor condition of the nineteenth-century Museum of Zoology.[6]

The first post-war plan for the New Museums Site was drawn up at the invitation of the university in June 1956 by Murray Easton, a soft-modernist architect of the pre-war generation. He tentatively offered a scheme 'on American lines, that is to say, based on the adoption of wide structures with offices and research rooms on the periphery surrounding large open teaching or other laboratories. The central spaces are, of course, without any natural lighting and must be air-conditioned.' Easton appeared to favour this option, but indicated 'that such an arrangement was unlikely to find favour at Cambridge, in spite of its advantages in providing maximum floor space'. Accordingly he recommended instead tight courts 'linked by openings sufficiently wide to provide glimpses from one to the other.'[7] The court, Easton appears to have felt, was so important to the identity of Cambridge that it was to be extrapolated from its collegiate roots in medieval residential architecture to comparatively recent buildings like laboratories and lecture theatres. However, Easton's courts would have risen an undomestic seven storeys.

The rejection of Easton's scheme is not explained in the archives, but Sir Leslie Martin seems the likeliest opponent. Martin arrived as first Professor of Architecture in Cambridge in 1956, after Easton's appointment, and from the later 1950s his power over academic architectural patronage was to drive traditionalist and soft modernist architects out of the prestigious boom in university work. Martin promoted instead his own preferred modernists including Lasdun, whom he recommended for the University of London redevelopment in Bloomsbury, the University of East Anglia, and two jobs at Leicester University. The New Museums Site appointment may already show his power: in 1959 he produced a model of a replanned New Museums Site 'intended to demonstrate that a central site such as this could be made to yield more usable floor space if at the outset an overall plan was agreed and followed'.[8] Named 'Scheme C' (there is no mention of schemes A and B), Martin's proposals were to inform Lasdun's on his appointment a few weeks later.[9]

Martin's name recurs throughout the 1960s history of the New Museums Site development: he was on the Financial Board Committee for the Redevelopment of the New Museums Site; he repeatedly supported Lasdun in crises (it would be a 'disaster if DL[asdun] [were] not [the] architect', and 'important that DL is to be architect and to be satisfied with solution'); he argued in 1963 for a fifty-year master-plan for all central science areas; and even sat on the Royal Fine Art Commission (RFAC, the government's influential design review board) when it judged Lasdun's proposal – though he stresses to the Cambridge committee that, although present, 'he himself had taken no part in the proceedings'.[10] As well as Martin's influence, Lasdun may have been selected because of his existing relationship with the university as architect of Fitzwilliam House (later College).

However he got the commission, Lasdun's planning brief was broad but complex: 'that the site is made to yield as much useful accommodation as it can consistently with its amenities and sound planning, and that the different stages of the redevelopment are planned in such a way as to interfere as little as possible with the teaching and research programs of the departments concerned'.[11] No mention here of aesthetics, but Lasdun had throughout his career positioned himself as an art architect, so the university's decision to employ him rather than architects who presented themselves more technocratically implies that they wanted the scheme to be well-received by architectural critics. Obvious motives for this appointment might include the desire to reflect institutional prestige through architecture, or the hope that a respected architect's name might smooth the passage through planning of a potentially controversial project.

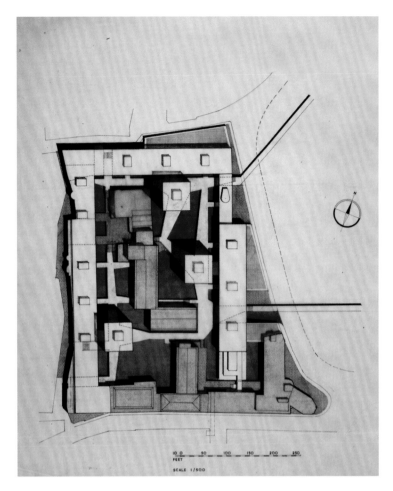

Lasdun's solution, first presented to the clients in June 1960, arose from the appropriately scientific-seeming basis of a statistical questionnaire investigating present and future needs of the site's departments in terms of 'population and movement' now and on ten years.[12] Lasdun proposed a medium-rise periphery block screening high towers within, all raised above a semi-basement service road and parking. This is strikingly similar in its principles to Leslie Martin's Scheme C, just as Lasdun's design for the University of London adopted Martin's previous outline block-plan.[13] High towers on small footprints would minimise disruption to research by decanting the activities of neighbouring buildings into them before replacing lower buildings, meaning each department need only move once.[14] Lasdun had developed this system of staged decanting for rehousing residents on the sites of his Bethnal Green housing estates.

The design was never detailed, but from Lasdun's models, drawings, and design report, its outlines are clear. Designed during the preparation of the 1963 Buchanan Report on *Traffic in Towns*, Lasdun's circulation was absolutely of its moment. The Smithsons' 1957 Berlin Hauptstadt Competition scheme shows visionary optimism that reinforced concrete had freed planning from the ancient dominance of ground-level circulation. Multi-level circulation promised free and separate movement of cars beneath and pedestrians above. The New Museums Site would have had no ground level at all: Lasdun followed Martin's Scheme C in proposing to excavate the entire site to a depth of 7–10 feet, above which 'pedestrian movement is restricted to elevated walkways, forming a web of natural routes between buildings six feet above street level'.[15] These, he hoped, could be 'designed to provide amenity and opportunity for social intercourse, equal to that associated with a court'.[16] In addition to these social benefits, the pedestrian separation would make service vehicle movements safe and inconspicuous, and provide

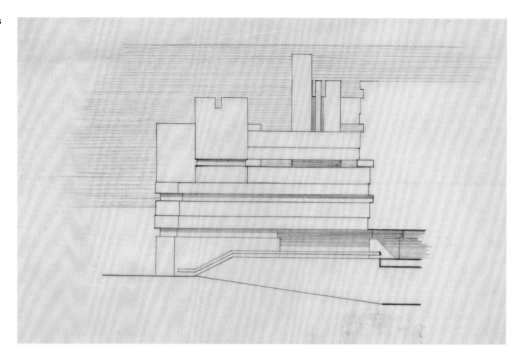

parking for 300 cars, 1400 bicycles – the latter distinctively Oxbridge at a time when most transport planning treated bicycles as no less picturesquely obsolete than ponies and traps. Presumably, as with the superbly Piranesian service roads at the Architects' Co-Partnership's Essex University or Lasdun's own University of East Anglia, this semi-sunk vehicle area would have been magnificently expressive, hard-textured, and dwarfed with thrilling dominance by the towers.

Lasdun's scheme grew stronger and more expressive: upper floors were cantilevered out, while towers and lower blocks alike were boldly modelled, the towers vertically to emphasise their height, the lower blocks generally in horizontal counterpoint. The surviving designs indicate a creative process involving repeated re-drawings of similar internal dispositions with different external treatments. This is one of the last designs in which Lasdun used this technique, derived directly from Carl Ludwig Franck's multiple elevation studies for Lubetkin.[17] Shortly after resigning the New Museums Site commission, Lasdun adopted balsa working models as his main design methodology.[18] The two-dimensional design technology, however, was used here to produce as sculptural a scheme as possible, pulling out decks from the cores of the lower buildings, and, as Kahn had done at his highly influential Richards Laboratories in Philadelphia, externally expressing services and access on the high towers in such a way as to sculpt their surfaces and emphasise their verticality.[19] It was with the first publication of Lasdun's scheme in 1960 that the project went from a private architectural exercise to a controversial expression of contested changes in the university's identity.

In discussing the representative force of the New Museums Site one is confronted with messy data. Firstly, the relations between university, City Council and County Council were barely civil, and unrelated projects were traded against each other like hostages. The County Council, for example (which Dowson recalls as 'absolutely ghastly'), threatened that 'the attitude of Jesus College over the King Street car park might adversely affect the reception given to the University's proposals'.[20] Similarly, Lasdun's development plan proposed retaining unloved Edwardian and Victorian façades, to forestall potential road-widening demands by the planners.[21] Chamberlin, Powell and Bon's failure to provide the University Development Plan commissioned from them was exploited by the County Council as a reason to reject individual university proposals, citing potential traffic problems if overall density rose unplanned.[22]

If the County Council was innately hostile to the scheme, its own future users seem to have been curiously uninterested, at least in its representative qualities. C. P. Snow's famous analysis of British intellectual life as damagingly polarised between scientific and artistic cultures was first aired in Cambridge in 1959, and a meeting of the University Senate two years later seems almost designed to illustrate his point. In a discussion of the Sidgwick Site development for the arts and humanities successive speakers voiced elegantly-phrased, culturally-contextualised opposition to a relatively modest next stage of the development. When the New Museums Site proposal, in its high-rise entirety, was debated, the users were represented largely by an academic working on the site:

> I welcome Mr Lasdun's proposals because, by providing for tall buildings and adequate car parking space, they offer the prospect of uncongested scientific development. [...As things stand,] one can easily envisage a future when, nearly all of the assistants having come to work in their cars, the lecturers who arrive on the [New Museums Site...] slightly later will be unable to commence their duties because they continue to circumnavigate the site in search of a place in which to park.[23]

If its putative users did not show much interest in the representative aspects of the project, however, the architects do appear to have done so, at least subconsciously. Initially Lasdun's tallest tower was to be 190 feet – Cambridge's highest building and a major alteration to the skyline.[24] Nor was its height unavoidable: Lasdun himself recorded that with less satisfactory planning within the site it would have been possible to achieve the same amount of accommodation without towers.[25] Rather, Lasdun wished to change the Cambridge skyline. One reason was purely formal: he told the RFAC that 'the skyline of Cambridge was uninteresting'.[26] Indeed, to this day the crematorium chimney of the suburban hospital is the most prominent landmark. In his presentation report on the scheme, where Lasdun discussed eight overlapping questions on the appropriateness of high buildings, another aspect is mentioned. Question two is 'has its position any positive visual or civic significance in relation to the town as a whole?'[27] The introduction of 'civic' significance suggests that the purpose of buildings is a factor in deciding whether it is appropriate to build them high.

Fig 4. Photograph of a
model of Lasdun's
unbuilt scheme, showing
Kahn-like externalised
structure and service
towers (RIBA Robert
Elwall Photographs
Collection)

Perhaps it was this double conviction that his towers would be both beautiful and appropriate which led Lasdun to choose such an apparently confrontational main image to illustrate the scheme at the time and subsequently: the towers are shown dominating and significantly altering the famous view of King's College from the Backs. If he were attempting to minimise the perceived impact of his towers, this would be the view to conceal most assiduously from the public, and his fondness for it must indicate that the towers were intended to make as big and stylistically-contrasting a contribution to the famous vista as Gibbs's Fellows' Building had done over two centuries earlier.

Lasdun nowhere stated explicitly why he felt science towers were of such 'civic significance' as to be the tallest buildings in town. In his engagement with historical architecture in Cambridgeshire, however, his comparisons – at an explicit level purely formal – can be read as having an interesting unifying theme to them: he repeatedly compares the New Museums Site towers to important medieval religious buildings. In his archive is a photograph of an early-modern engraving of Cambridge showing the city's skyline dominated by turreted church and chapel towers; and his office types up a note from his friend the amateur architectural historian J. H. V. Davies, recording the provision in the will of Henry VI for building a tower of 120 feet at the west end of the chapel, with 'small tourettes over that, fixed with pynacles'.[28] The silhouette and prominence of Lasdun's towers would have echoed these Gothic precedents. In discussing his turrets with the RFAC, Lasdun justified them (with telling vagueness in the functionalist defence) as:

> for lift over-runs, staircase escape and general technical requirements, but equally important as the functional considerations was the profile of the tower. Lord Bridges was particularly interested in this argument and seemed satisfied when DL showed the difference between form and profile, illustrating the point with Ely Cathedral.[29]

It seems probable, too, that as an admirer of Hawksmoor and occasional client of illustrator Gordon Cullen, Lasdun would have known Cullen's 1955 illustration of

Hawksmoor's unbuilt scheme for a tower in King's College.[30]

Not a believer in any particular faith, Lasdun's interest in these medieval neighbours may have been more formal than programmatic, but the comparison is still suggestive. The medieval churches and chapels he cites dominated the skyline of Cambridge and Ely just as the institutions they housed and represented dominated the intellectual life and cosmological understanding of their day. Lasdun's towers, which were to contain among others the prestigious Physics Department, could be seen as expressions of the supremacy of scientific cosmology in the twentieth century, and particularly of the contribution of Cambridge Physics. It is a curious irony that the strongest objections to Lasdun's scheme from within the university came from Corpus Christi College, upset at the way that Lasdun's towers would dwarf their chapel tower.[31]

This framing of Lasdun's proposals in a longer architectural tradition was shared by the RFAC. The fellow modernist architect Frederick Gibberd disagreed with Lasdun's sense that the skyline of Cambridge was 'uninteresting', leading to 'general muttering about the relative skylines of Oxford and Cambridge'.[32] This frame of reference, comparing England's old, elite universities, gives a glimpse of the criteria against which the RFAC judged – and in the event approved – Lasdun's scheme.

Lasdun must have known that his towers' height would attract opponents; it is an indication of the importance he attached to them that such a proficient manager of public opinion should risk such opposition. Sure enough, those against Lasdun's towers framed the debate like the RFAC, in terms of alteration of historical views and 'character'. In their hostility to the development, the County Council called in Thomas Sharp, one of the originators of 'Townscape' and its associated priorities of visual planning for the creation and retention of a *genius loci*.[33] Sharp, who hated tall towers for their tendency to intrude unplanned on views which had been formed by centuries of piecemeal change, threw himself energetically, and with characteristically zealous polemicism, into the battle. His view was that the aggressive omnipresence of the towers arose from architectural egoism: 'the real reason for the proposed towers was that the architect or the University liked them'. Sharp and those who agreed with him proposed

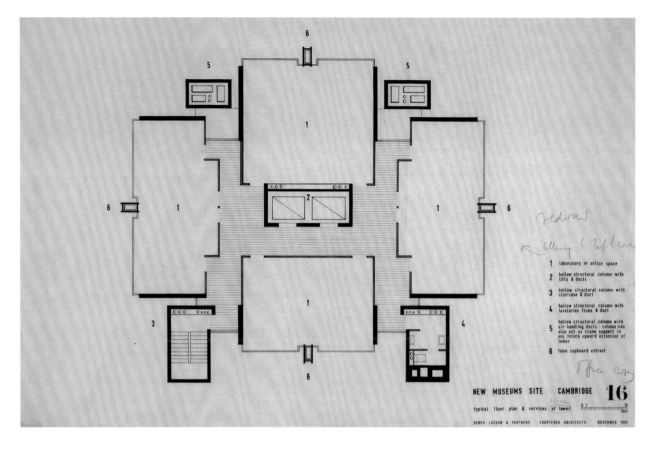

Within the figure (legend):

1 laboratory or office space

2 hollow structural column with lifts & ducts

3 hollow structural column with staircase & duct

4 hollow structural column with lavatories flues & duct

5 hollow structural column with air handling ducts : column can also act as crane support in any future upward extension of tower

6 fume cupboard extract

NEW MUSEUMS SITE   CAMBRIDGE   16

typical floor plan & services of tower

DENYS LASDUN & PARTNERS   CHARTERED ARCHITECTS   NOVEMBER 1961

Fig 6. A plan of one of the towers in Lasdun's unbuilt scheme, showing the externalisation of much of the service and access as attached turrets, like Kahn's Richards Medical Laboratories (RIBA Drawings and Archives Collections)

that the 'character' of Cambridge as a 'historic' city was in danger from the towers. 'The University has no special licence and their buildings are not in a special category which placed them outside the precepts of neighbourliness.'[34]

Although neither side explicitly engages the other in its own terms, an opposition can be constructed between the conservationists' leading priority, which was to retain traditional continuity in views towards and within Cambridge, and Lasdun's desire to provide a heroic architectural expression for the departments which were making the most exciting discoveries of the day. Two notions of the university were thus in conflict: on the one hand, the notion of the university as a body of buildings which house and protect a scholarly tradition valuable for its continuity and antiquity; on the other hand the idea that the essential quality of the university is its research and teaching, and the physical fabric ought to adapt proudly and assertively to its fast-changing needs. The physicists, for example, seemed willing to demolish the buildings in which some of science's greatest discoveries had occurred, whilst many humanities academics fought the move to the Sidgwick Site.

The public debate became extremely nasty. Sharp published mock-ups of Lasdun's towers, inventing detailing for them that was inconceivably ugly for Lasdun, who promptly investigated suing him.[35] So hard did Lasdun try to get a preview and right of simultaneous reply to an article by the architectural journalist Derek Senior in the *Architects' Journal* that Senior accused him of 'a venal ruse', and 'deliberately offensive lies'. In reply came a letter from Lasdun's solicitors threatening an action for defamation.[36]

Whilst Sharp's tactics were certainly successful in calling media attention to the proposals and the controversy which they had stirred, they were regarded as a mixed blessing by the City Council, whose representative would apparently have been 'really rather horrified if Thomas Sharp was brought into the enquiry'.[37]

The controversy led to the scheme being called in for a public enquiry early in 1964.

Lasdun did not attend, being represented by Harry Pugh from his office. The enquiry concluded that Stage 1 of the scheme could go ahead subject to a limitation of 80 feet on the height of the towers, but this was increased to 110 feet (the height of Lasdun's design submitted for planning) by the minister, subject to approval of the final designs by the local planning authority.[38] But by this time the pressure of the university's Major Building Schedule was high – Stage 1 had to go on site by the end of 1965 or lose its funding.[39] Lasdun resigned as the architect of Stage 1, citing as reasons his busyness with UEA, his ill health at the time and the excessively tight schedule (he had given a last possible date to begin detailing, and his deadline had been missed through the lateness of the minister's decision).[40] It seems almost certain, additionally, that he was disenchanted with a project now so damagingly controversial. In particular Susan Lasdun, the architect's widow, and his late assistant John Hurley recalled that he was concerned that if he built Stage 1, with only one of the three proposed towers, it would not be in itself a satisfactory building. They both reported that Lasdun resigned when unable to get an assurance from the university that the other towers would eventually be built. This is supported by Lasdun's own earlier memorandum in which he refused to commit himself to the towerless scheme for which Leslie Martin was asking. He records in his usual third person that:

> DL... saw [Leslie] Martin who still agrees, at least to his face, that the
> scheme was the right one, but there can now be no towers if the University are,
> in fact, to build anything at all on this site in the final program for 1964.
> DL said quite emphatically he would not build anything he did not believe to
> be right and Martin agreed.[41]

When Lasdun resigned in May 1964 his master-plan remained live, so Leslie Martin insisted that 'the choice of [Stage 1] architect must be acceptable to Mr Lasdun', and they together drew up a shortlist of architects.[42] The first choice, Farmer and Dark, rejected the job partly because the timing was too tight, and partly because they did not like the overall shape of Stage 1 as it was left after the planners had finished with it: 'our joint reaction to the present layout (as opposed to Lasdun's original scheme with high towers) is that the present tower block, being only 30 feet higher than the large adjoining mass, ceases to be a tower'.[43] Lasdun had been at Rugby School with the letter writer, Bill Henderson of Farmer and Dark.[44] The Financial Board was impressed by their terms of refusal, with its treasurer writing to the President of Queens' College that 'my immediate reaction to the letter is that this is a firm which we ought to keep in mind for future occasions'.[45]

The second choice was altogether more surprising: Arup Associates. The surprise lies not in their appropriateness – they were an exciting new practice that had had commissions in Oxford and Cambridge colleges, and were already on site with a very successful laboratory commission for the University of Birmingham (which the committee researched).[46] Rather the surprise lies in the hostility which both Derek Sugden and Philip Dowson of Arup Associates recall Lasdun as having had towards their firm.[47] Lasdun, Spence and other architects, they recall, were very upset when Ove Arup, the great engineer, set up the experimental practice to provide all architecture, engineering and quantity surveying in an integrated design team and contract. Arup explained the new practice as 'a study of collaboration. It is like a lab inside our organisation [Ove Arup and Partners] in which we hope to develop new ideas, which incidentally should make us more fit to give the best possible advice to those architects who wish us to help them with their structural problems'.[48] Yet Dowson feels he was initially 'condemned for being a blackleg by the RIBA'.[49] Lasdun appears to have responded by breaking his career-long association with Ove Arup and Partners, using Flint and Neill for his next major project, the National Theatre.

It is an interesting sidelight on the relationships between architects and engineers that leading architects should have been so very upset by this new practice. Architecture of the 1960s was so expressive of its engineering that architects seem to have been particularly sensitive about these new rivals – more so than by competition from within the conventional professional structure.

Nevertheless, despite the strength of Lasdun's apparent hostility to the new practice, he must presumably have agreed to their being approached as possible successors for the Cambridge job – indeed, he later recorded that 'we recommended the appointment of Arup Associates', and Arup Associates took up the challenge.[50]

Dowson, the lead architect for Arup Associates, approached the project as a political as well as a design challenge, seemingly learning from Lasdun's difficulties. He promptly met the heads of each university department to be affected by the project, and liaised with City and County planners; perhaps more importantly the team replanned the accommodation into a less high-rise building.[51] Largely by cutting circulation space, Arup Associates saved seven per cent of the gross area yet created a similar room area, and by slightly bulking-up the building they kept the towers to around eighty feet.[52] The price paid by the finished project for this efficiency is rather tight circulation spaces.

In terms of its representative power, the New Museums Site never came to be the Piranesian celebration of science envisioned by Lasdun. The 'squalid jumble' which he had been employed to rationalise mostly survives, with Arup Associates' building pushed awkwardly into one corner. Its pedestrian deck never linked up with raised circulation within the site, let alone to the mixed use Lion Yard development outside the site as hoped, and the brick podium facing the street front seems defensive. In this, the New Museums Site echoes the unfulfilled hopes of 'the white heat of the [technological] revolution' which Harold Wilson had promised would shape Britain. The early ambition of the project gave way in the 1970s to an enforced acceptance of economic limitations, and uncertainty about or rejection of the 1960s utopianism which had cheerfully erected so many Stage 1s with blithe confidence that indefinitely-continuing redevelopment would eventually extend their circulation decks round entire town-centres.

If the overall planning of the New Museums Site represents unrealistic 1960s optimism, the execution of the building by Arup Associates reflects a more positive outcome of that decade's energetic architectural self-confidence. As Dowson wrote, the construction 'could hardly have been more difficult having practically no access, surrounded by hyper-sensitive scientific equipment and scientists and sitting on a river'.[53] The tightness of the design schedule and the pre-existing, angry public controversy heightened the difficulties. Yet Arup Associates, led by their chief architect Philip Dowson, and with Derek Sugden as their leading engineer, seem to have relished the challenge. Architects, engineers (structural and mechanical) and quantity surveyors collaborated closely from the outset on Arup Associates' projects, and Dowson recalls design-team retreats at his house in Suffolk, where intensive discussion and design, with many models, would resolve problems fast. Engineers, according to Sugden, contributed extensively to detailing, though some aspects were dictated by the architects, notably the lead cladding, which Dowson remembers the engineers as never understanding.[54]

The result is a well-made building which is unmistakably under close aesthetic control. The requirement to minimise site assembly space and avoid vibration were turned into excuses to explore structural prefabrication off-site. By ensuring that the columns carried only vertical, not lateral thrusts, they could be made ostentatiously slender, a boney elegance echoed by the whale skeleton hung on the deck level. This conspicuously exposed structural engineering then became an advertisement for, or representation of, Arup Associates' unusual collaborative process, with the end result beautifully made through careful on-site supervision by a site engineer.[55] The massing is clear, and robust-looking detailing is consistent at all scales, including inside the elegant and nicely-lit Zoology Museum in the podium. As Dowson said, 'I want always to know that a building, when complete, can be cut in half and its whole anatomy laid open to

reveal a consistency between the main aspects and the smallest detail, between the idea and the execution.'[56]

Above all, the building seems to represent its scientific purpose in its imagery. Whilst the extensive exposed concrete and areas of lead cladding suggest the tag 'Brutalist', as in many such buildings of the mid- to late-1960s it shows signs of its designers engaging with High Tech ideas and images. The skinny legs and bulky thorax of this building echo the improbable zoomorphic doodles of Archigram, and the plug-in quality of the towers and above all the servicing solution are also closely related to High Tech organisational dispositions. The carrying of services in the interstices of doubled or quadrupled structural elements (a 'tartan grid') is characteristic of Arup Associates, as in Dowson's remarkably High-Tech-sounding statement of 1966 that in some of their work they thought of structure 'mainly as support for the services'.[57] Developed by Arup's engineers in collaboration with Lasdun at UEA and refined at Birmingham by Arup Associates, this was to be a major influence on the thinking of High Tech architects like Barry Maitland, and resembles the thought processes of Norman Foster or Richard Rogers in the later 1960s.[58]

This is one of Arup Associates' most punchy and exciting buildings, mysteriously underplayed by them in their own publications, and likely shortly to become a live conservation issue, after an advertisement of December 2011 sought architects for alterations.[59] It is at the time of writing un-listed and strangely underrated, but remains one of the most exhilarating and attractive pieces of high Brutalist architecture in Cambridge.

This article has examined what the successive schemes for post-war replanning of the New Museums Site represented to a variety of contemporaries. Lasdun's proposals, if built, would have staked an immense and assertive claim to the centrality, physical and intellectual, of science to the life of Cambridge. Arup Associates' eventual building, though excellent, makes a smaller claim in its less inescapable profile (its smaller towers are only stubbily visible from a number of open spaces around Cambridge). Lasdun and Arup Associates each engaged with contemporary architectural theory, and each sought an architecturally distinguished design, whilst attempting to maximise flexibility in the face of the rapidly changing demands of cutting-edge scientific research and more gradual evolutions in teaching. Yet beyond the representative dimension was this in fact the best approach for the research functions of the New Museums Site? These architecturally driven proposals are nothing like the built infrastructure of the government's nuclear research, for example. Rather than attempting to produce a cleverly serviced, flexible shed, nuclear research programs tended to build the cheapest enclosure they could for each successive generation of machinery and infrastructure despite vast budgets. These sheds were highly specific and expendable, rapidly becoming obsolete, but as they were built only for one purpose, they were likely to perform it well.[60] When, in 1974, Physics left the New Museums Site, it did something similar, moving to cheap, unglamorous CLASP prefabs on a substantial green field site outside Cambridge. The important research of the Cavendish Physics Laboratory has since been housed in a building which looks like a system-built school, and despite its national priority the nuclear weapons research project was pursued in an array of shabby brick huts and sheds. It is strikingly clear how far removed the architecture of the highest technology was from High-Tech architecture. Leading scientists and engineers derived their prestige from equipment and results, not buildings, and so cared more about what their buildings did than what they represented. High Tech architecture was for low-tech organisations where cultural capital was derived from the soft power of architectural avant-gardism – organisations like art galleries and insurance brokers.

1. Wayne Cocroft and Roger Thomas (P. S. Barnwell, ed.), *Cold War: Building for Nuclear Confrontation 1946–1989*, Swindon, English Heritage, 2003, pp.236–7.

2. Elain Harwood, 'The Churchill College Competition and the Smithson Generation', in Louise Campbell ed., *Twentieth Century Architecture and its Histories*, London, SAHGB, 2000, 37–56 (p.38).

3. Planning Inspector's Report by W. Riley on New Museums Site Planning Enquiry, 28 February 1964 (henceforth 'Planning Inspector's Report'), p.2, FBM687/8, Cambridge University Library Special Collections (CUL).

4. Brian Pippard, 'The move to West Cambridge', in *A Hundred Years and more of Cambridge Physics* (Cambridge University Physics Society, third edition 1995), available at http://www.phy.cam.ac.uk/history/years/westcam.php.

5. Philip Dowson interviewed at his house in Kensington by the author, 12 January 2012.

6. 'Report of the Committee appointed by the Council to consider the provisional assignment of accommodation on the New Museums Site when the new buildings for the Chemistry Departments on the Lensfield Site begin to be occupied', 13 May 1952, UAR:BA281:R2656, CUL.

7. Murray Easton, report on the New Museums Site, June 1956, pp.1–3, FB687/F/2, CUL.

8. 'Note of a joint meeting of Financial Board Committee on Sites and Needs and General Board Committee on the future use of New Museums Site', 28 November 1959, FB687/F/1(220/C/1), CUL.

9. Scheme C, PB898/4(5), RIBA Drawings and Archives Collections (henceforth RIBA).

10. 'F. B. Cttee [sic] for the Redevelopment of the New Museums Site', FBM687/8, CUL; for Martin's support for Lasdun, memorandum of meeting at Cambridge, 28/5/1963, LaD/37/4, RIBA; for Martin's scheme for Old Addenbrooke's Site and Downing Site, see Minutes of meeting of Financial Board Committee on Sites and Needs, 14/2/1963, p.1, FB687/F/8, CUL; for Martin and RFAC, unconfirmed minutes of meeting, 16/1/1964, FBM687/1:FB(NMS)(63)2, CUL.

11. Letter A. Parnis (of the Financial Board) to Lasdun, 15/1/1960, 687/F/2, CUL.

12. Denys Lasdun & Partners' report, 'Proposed Development of the New Museums Site', June 1960, p.1, FBM687/10, CUL.

13. Note on an early briefing document, 'Programming based on adaption of Martin's scheme', LaD/36/3, RIBA; For London, PA2106/1(1–3, 12), DR42/7(4–11), RIBA.

14. Minutes of NMS Committee meeting 6 May 1960, FBM687/1, CUL.

15. For Martin's proposal, Note of a joint meeting of Financial Board Committee on Sites and Needs and General Board Committee on the future use of New Museums Site, 28 November 1959, FB687/F/1(220/C/1), CUL.

16. Denys Lasdun & Partners' report, 'Proposed Development of the New Museums Site', June 1960, p.2, FBM687/10, CUL.

17. John Allan, *Lubetkin: Architecture and the Tradition of Progress*, London, RIBA, 1992, p.387.

18. Barnabas Calder, 'Medium or message? Uses of Design and Presentation Models by Denys Lasdun and Partners', in Hilde Heynen and Janina Gosseye, eds., *Proceedings of the 2nd International Conference of the European Architectural History Network*, Brussels, EAHN, 2012, pp.452–456; Lasdun's model-maker Philip Wood interviewed by author, 15/6/2012, forthcoming on RIBA's *Lasdun Online* website, summer 2014.

19. E.g. PB898/4(11–12), RIBA.

20. Dowson interview; Minutes of meeting of Joint Committee on the Cambridge Development Plan, 21/1/1961, 687/F/5, CUL.

21. Copy of letter Lasdun to Phillips (chair of New Museums Site committee), 5/5/1961.

22. Planning Inspector's report, p.3, FB(NMS)(61)6, CUL.

23. Report of meeting of the Senate, 2/5/1961, p.5, FBM687/1:FB(NMS)(61)5, CUL.

24. Planning Inspector's report, p.5.

25. Planning Inspector's report, p.2.

26. Lasdun memorandum, 13/3/1963, LaD/38/2, RIBA.

27. Denys Lasdun & Partners' report, 'Proposed Development of the New Museums Site', June 1960, p.2, FBM687/10, CUL.

28. Photograph, LaD/38/1, RIBA; Memorandum 'Extract from: King Henry VI's Will', transcribed 13/11/1962 from letter Davies to Lasdun, 10/7/1962, LaD/38/1, RIBA.

29. Lasdun memorandum, 13/3/1963, LaD/38/2, RIBA.

30. David Roberts, *The Town of Cambridge as it Ought to be Reformed : The plan of Nicholas Hawksmoor interpreted in an essay*, Cambridge University Press, 1955. My thanks to Otto Saumarez Smith for drawing this to my attention.

31. Report of meeting of the Senate, 2/5/1961, p.5, FBM687/1:FB(NMS)(61)5, CUL.

32. Lasdun memorandum, 13/3/1963, LaD/38/2, RIBA.

33. John Pendlebury and Erdem Erten, eds., *Alternative Visions of Post-War Reconstruction: Creating the Modern Townscape*, London, Routledge, forthcoming.

34. Arguments summarised in Planning Inspector's report, pp.10–11.

35. Memo of visit by Michael Brawne to 'Mr Megarry's Chambers', 7/2/63, LaD/37/4, RIBA.

36. Letter from Senior to Lasdun, 22/10/1961; letter from Roche, Son and Neale to Senior, undated draft, c. October 1961, LaD/38/1, RIBA.

37. Memorandum of conversation between Phillips and Michael Brawne of Denys Lasdun & Partners, 30/1/1963, reporting meeting with County Council representative, LaD/37/4, RIBA.

38. Planning Inspector's report, p.17; Letter W. M. Schwab on behalf of Minister of Housing and Local Government to Mills (Director of Estates Management), 27/4/1964, FBM687/11, CUL.

39. Extract from *University Reporter* 9/12/1964, 3b, UAR:R2656 Box 281, CUL.

40. Minutes of meeting 25/5/1964, p.1, FB(NM)(63)2, CUL.

41. Lasdun memorandum, 30/4/1963, LaD/38/2, RIBA.

42. Minutes of meeting 25 May 1964, p.2, FB(NM)(63)2, CUL.

43. Letter W. A. Henderson to R. E. Macpherson (treasurer of CU Financial Board), 11/5/1964, 687/F/11, CUL.

44. Letter Henderson to Lasdun, 6/1/1965, LaD/241/6, RIBA.

45. Letter Macpherson to President of Queens' College, 13/5/1964, 687/F/11, CUL.

46. Anonymous, undated, but seen by the committee 2/7/1964, 'Notes on a visit to Birmingham University to see the building being erected by Arup Associates', FB687/F/11, CUL.

47. Derek Sugden, interviewed by author at his house in Watford, 2 November 2011.

48. Ove Arup's open letter to architects on the foundation of Arup Associates, 8/10/1963, reprinted in Michael Brawne, *Arup Associates: The Biography of an Architectural Practice*, London, Lund Humphries, 1983, p.7.

49. Dowson interview.

50. Memorandum 21/11/1968, LaD/38/2, RIBA; Letter Dowson to Mills, 21/5/1964, FB687/F/11, CUL.

51. Minutes of meeting 25/5/1964, p.3, FB(NM)(63)2; minutes of meeting 25/11/1964, p.2, FBM687/1, CUL.

52. Minutes of meeting, 25/11/1964, pp.2–3; FBM687/1, CUL.

53. Philip Dowson, 'Architects' Approach to Architecture', *RIBA Journal*, vol.73, no.3, March 1966, pp.105–15 (p.112).

54. Dowson and Sugden interviews.

55. Sugden interview.

56. Dowson 1966, op. cit., p.109.

57. ibid., p.105.

58. For Maitland, see Barnabas Calder, 'Castles, Cows and Glasshouses: The Burrell Collection architectural competition,' *Twentieth Century Architecture*, vol.10, 2012, p.43.

59. http://www.architectsjournal.co.uk/competitions/cambridge-university-seeks-architect-for-new-museums-site-building/8623910.article, retrieved June 2012.

60. Wayne Cocroft, 'Cold War Architecture', lecture given to Cambridge MSt in Building History, 24 April 2012.

11
Modernising Some of Oxford's Listed Twentieth-Century Buildings
Alan Berman

Fig 1. Landing at
Blackhall Road
(Andy Spain)

Dilemmas and Dislikes

Oxford colleges are the best of clients and the worst of clients; they are unlike any other and working for them is a very particular experience. What makes them so unusual is their independence and governance structure. Distinct from the universities of Oxford and Cambridge, and from all other universities, the colleges themselves are wholly independent, self-governing private institutions, able to spend their money (though not all are wealthy) for whatever purpose their governing bodies of some forty Fellows wish, according to the personal agendas of whatever individual or faction carries the day. Over 25 years we have worked for 14 Oxford colleges and one in Cambridge. All in principle have this same decision-making structure but they are, by virtue of the different personalities of the Fellows, all very different. When it comes to buildings and architecture some are wonderfully open, enlightened and realistic while others, notwithstanding their enormous collective brainpower, are deeply conservative and suspicious of anything modern: knowledgeable of course, but occasionally narrowly opinionated, unworldly and impractical. Some are convinced that the whole construction industry is determined to 'rip them off' and that buildings can be purchased for the same price as sheds at B&Q. We are fortunate to have worked for many of the former, and they approximate to the dream client. What is relevant here is that there are also those who are viscerally opposed to modern design.

When working on Oxford's mid-twentieth-century buildings the practical issues are no different to those encountered elsewhere. In matters of design there is, however, an extraordinary schizophrenia about things 'modern'. While they may be conducting research at the forefront of modernity, Oxford college dons are at the same time cocooned in an unchanging carapace of everything old: ancient stone walls and the comfort of sometimes wealthy institutions shut out the contemporary world, with quiet quads where nothing changes and nothing jars – except where a mid-twentieth-century concrete monster rears its head. Even here, the buildings of that post-war optimism that were part of building a 'new' Britain have made their presence felt.

At the time the passion of the sponsors and designers of these buildings – indeed the whole construction industry – was undeterred by their lack of knowledge of the new materials and building methods deployed in the rush to expand university provision, building fast and building cheap. Oxbridge colleges, along with the new and expanding provincial universities, became the field in which many of the finest young architects cut their teeth, producing buildings the likes of which had not been seen before. In the Oxbridge milieu these buildings were radical red flags to the conservative bulls. And so they remain still, largely – but by no mean universally – unloved.

Berman Guedes Stretton works on listed buildings from all periods, and in Oxford and Cambridge, environments dense with historic buildings of the highest order, the commonly agreed assumptions of what constitutes 'the valuable and good' in architecture and heritage means that funds are found for the repair, restoration and retention of traditional buildings, where the colleges generally accept their roles as guardians of their rich built heritage. But when it comes to the products of 1960s Modernism they question whether to spend their money on these 'monsters' – why would one possibly do that? At a meeting to discuss potential changes to a listed building by Howell, Killick, Partridge and Amis, one Fellow vehemently remarked, 'now get my position on this building clear: Semtex is the only solution'.

One challenge that we face is making the case for the appropriate level of expenditure to ensure proper renovation in order, at the least, to stem the deleterious effects of continuous 'patch and repair' attitudes that exist in many a college finance committee. It sometimes seems they have a positive mission to use inadequate maintenance to ensure a building's demise. When modernising older listed buildings we can find ourselves supported by college clients ranged against resistant heritage officers, yet when dealing with a modernist building we can find ourselves allied with the officers confronting an obdurate client who argues with Messianic zeal for demolition or defacement. And of course argument is the stock-in-trade of the academic, and no planning official or architect is going to beat an Oxford don in debate.

These esoteric issues that colour the Oxford context add a challenging layer to the many issues involved in renovating these buildings. The practical issues are well known and no different from the problems of twentieth-century buildings elsewhere: poor thermal performance, extensive cold bridging, basic services that relied on new technology at the time which, while excellent in principle, was often based on inadequate construction knowledge of new materials and sometimes on low budgets. Where personal preferences carry so much weight, an individual's dislike for these buildings can be successfully hidden beneath the banner of a poor energy rating: high energy bills make an excellent case for demolition. We are in the midst of such an argument at present.

Three houses at Blackhall Road, designed by Michael Powers of the Architects' Co-Partnership in 1962 and listed grade II, serve as examples of the nature of the work entailed when dealing with such buildings. So too do buildings at Wolfson College, designed by Powell and Moya in 1967 and recently listed grade II, where we have worked over many years. It is very important to make clear that this completely new college is very much loved by the Fellows: it is a pleasure and a privilege to work with clients who so cherish this unashamedly modernist work. In these and similar college projects, we are faced with the repair and renewal of the fabric and services, as well as modernising the accommodation and facilities to meet today's needs. The work we generally encounter will include:

- Improving the thermal performance of roofs, walls and windows
- Addressing cold bridging where structural elements are an important part of the architecture
- Improving facilities such as *en suite* bathrooms and shared kitchens
- Renewal of safe electrical installations and providing more power and data cabling
- Renewal of often furred up pipe-work, inefficient boilers and water storage
- Buried services inaccessible for maintenance
- Poor sound separation
- Remedying roof drainage systems built with insufficient falls
- Improving poor standards of construction

Some of these matters are unique to buildings of this period and solutions have to be developed to suit the particulars of the design, while in others there are readily available answers – but in all cases the work has a potentially damaging effect on the fabric. In order to help decide what will be acceptable in relation to the architectural value (I hate the politically correct term 'heritage value') of any element in question,

Fig 2. Exterior of Blackhall Road (Andy Spain)

we use an informal matrix for prioritising different aspects of the work. This allocates a rating to each of the operations appropriate to both the scope of the project and the nature of the historic fabric, with the aim of achieving the most benefit for the least disruption. This assessment will include some of the following:

- The extent of the need for repair and its necessity to the future stability of the building;
- Non-compliance with current regulations – most particularly fire and safety;
- The extent of the need for spatial reorganisation of facilities – whether it is critical for the future viability of the building;
- Environmental comfort;
- Energy use;
- Accessibility for wheelchair users;
- Accessibility or visibility of the building for public benefit.

These issues arise on all buildings of architectural and historic merit, and the perennial tension between priorities involves a fine balance of judgement, in which the attitudes of clients with strong views have to be carefully weighed up.

One example of such a debate concerns the access decks at Wolfson College. Stretching the length of the long wings that thrust magnificently into the landscape,

Fig 3. Staircase at
Blackhall Road
(Andy Spain)

the corridors are semi-enclosed outside spaces, partially protected on one side from wind and rain by a rhythm of wide vertical glass louvres with gaps between each one. This means that the accommodation ranged along one side of the corridor has an extensive external wall area. Built with scant insulation, the heat loss of the building is enormous. The easy answer is to enclose the corridor by infilling the gaps in the glass louvres so that the corridor acts as a thermal buffer. The alternative is to insulate the walls in the flats, which would require massive disruption to every bathroom and kitchen. From an environmental point of view enclosing the corridors is the correct answer, whereas insulating the rooms would have minimum architectural impact. The matter was debated at some length but was never put to the test because the building became listed. I have, only half-jokingly, been asked by one college client, 'whose side are you on?'. We have been told openly in one case that we were not appointed because it was clear we would be too determined to protect a 1960s building from alteration.

The renovation of two of the Blackhall Road houses (Anna Aligne was the project architect) illustrates some of the issues with which we have had to deal. (The third house will be renovated when the lease expires.) It was easy to see how someone might take against the houses, as they were externally overgrown with creepers, the concrete over the front doors was badly spalled and stained, and the grey calcium silicate bricks were weathered and festooned with wires. They had been empty through the winter and, inside, the aging paintwork, and 'tide' marks where pictures had been removed contributed to making the houses seem cold and uninviting – not ideal conditions for showing off the fair-faced grey brickwork and black quarry tile floors. To the future tenant this hardly suggested a cosy Oxford home, set for study and comfortable academia. Having been allocated the house the future occupant had instructed works to 'traditionalise it' by plastering over the fair-faced brickwork and applying moulded cornices and other works to erase the original modernity. A planning officer stopped the works and BGS was asked to attempt a resolution. I found myself having to write to my good client, the Bursar, who would make the final decision and who, I suspect, is not a great lover of the building, making a robust case to protect it. I suggested that the college was surely sufficiently conscious of its role as guardian of historical continuity that it should persuade the future occupant that as a temporary resident of a building considered architecturally valuable by a national body he had no right to change it because it did not suit his personal architectural preferences. It was a tricky moment in our relationship with the college – an instance of that additional political dimension that we encounter when working in Oxford.

Despite the absence of comprehensive records it was not difficult to develop an understanding of the significance of these houses. Almost entirely intact, they are exemplars of the best work of the period, manifesting in all respects the contemporary attitudes of domestic planning. We could obtain no original drawings but had a set of surveys from 1971 when a small extension was added so sensitively that it looks as if it was part of the house. The success of this early extension was one factor in deciding that we should go against one of the guiding principles considered essential to successful restoration: that interventions and replacements in historic buildings should not attempt to match the original but remain distinctly visible from the original fabric. We attempted wherever possible to ensure that the work of repair should be invisible and that the house should appear as close to its original state as possible. While well aware that in older buildings the 'palimpsest' of past changes adds to their quality it is interesting to note that this rule is not followed in many restorations of modernist buildings. Here there was nothing in recent changes that added to the architectural, historic or social value of the buildings, and everything was to be gained by returning the buildings to their original state.

Using our matrix we assessed the extent to which this 'scraping' away would be deleterious to the fabric and established a schedule of draft proposals for discussion with

Fig 4. Living area at Blackhall Road (Andy Spain)

the historic buildings officer. From the published literature we learned that the changes that had been made were relatively superficial and limited: the original matchboarded pine ceilings had been plaster boarded, the kitchen units had been replaced, and some of the bathroom fittings and the vanity units had been changed, but most of the distinguishing architectural features remained.

The planning of the rooms on the ground floor followed the Frank Lloyd Wright arrangement of a sequence of rooms that open to each other, revolving around a central core of fair-faced brickwork containing an open fireplace to the living room, and a partly circular staircase – the pivot of the whole plan. For privacy the ground floor rooms are separated but in order to retain the sense of spatial flow the architects used glass screen walls and doors in chunky timber framing, and a timber sliding door that appeared to have been unused for many years. Internal walls are in some places the exposed calcium silicate bricks used on the outside, and in others white panels of plaster framed by timber skirting and cornice rail. The original timber windows were in good condition; interestingly they provide relatively good thermal performance as they were built with outer and inner opening lights.

Throughout the house the unpainted timber doors, frames, and extensive fitted cupboards had been almost blackened by many layers of dark polyurethane varnish obscuring the timber grain, and making the corners lose their crispness. We agreed that it was important to rejuvenate them so that their appearance as a 'natural' material was brought into line with the original design intent which used materials in their raw uncovered state. Where it is so often wrong to 'scrape' away the layers of the past, in this instance it seemed appropriate – but we did not scrape to the extent that the timber looked quite new.

The ceilings posed more of a quandary about going back to the original or leaving the change in place: in some rooms ceilings were the original pine boarding and in others more recent white painted plasterboard. By reference to the original design we concluded that the lines of the boarding and the continuity of material throughout all the ground floor rooms was an important element that reinforced the flow of the spaces. By removing a small amount of the plasterboard we discovered that it could be removed with virtually no damage to the original timber. Restoring the original ceilings was therefore simple but significant.

The fair-faced brick walls were a challenge, as these had been damaged by the many cables, switch plates and socket outlets that had been surface fixed over the years. Where their removal left small screw holes these were filled with a grout that was easy to lose in the grey flecked bricks and cement mortar. However, where bricks had to be replaced, because of damage or where rewiring had to be installed, we had a more difficult task, not least because the same calcium silicate bricks are no longer made. The introduction of many more power points meant replacing original switches and socket points in the walls, as the existing ones were now considered unsafe. These had originally been wired within the brickwork. We minimised the difficulty by locating as many of the new and replacement outlets in the plastered walls as was practical, so that all new wiring could be hidden. Where we were left with a few bricks that needed replacement we took bricks from an invisible area in the original garage. The plastered walls had a particular finish that we needed to emulate after the chasing: a slightly textured rough but not sharp render which the builder managed to replicate after experimenting with different trowels.

Having determined that we wanted to match any new work to the old, rather than articulating it clearly as being of different period, the project depended in large measure on the quality of the workmanship. We are lucky in Oxford to have skilled tradesmen used to working on such buildings and contractors who understand the need for preparing repeated trials to obtain the right result. Working with such contractors is another pleasure of our work in Oxford.

Fig 5. Wolfson College
(James O. Davies/
English Heritage)

Determining the best method of repair for the spalled external concrete took a great deal of trial and error after discussion with officers from the Twentieth Century Society and Oxford City. Three methods were considered:

1. Repair mortar with 'coloured' mineral covering only the area of repair;
2. Use the same materials but covering the repair and the whole of the surface in which the repair has been made;
3. Use purpose mixed mineral restoration mortar as a 2–3mm finishing coat over the whole area after a strong repair mortar.

In the end we did both one and three.

While obtaining a good colour match is important, re-establishing the original texture of the rough-sawn, timber-finished concrete is possibly even more so. Given that the concrete will weather unevenly, particularly on such a confined site with overhanging trees and rain 'shadows' from adjacent buildings, if the correct texture could be achieved then weathering discoloration over time would be of the same order as the original, making the repair nigh invisible. We used J. Gilchrist Wilson's marvellous book *External Concrete Repairs* – published at the same time as the design – which enabled us to specify the correct boarding for the shuttering.

Other matters of upgrading were relatively straightforward: parapets allowed us to install additional insulation when recovering the roof; the timber window sections were

sufficiently large to allow the replacement of the single glazed units with double glazed on the outer windows – thereby effectively creating triple glazing; and much of the original pipe work was surface mounted so the new plumbing installation posed no difficulty.

Having completed the project it was a great credit to our project architect Anna Algne and builder Jonathan Ward that we received a letter of appreciation about the work from the professor who had been so adamant about altering the house.

I have no doubt that some of the techniques we have used break the rules and purists would have done the work differently, but one of the lessons we have learned from working on buildings of this period is how relaxed the designers appeared to be about finding expedient solutions to problems as they arose. In many cases of course this was because these buildings, in the timescale of the history of building, were new and experimental, and indeed sometimes left a legacy of problems, but at the level of design the obsessive rigour and purism that today dictates that all details should be consistent seems not to have existed – the buildings have a vibrancy that comes from flexibility of mind and invention. These buildings, designed by masters of architecture, are a perennial and fascinating learning experience. It might seem odd for architects to be happy to leave a project with their work invisible, but it is enormously satisfying to work to ensure the continuity of these superbly designed buildings, and also to try to turn the tide and make them more loved than they are.

About Twentieth Century Architecture

Twentieth Century Architecture is the academic journal of the Twentieth Century Society, a registered charity founded in 1979 as the Thirties Society. Its chief aim is to promote interest and support for buildings of quality and their related artefacts, including murals, sculptures and landscapes, created after 1914 across the United Kingdom. Much of this advocacy is realised through education. It also advises local authorities, campaigners and policy makers, assessing listed building applications and buildings at risk, while also proposing new additions to the statutory list.

Through visits, lectures, conferences and publications, including the thrice-yearly magazine for members, *C20*, it challenges prejudices and misunderstandings, and promotes public appreciation of buildings in all the styles current since 1914. The Society recognises no end date for its activities and performs an important function in persuading decision makers that the most recent heritage is often the most endangered.

Each issue of *Twentieth Century Architecture* focuses on a different theme, and contributes to the growth of popular and academic understanding in its field. Articles in the present issue have been peer-reviewed, and for Journal 13, *The Architecture of Public Service*, 2015, contributions have been invited through a call for papers. In addition, the Twentieth Century Society provides the editorial leadership for the series of monographs Twentieth Century Architects, now being published by English Heritage and previously by the RIBA. Eleven titles have so far been published.

The Journal, which is now intended to become an annual publication, is sent free to all C20 members. It is supported by grants and donations from a number of charities and educational trusts, as well as from individuals. New donations are always very welcome. A stock of some back numbers is available for sale (see amazon.co.uk) and the contents of earlier issues are available on the academic research website, JSTOR.

For further information and details of how to join the Society, see *C20society.org.uk*.

Elain Harwood
Alan Powers
Editors